# The Prime-Time Presidency

# The Prime-Time Presidency

## The West Wing and U.S. Nationalism

TREVOR PARRY-GILES AND
SHAWN J. PARRY-GILES

UNIVERSITY OF ILLINOIS PRESS
Urbana and Chicago

© 2006 by Trevor Parry-Giles and Shawn J. Parry-Giles
All rights reserved
Manufactured in the United States of America
1 2 3 4 5 C P 5 4 3 2 1

♾ This book is printed on acid-free paper.

Library of Congress Cataloging-in-Publication Data
Parry-Giles, Trevor, 1963–
The prime-time presidency : the West Wing and U.S. nationalism /
Trevor Parry-Giles and Shawn J. Parry-Giles.
p.   cm.
Includes bibliographical references and index.
ISBN-13: 978-0-252-03065-9 (cloth : alk. paper)
ISBN-10: 0-252-03065-6 (cloth : alk. paper)
ISBN-13: 978-0-252-07312-0 (pbk. : alk. paper)
ISBN: 0-252-07312-6 (pbk. : alk. paper) 1. West Wing (Television
program) I. Parry-Giles, Shawn J., 1960– II. Title.
PN1992.77.W44P37      2006
791.45′72—dc22      2005021529

*To Samuel B. and Eliam T.*

# Contents

# Acknowledgments

OUR INTEREST in *The West Wing* began, like so many other avid viewers, with the show's debut in 1999 and has not waned since. Our academic interest in the program began at almost the same time, and along the way numerous individuals have contributed to our thinking about the program, the issues it raises, and its ideological meaning for U.S. political culture.

Shawn's interest in matters of nationalism began with an independent study at Monmouth College that brought together several scholars from various disciplines (art, communication, English, government and politics, and history) as well as several undergraduate students interested in cultural studies. She thanks those scholars for their discussions related to theories of nationalism and globalism, particularly Farhat Haq, Cheryl Meeker, Jan Stirm, and Simon Cordery.

Shawn's study of nationalism expanded once she came to the University of Maryland and was invited to participate in two summer programs as part of the International Institute in Women's Studies, "Theories and Practices of Difference" and "Commonality," sponsored by the Department of Women's Studies and the Curriculum Transformation Project. First, she thanks Claire Moses for her mentorship and for inviting her to become an affiliate faculty member with women's studies. In addition, she thanks Seung-kyung Kim and Deborah Rosenfelt for inviting her to participate in the summer conferences and Bonnie Thorton Dill for her insights on matters of intersectionality. Finally, she acknowledges two graduate students from women's studies—Luh Ayu Prasetyaningsih and Na-Young Lee—with whom she worked on an independent study project related to theories of gendered and racialized nationalism. Conversations that took place during such interactions helped her formulate several of the arguments about nationalism that appear in this volume.

We also thank several faculty members at the Department of Communication for their on-going conversations regarding *The West Wing:* James Klumpp, Mari Boor Tonn, Linda Aldoory, and Joseph McCaleb. We are also indebted to Edward L. Fink for his support as chair of the Department of Communication. We thank Bjørn Stillion Southard for his tireless research efforts in locating and retrieving many of the primary sources cited in this book.

We also acknowledge those who reviewed and/or reacted to versions of this project in its initial stages of development, including Karlyn Kohrs Campbell, Dana Cloud, Sharon Downey, Christine Harold, and John Murphy. We are also indebted to the feedback of Vanessa Beasley and Bonnie Dow at the manuscript stage of this project for reviews that were insightful and instrumental to refining theories linked to the study of the media, feminism, and the history of U.S. nationalism. In addition, they were generous and careful in their reading of our analysis of *The West Wing,* making sure that our discussion of the text was argued and evidenced sufficiently even if they disagreed with our interpretations.

Kerry Callahan at the University of Illinois Press has been gracious, patient, and very encouraging of our project. Everyone at the University of Illinois Press has been helpful and supportive in the final production of this volume, and we are grateful for their work.

Finally, we are most indebted to our children—Samuel B. and Eliam T. Parry-Giles—for their patience with a project that spanned several years in their young lives. Even though they are not fans of *The West Wing,* they endured endless hours of conversation about it and tolerated the constant viewing of current and past episodes. Research and teaching is our profession, but our passion and inspiration derives from our lives with these two great kids.

The Prime-Time Presidency

# Introduction:
# The Presidency, Prime-Time Popular Culture, and U.S. Nationalism

> Let me tell you something. We can be the world's policeman. We
> can be the world's bank, the world's factory, the world's farm.
> What does it mean if we're not also. . . . We've made it into the
> New World, Josh. You know what I get to do now? I get to pro-
> claim the National Day of Thanksgiving. This is a great job.
>
> —President Josiah Bartlet, "Shibboleth"

ON DECEMBER 13, 2000, millions of Americans turned to their television sets at 9:00 P.M. EST to view a program about presidential politics. NBC
promised viewers that Wednesday evening a gripping and insightful exploration of an assassination attempt on senior White House staff members. Not
only were eager viewers to learn about the psychological toll of presidential assassinations but they were also to experience, as they did every week, a behind-
the-scenes glimpse of what life is like in the West Wing.

Those millions of viewers that cold winter night may have been disap-
pointed when their weekly encounter with presidential politics on *The West
Wing* (*TWW*) was replaced by the "real" politics of Campaign 2000. Instead
of the soothing, surrogate presidency of Josiah Bartlet, viewers saw instead
the compelling oratory of Vice-President Al Gore and Texas Governor George
W. Bush as they responded to the Supreme Court's decree halting the Florida
recount. The strange coincidence of December 13, 2000, when the quest for
the presidency preempted the dramatic exercise of presidential politics on
*TWW*, points to the powerful collusion of reality and fiction in contemporary U.S. political culture.

Americans are increasingly finding fictionalized representations of presidents and the presidency in literature, film, and on television. In the 1990s alone, thirty-one films featured presidents or members of their family prominently, from box office successes like *Dave* and *Air Force One* to less popular but more artistically adept films like *Jefferson in Paris*.[1] These fictionalized presidents, as well as those found in many novels and on television, regularly engage serious issues and define presidential leadership in powerful and meaningful ways, reflecting the cultural preoccupation with this institution and its place in our national culture.[2] Sometimes the depictions are humorous, other times quite serious. But whatever their tone and purpose, such fictionalized depictions of the U.S. presidency provide a commentary on the nature of presidential leadership.

A fictional depiction of the presidency offers what we have previously called a "presidentiality," or a discourse that demarcates the cultural and ideological meaning of the presidency for the general public. Some presidentialities are fictional, some are not, and the presidency's meaning emerges from the many different voices and divergent texts that use as a referent the office of president of the United States and the individuals who hold that office. A given presidentiality is thus responsive to context and collective memory, and it defines, in part, the national community by offering a vision of this vital office of the U.S. political system. Given its constitutive character, each presidentiality invites the continued scrutiny of the ideologies and boundaries that circumscribe the presidency and presidents in U.S. political discourse.[3]

Created by Article 2 of the Constitution, the U.S. presidency has developed over two centuries and continues to evolve. Presidents are the men who have occupied this office and the women and men who will eventually assume the role. In addition, the presidency is, arguably, the most important and symbolically meaningful institution of the U.S. system of government. No other branch of the federal government—not Congress, not the federal courts—is the focal point of public discussion, cultural angst, or political hope in the same way.

Simply put, individuals who occupy the presidency embody the national polity. "The president became the most visible landmark of the political landscape, virtually standing for the federal government in the minds of many Americans," notes political scholar Fred Greenstein.[4] These leaders thus represent the United States internationally and become the expression and receptacle of communal ideology. On a symbolic level the president also functions as a "signifier," Anne Norton concludes, and in this role "the President calls up not only the American nation, the government, the executive branch, and the triumphant party (already a rich—and variable—assemblage of images) but the mythic and historical associations that attach to the office and to its past and present occupants."[5]

But neither its institutionality nor its history fully defines what the presidency means. A complete understanding of the nature of presidential leadership and the relationship between presidents and their publics demands attention to discourses about the executive branch that circulate outside political campaigns, the news, and the academy.

Many presidential commentators who assess the nature of the institution and individual presidents ignore the symbolic importance of the presidency as a cultural force in U.S. political life. Their focus, rather, is on leadership, greatness, and strength as barometers of institutional/political power rather than on the depictions of the presidency in cultural life or the impact of such depictions on questions of national identity, governmental performance, or presidential behavior.[6] Consider, for instance, political scientist Stephen Skowronek who masterfully rereads presidential history and discerns "the politics that presidents make." His telling of this history is, as might be expected, a search for the *"institutional* logic of political disruption" as he challenges sacrosanct notions of structural order to reinscribe a vision of the nation's chief executives.

Taking nothing away from Skowronek's important work and the work of so many others, we suggest that to completely appreciate the ideological meaning of the presidency requires engagement with the vast collection of discourses that also figure in the cultural meaning of the office and the people who occupy it.[7] In other words, and borrowing from Bruce Miroff's definition, we see the U.S. presidency as a "spectacle" in which "particular details stand for broader and deeper meanings."[8] Understanding that spectacle completely means critiquing the various texts that contribute to its construction, whether they emanate from the White House itself, from the CNN Center in Atlanta, or from the Warner Brothers' back lot in Hollywood.

## Mimetic Presidentialities in Popular Culture

Foretelling the increased attention to the aesthetic dimensions of rhetoric, Thomas Farrell argued in 1986 that "rhetoric is the only art responsible for the imitation and expression of public thought."[9] As a powerful and accessible rhetorical form, popular culture is intensely influential in its imitation of public life—it functions, in Farrell's words, as a "rhetorical resemblance." Increasingly, rhetorical forms that are technologically sophisticated and highly mimetic in their portrayal of public thought dominate postmodern culture. Popular culture engulfs contemporary life and has come to possess a central role in the definition and expression of political culture as well.

The ancient concept of mimesis begins to explain the meaning of fictionalized presidencies emanating from popular culture for contemporary political discourse. Mimesis refers to the ability of a discourse to imitate, or copy, actual experience. The mimetic experience is a meaningful one, generating "a world of appearances, of semblance, and the aesthetic." Although it might be tempting to dismiss mimetic renditions as mere replicated fakery because they belong "to a nonempirical order of knowledge," such dismissal would be a mistake.[10] The mimetic process creates a material reality and ultimately "designates not a passive process of reproduction but the process of creation, representation, or enactment."[11]

Mimetic representations of the presidency frequently offer audiences new realities of this political institution or new renditions of the biographies of the men who have served as America's chief executive. Such representations work precisely because of their ability to approximate a reality of the presidency that is persuasive and credible—they are, in other words, mimetically efficacious.[12]

Fictional presidencies vary greatly in their mimetic capacity, and that variance explains the relative power of some such representations to influence larger meanings of the presidency and the relative weakness of others. For instance, Jack Nicholson's president in *Mars Attacks!* is clearly a caricature, and the part is written largely for comic impact. As such, this portrayal would be mimetically distant from the reality of the presidency for most viewers. Harrison Ford's president in *Air Force One* displays more of the behaviors and nuances of "real" presidents but is still mimetically distant in his role as action hero when he saves an airplane full of people from Russian terrorists. Other fictional presidents, such as Morgan Freeman as President Tom Beck in *Deep Impact* or Michael Douglas as President Andrew Shepherd in *The American President,* behave in more conventionally "presidential" ways and may be said to be closer imitations of the reality that most viewers understand.

These portrayals are really several steps removed from the reality of the presidency. They are representations of representations in that for most citizens the presidency is only and always a representation, an image of a reality that can never be known. In this way, when film and television depict a fictional presidentiality they are adding yet another representational text to the range of representations of the U.S. presidency and function as another example of the hyperreality of American politics.[13] Nonetheless, popular culture, as it represents political activity and the presidency in American politics, must strive for a high degree of perceived mimetic verisimilitude to secure audience acceptance. As Lee Sigelman notes, the "mimetic aspect is the key to the popularity and the political significance of the Washington novel."[14] The same is true of portrayals of presidential politics in film or on television. There must be a certain plausibility to a fictional depiction of the presidency, a believability in the characterization of the president and his staff, for the text to function as a compelling and ideologically relevant reflection.

Our purpose is to examine the presidentiality emergent from the NBC drama *TWW*. Recognizing the power of television in the formation of cultural beliefs about the presidency, we take *TWW* seriously as a meaningful discourse about presidential leadership and identity.[15] Increasingly, as Murray Edelman notes, "Politics now has to be seen as multivocal and manipulable." Politics comes from a variety of sources; political meaning is derived from a myriad of texts and discourse. We agree with Edelman when he concludes that the "meaning of every action, claim, promise, and threat is contingent on its level of abstraction, the plans of the actor or speaker, and the audience's aspirations, anxieties, and fears, themselves at least partly learned from works of art."[16]

Certainly, given its reach and popularity, the political messages broadcast in television programs like *TWW* have more impact than other forms of artistic politics—paintings, museum exhibits, and literature, for instance. As Allen McBride and Robert K. Toburon remind us, "The images that are saved and broadcast on magnetic tape [on television] provide clues about the cultural bias of our society in social, political, and economic terms."[17] From the talk shows on twenty-four-hour news networks to the Sunday morning news programs, from C-SPAN to prime-time serial drama, Americans learn about politics and understand their political culture via television.[18] Indeed, as political scientist Diana C. Mutz remarks, when trying to understand political communication fully, "the traditional distinctions between news and entertainment content are no longer very helpful."[19]

Although there is forever a tendency to diminish and degrade the role of television in social and political life its increasing presence as a popular and artistic discourse demands continual criticism without jaded cynicism.[20] Unlike other artistic discourse, television is decidedly a medium that must by definition express dominant cultural perspectives to be successful. This perspective reflects the formulation of television as a cultural forum articulated by Horace Newcomb and Paul Hirsch in 1987, when they concluded that the focus of television criticism might profitably be "the cultural role of entertainment" that works parallel with "a close analysis of television program content in all its various textual levels and forms."[21] Seeing television in this way validates its central importance as a source of symbolic action and meaning for a community, as a serious medium of cultural understanding.

Taking television as a cultural forum also motivates analysis of the nature and valence of the meanings emergent from texts in that forum. Television's programming is complex, with a range of options for viewers that Newcomb and Hirsch could hardly have envisioned. Channel proliferation alone means that the forum is bigger and broader, with an array of programming that is almost overwhelming. Newcomb and Hirsch could speculate that "it would be startling to think that mainstream texts in mass society would overtly challenge dominant ideas," but such a possibility is more likely today, given the alternative channels, oppositional programming, and polyglot of voices that frequent the airwaves.[22]

At the same time, much television programming still puts forth a largely dominant message, a "commonality of viewpoints and values" that Larry Gross identifies as "mainstreaming" in conventional television fare.[23] Mainstream discourse embodies a dominant ideological perspective even as it contends with oppositional perspectives and orientations. With an ever-expanding range of channels and technologies, television has the potential, notes John Street, to be the "site of the liveliest and most radical of political exchanges, certainly when compared to the political discussions which are heard in many representative assemblies or which litter daily newspapers."[24] From this negotiation emerges the cultural force of television's discourse, where "contemporary images and narratives appear to be crystalising around distinctive clusters of meaning."[25]

The challenge for a television critic is to navigate the uncertain terrain between television's tendency to mainstream its message to achieve popular success and the occasional articulation of opposition and divergence in the televisual text. The television critic thus explores what Sarah Projansky calls the "media's intricacy" to offer an argument about meaning.[26] Indeed, a television critic enters the stream of conversation that flows through and around the discourse, offering another perspective, a new argument, an alternative reading that embraces the "socially situated" communal readings of television that occur all the time.[27]

From a critical standpoint, then, entertainment television is an art form with considerable reach that, in the case of *TWW*, offers a popular, critically acclaimed, and compelling vision of the U.S. presidency.[28] This vision is complicated, offering viewers messages about the presidency that are rich in detail, often contradictory, and filled with ideological meaning for U.S. political culture.

## The West Wing and the Contemporary U.S. Presidency

NBC debuted *TWW* on September 22, 1999. Just seven months earlier the U.S. Senate acquitted President Bill Clinton of impeachment charges brought against him by the House of Representatives. In a little over a year Americans would vote for Clinton's successor, and at this early stage in 1999 candidates were already soliciting supporters and raising campaign funds. Of course, the 2000 election would prove to be one of the most memorable in U.S. history. Almost two years later two airplanes would fly into the World Trade Center in Manhattan, another into the Pentagon, and yet another into a Pennsylvania field, and more than three thousand individuals from around the world would perish in a tragically remarkable terrorist attack. Soon thereafter the United States embarked on a global "war against terrorism," including military invasions of Afghanistan and Iraq. But in the autumn of 1999 all that still lay ahead. When *TWW* had its debut the economy was robust, terrorism seemed remote and occasional, and the U.S. presidency was in considerable flux.

The uncertainty about the role, scope, and power of the U.S. presidency in the late-twentieth and early-twenty-first centuries was not just the result of Bill Clinton's impeachment. Rather, it emerged from a shifting political environment that encouraged reassessment and realignment about the place of the presidency in U.S. political culture. By the end of the twentieth century, claims Miroff, "the image of the presidency [had] grown more hollow" as a result of a "postmodern spectacle" encouraged by Bill Clinton that left Americans with a sense of "unease."[29] That postmodern spectacle was the predictable consequence of a rapidly developing "rhetorical presidency" that expanded over the span of the twentieth century and significantly altered the nature of this institution.

The rhetorical power of the office, according to Jeffrey Tulis, is a constitutive force that puts forth, from the bully pulpit of the rhetorical presidency, a vision of U.S. national identity through the very discourse used.[30] Beginning with William McKinley, and flourishing under Theodore Roosevelt and Woodrow Wilson in particular, the early rhetorical presidency was an institution less concerned with parochial matters of patronage and governmental administration and more with securing the assent of the broader public through rhetorical appeals and public performance.[31] The result of this shift was that presidents became more overt in their political actions, reaching out to larger and larger audiences as they sought to affect public opinion about important issues of public policy.[32] A notable early example of the shift was

Woodrow Wilson's journey across the country to persuade Americans of the wisdom of his League of Nations proposal.[33]

Over the span of the early to mid-twentieth century the rhetorical presidency produced an institution with greater power, increasing levels of influence, and a more heroic image in the minds of many Americans.[34] Assorted observers noted this rising influence and wrote of the "imperial" presidency and the growth of "presidential power."[35] With two world wars, the depression, and the cold war providing exigencies that demanded strong executive responses, the powers of the presidency centralized, particularly in comparison to the waning powers of Congress. During this period, unlike any other in the history of the United States, the presidency was the focal point of governmental activity, public identification, and national identity. From this position of power, presidents, Erwin C. Hargrove maintains, help "'teach reality' . . . through rhetoric," which "involves the explanation of contemporary problems and issues but, at its best, must invoke and interpret the perennial ideals of the American national experience as expressed in the past and present, and as guides for the future."[36] In the process, Mary E. Stuckey suggests, presidents tell "us stories about ourselves, and in so doing . . . tell us what sort of people we are, [and] how we are constituted as a community."[37]

By the later decades of the twentieth century, however, presidential power and the symbolic role of the presidency had shifted for a variety of reasons. First, specific presidents diminished their own power—and to some degree the power and role of the office—with their misdeeds. Lyndon Johnson's prevarications about the Vietnam War and Richard Nixon's malfeasance in office and abuses of power did much to intensify public mistrust of presidential power.[38] Although Jimmy Carter returned a sense of honesty and morality to the White House, his presidency still failed to adequately address national problems, resulting in his ouster after just one term. Ronald Reagan's restorative presidency was marred by the Iran-Contra affair and Bill Clinton's by a constant barrage of scandal and investigation, some generated by partisan opponents, some by Clinton's own actions, and some by an overeager, adversarial press. In short, presidents from Johnson to Clinton made mistakes, committed crimes, or mishandled national problems so as to erode public trust in the presidency and diminish the stature of the institution.

Second, between the end of the cold war and the attacks on the World Trade Center and the Pentagon in 2001 the national exigencies facing the country seemed less severe, making a strong executive less necessary. Restoration of the constitutional framework of three relatively equal branches of government was reasonable when the threat of nuclear annihilation diminished. Kenneth Walsh remarks that the end of the cold war meant the "President is no longer the final arbiter of an ultimate conflagration," resulting in a "diminution of the presidency itself."[39] In short, before the September 11 attacks the commander-in-chief role of the presidency, unique within the constitutional system, was less important for the health and status of the nation.

A third reason for the decline of the U.S. presidency emerges from social and cultural changes in the later part of the twentieth century—changes that affected the definition of the presidency. Intellectually, the period can be labeled the "postmodern turn" and is characterized by a questioning of long-held truths, a challenge to powerful narratives and ideologies, and a tendency to interrogate the orthodox and the certain so as to manifest new outlooks on social life. Accompanying a postmodern intellectual shift was an increasing level of intrusion by journalists and a proliferation of media outlets because of cable and Internet technologies.[40] As more and more journalists probed presidents and their families about increasingly diverse topics, lessening further the public/private distinction so critical to presidential power, the influence of the presidency declined.[41]

While dominant narratives in science, religion, philosophy, and the humanities were under a postmodern assault intellectually, so, too, were the narratives and norms governing political institutions and the people who control them. This tendency was manifest in revisionist histories and biographies that emphasized unsavory or scandalous behaviors by mythologized political heroes. Americans came to learn of Thomas Jefferson's relationship with one of his slaves, of Abraham Lincoln's bouts with depression and possible gay relationship with an associate, of Franklin Roosevelt's long-standing affair with a secretary and Eleanor Roosevelt's rumored lesbian relationships, and of John Kennedy's dependence on pain medication and his sexual appetites bordering on the insatiable.

The postmodern challenge to the U.S. presidency was one that beckoned journalists and historians alike to attack and erode foundations at the basis of the rhetorical presidency—a distance from the people, a level of privacy for the president, and a sense of trust in the individual and the institution. Richard Waterman, Robert Wright, and Gilbert St. Clair in 1999 concluded that "there are indeed serious problems with the state of the presidency as we come to the end of the twentieth century and get ready to embark upon a new millennium."[42] Yet even as the presidency was in decline, the rhetorical presidency still meant that the president and the office were of critical importance to political and communal affairs in the United States. It was in this atmosphere, at this historical moment, that NBC launched a television program focused on the U.S. presidency—*The West Wing*.

## *The West Wing*

Written almost exclusively, for four seasons, by Aaron Sorkin, *TWW* features the activities of the senior staff in Democratic President Josiah Bartlet's White House.[43] The primary characters in the show include the chief of staff, Leo McGarry; the communications director, Toby Ziegler; the deputy chief of staff, Josh Lyman; the First Lady, Abigail Bartlet; the deputy communications director/speechwriter, Sam Seaborn; and the press secretary, C.J. Cregg (Appendix B).[44] Other prominent characters include the vice president, John Hoynes; the president's daughter, Zoey; the president's personal assistant, Charlie Young; and the assistant to the deputy chief of staff, Donna Moss. Other characters appear regularly, including various high-ranking administration officials, military leaders, staffers and assistants, other members of the president's family, members of Congress, and journalists. The program is decidedly organized around the ensemble; narrative strands regularly involve different cast members and plots woven together in a given episode and over a span of several episodes.

Much of *TWW*'s action occurs in the "west wing" of the White House, although the characters are also portrayed in other settings around Washington and across the nation. Staging is motion-filled and constant.[45] The pacing works in conjunction with the program's serial narrative form. Often the show features plotlines that span several episodes or cannot be resolved by the characters. These plots will often overlap or bear some resemblance to one another. In this way one plot of a given story line may provide a "drama frame" for the central plot in the same narrative, as a news media frame that represents a "way of seeing an event."[46] Even if unrelated, subplots may frame major plotlines and offer cues and clarity about the primary plot of an episode, sometimes complicating narratives through their constructed interrelationships. Thus, a drama frame will often bolster the ideological meaning of a particular narrative.

Our analysis of *TWW* concerns the "first term" of the Bartlet presidency. We analyze the first eighty episodes of the program (and list them in Appendix A), from the pilot airing on September 22, 1999, through "The Long Goodbye," which aired on January 15, 2003. *TWW*'s first season spent considerable time establishing the characters and the drama's narrative parameters, a process that began with the pilot episode and continued for much of the premiere season. In the pilot, one of the show's main characters, speechwriter Sam Seaborn, sleeps with a woman who turns out to be a prostitute, a plotline that resurfaces throughout the season. Other recurring plots included the nomination of a Supreme Court justice, conflict between the president and vice president, the appropriate level of response to an attack on a U.S. military airplane, a crisis between India and Pakistan, gay rights, and drug use by the White House staff. The season ended with a cliff-hanger involving an assassination attempt on the president.

Beginning with the aftermath of the assassination attempt, the second season provided a history of the Bartlet presidential campaign via flashbacks in the season premiere. In the process, *TWW* gave its characters context and a biography that added depth to the narrative. The same flashback technique was also used at the end of the second season to provide a personal history of the president by focusing on his years in a New England prep school. The remainder of the second season, like the first, concerned a variety of issues and plotlines—from U.S. hostages in Colombia to a Justice Department suit against the largest U.S. tobacco companies, from racial tensions to a rescue mission for a tenuous, democratically elected government in Haiti. In addition to these real world concerns, *TWW*'s second season also addressed the president's multiple sclerosis and the attempts to keep it secret, a story line that would continue into the third season.

Much of the *TWW*'s third season addressed two connected plots—the revelation of the president's multiple sclerosis and an ensuing investigation by Congress and an independent prosecutor that took place in the context of the administration's reelection efforts. Lingering plotlines from the second season also included the mission in Haiti and the government's suit against tobacco companies. In addition, the third season raised new issues, specifically about the estate tax. It continued depicting the tension between the president and the vice president, and also showed the president receiving psychiatric counseling.

Because the third season began after the September 11, 2001, terrorist attacks, *TWW* also confronted the issue of global terrorism more directly than in previous seasons. The initial episode of the season, airing on October 3, 2001, was a special installment entitled "Isaac and Ishmael" that specifically addressed the issue of terrorism within the immediate context of the September 11 attacks (chapter 5). *TWW* also manufactured the fictional country of Qumar (a theocratic Muslim monarchy) in the third season and used this device to address issues of gender discrimination in the Muslim world and the problem of state-sponsored terrorism.

At the end of the third season the president ordered the assassination of an official from Qumar suspected of terrorist activity. The consequences of that decision dominate the fourth season's episodes, along with the final stages of the president's campaign for reelection. Over the twelve episodes of the season we address, the president participates in a single debate with his Republican opponent and easily wins reelection, even though leading up to the election there is considerable doubt and angst about the president's political viability. There are substantial depictions of political campaign activity and continued discussion of terrorism in the context of Qumar. This analysis ends just before the inauguration of Bartlet's second term in office.

Critically acclaimed, *TWW* has won numerous awards, including the 2000, 2001, 2002, and 2003 Emmy Awards for Best Drama, two Peabody Awards, several Golden Globe nominations, and three Television Critics Association Awards. *TWW* regularly achieves high ratings, especially among high-income viewers in the eighteen-to-forty-nine age group. Indeed, for its third-season finale *TWW* drew sixteen million viewers—a sizable audience even if a decline from the twenty million that saw the second-season finale.[47] By the fourth season the ratings maintained respectability although they were lower than the third season. In addition, *TWW* achieved a buzz such that it is among the shows that receive considerable media coverage, motivate conversation, and generate excitement. In the words of *George* magazine, *TWW* is "a zeitgeist show, a reflection of the tenor of our times."[48]

Much of the praise for *TWW* is for the show's alleged realism. Many commentators have noted that the drama portrays what the presidency is really like. Former White House Press Secretary Marlin Fitzwater, a *TWW* consultant, concludes that the program "very accurately portrays so many elements of presidential life—the frantic urgency about issues and decisions."[49] To achieve such verisimilitude the show's producers hired consultants and creative writers who have political and White House experience, including former White House Press Secretary Dee Dee Myers, Jimmy Carter's pollster Patrick Cadell, and journalist and former U.S. Senate staffer Lawrence O'Donnell. The result, as *Us* magazine noted in its preview of the program, is that such experts "help ensure accuracy on the set."[50]

Of course, *TWW*'s producers promote the realism of the program, and they received assistance from the news media's coverage of the show. *TV Guide* featured a cover story in July 2000 that profiled all of the cast members of *TWW* and their "real-life" White House counterparts.[51] *Brill's Content* even concluded that *TWW* "presents a truer, more human picture of the people behind the issues than most of today's White House journalists."[52]

*TWW* achieves its realism with well-publicized location shoots in Washington, D.C., occasional appearances of the C-SPAN or MSNBC logos or CNN anchors on *TWW* televisions, and a frequently self-indulgent seriousness about the show's topics and plotlines. It also had regular and publicized contacts with the Clinton White House.

With elaborate set design, location shooting in Washington, and discussion of actual political issues that appear in the news, *TWW* achieves an impressive level of mimetic verisimilitude. The show manipulates the time-space dynamics visually and through dialog to present an image of reality. In that sense *TWW* functions as a chronotope where, as Mikhail Bakhtin noted about the novel, "time . . . thickens, takes on flesh, becomes artistically visible; likewise, space becomes charged and responsive to the movements of time, plot and history."[53]

Some critics, however, are fixated on the realism, or its lack, in the program, holding the show to an impossible standard of accuracy. Myron A. Levine, for instance, faults *TWW* for not capturing every nuance, every potential plot, that characterizes real politics in the White House, such as "staff competition, factionalism, groupthink, and presidential isolation."[54] One could argue that *TWW* has tackled those issues, but more to the point is the unreasonable expectation that the show should be realistic. Other critics, for example, Donnalyn Pompper, praise *TWW* for its realistic depiction of presidential politics, noting that because it portrays the "backstory" of politics it allows Americans to "overcome political malaise and feel connected to the presidency in ways that formal journalism cannot facilitate."[55]

Lost in all of this criticism is the simple truth that *TWW* is a television show, a fictional drama. The mimesis of *TWW* is what matters, not its ability to completely portray the reality (whatever that is) of presidential politics. As Sorkin has remarked, "The appearance of reality is more important than reality."[56] Of critical significance is not the accuracy of its portrayal of life in the White House but its depiction of a presidentiality with ideological power for millions of viewers every week.

Precisely because of its verisimilitude, *TWW* has also been criticized for its political biases as commentators worry that viewers will accept the political viewpoint of the program as real and legitimate. Critics on the right see the program as a forum for the expression of decidedly liberal politics—an example of "political pornography for liberals," according to the *Weekly Standard*'s John Podhoretz.[57] For *The Atlantic Monthly*'s Chris Lehmann, the real danger of *TWW* is that it "lodges the structure of [Bill Clinton's] personality firmly in our collective unconscious, even while strategically erasing its substance."[58] Conservatives point out that *TWW*'s president is a Democrat from New England and that Republicans and other conservatives are frequently portrayed in negative ways. Although it might seem obvious for conservatives to complain about a prime-time television show featuring a liberal, Democratic president, *TWW* has also been criticized for offering an overly conservative message. Writing in *The Progressive,* Fred McKisack asserts that *TWW* demonizes Arabs and underrepresents minorities in the White House, and, he argues, it is time to "drop the pretense that this is somehow a pro-lefty, commie-lovin' roll-a-doobie."[59]

Debates about *TWW*'s realism or political orientation divert critical attention from the representational quality of the program—its capacity to offer a meaningful and powerful rhetoric concerning the U.S. presidency. This book confronts that dimension of the program directly, assessing how *TWW* works in a political culture where the presidency is still a forming, ever-changing institution.

## *The West Wing* and U.S. Nationalism

Our central premise about the ideological influence of *The West Wing* is that the drama reflects the ideological history and contestations of U.S. nationalism from the country's inception through its contemporary conflicts. On one hand, we situate the drama in the sweep of commitments to nationalism prevalent in U.S. history and politics. On the other hand, theories of nationalism, as they intersect with scholarship on romance, gender, race, and militarism, are a critical lens through which to examine this political text. In so doing we move beyond stale debates about *TWW*'s realism or specific politics. Instead, reading *TWW* for its nationalistic connotations and implications demonstrates how popular culture sustains and challenges existing conceptions of U.S. nationalism through presidential depictions, shaping the meaning of what it means to be an American and the identity of the United States as a nation-state.[60]

We work from the belief that nations are primarily rhetorical constructions—what Benedict Anderson famously called "imagined communities." The critical task in understanding such communities is not discerning their geographical boundaries or constitutional essence but discovering how they are constructed. In the process, the analysis of nationalism recognizes, as M. Lane Bruner notes, that there is a "never-ending and politically consequential rhetorical struggle over national identity" and that struggle results in the articulation of a "national character."[61] In other words, to quote Anderson, "Communities are to be distinguished, not by their falsity/genuineness, but by the style in which they are imagined."[62] In the United States the presidency is central to this rhetorical, imaginary process. As Vanessa Beasley argues convincingly, "The rhetorical presidency can be understood as an institutional response to the United States' diversity. Rather than 'going public' solely to promote specific legislative or policy measures, chief executives may have also used the bully pulpit to 'form a mass' out of an increasingly diversifying American people."[63] We consider one discourse in the imaginary of the United States and seek to explain how that discourse, *TWW,* defines and shapes a vision of U.S. nationalism, articulating a struggle over the constitution of the U.S. national character.

The sense of nationalism that creates and binds a given community is constructed in a variety of ways by a range of public institutions and voices. The polyglot of nationalistic texts continues to expand as technology proliferates. More and more voices compete to define nations from a range of channels and media, confirming Anderson's conclusion that "we are faced with a world in which the figuring of imagined reality was overwhelmingly visual and aural."[64] Just as the U.S. presidency is an institution defined by a range of discourse from news to popular culture, so, too, is U.S. nationalism emergent from the interplay of an array of texts. Tamar Mayer suggests that the "'ideal' nation and its 'model' members are represented in arts, literature and the media, in public speeches and in the writings of the nation's leaders—in every medium through which the nation is mobilized."[65]

In many ways texts of nationalism typically offer a mythic ideal of individual and collective identity. That is especially the case in times of crisis or uncertainty. Moreover, such nationalism may employ nostalgic images of the past or jingoistic visions of the present to solidify support for the nation and reaffirm collective identity. "In times of change or crisis," Jean Pickering and Suzanne Kehde conclude, "nations look to the past and infer a narrative that erases all confusion and contradiction . . . [and offer] a mythic national identity that, Platonic fashion, has presumably always existed." Such images are not monolithic or simplistic, Pickering and Kehde note, but will emerge from serious writers and others who produce even the most sophisticated cultural artifacts.[66]

Because nationalistic texts are not unified, especially those that emanate from artistic or cultural venues, the analysis of such texts must account for and appreciate their polyvalence.[67] In calling *TWW* a nationalistic text we are not suggesting that it presents a single, patriotic, pro-American vision of the United States, although such messages are frequently present in *TWW*. Rather, we embrace the show's complex nationalism and tendency to offer a multifaceted sense of U.S. national identity.

Seeing *TWW* as a nationalistic text calls attention to the ways in which the discourse constructs a specific vision of the United States, "Americanness," and the presidency within this historical and ideological context. The intersectional construction occurs on several different levels that transform over the duration of the drama. Beginning with an examination of presidential romance and nationalism, we progress to an examination of the gendered, racial, and then militarized implications of U.S. nationalism as reflected in *TWW*. As each chapter progresses we assess the intersectionality of these nationalistic discourses.[68]

In chapter 1 we explore how *TWW* offers a multilayered, romantic vision of the U.S. presidency. Highlighting how the show functions mimetically to reconstruct a vision of the presidency, we emphasize how *TWW*'s romantic vision of the presidency is complex. Specifically, *TWW* is not content to offer a one-dimensional president who works heroically to achieve a greater good or who is blatantly and obviously corrupt. Instead, *TWW* displays a presidential administration that often behaves heroically and rehabilitates politics through a commitment to public service and communal progress. Simultaneously, the "backstage" position of *TWW* offers a vision of a president confronting personal insecurities, family crises, staff dramas, and physical infirmity. In this way *TWW* both bolsters and undermines its romantic portrayal of the presidency and complicates its nationalistic message. Viewers are reminded that just as the presidency is a site of nationalistic meaning, and that this president and his staff represent the best of U.S. idealism and romance, the humanity and idiosyncrasies of individual leaders also mitigate the presidency's unified nationalism.

A central component in the construction of U.S. nationalism is the consistent depiction of gender roles and a decidedly masculine vision of the U.S. as a nation. Our goal in chapter 2 is to examine the gendered and romantic nationalism of *TWW* with a particular focus on how the program articulates a specific vision of nationalism ordered by gendered norms and historically rooted gender roles. Some critics applaud *TWW* for its depiction of women, noting that these women are frequently portrayed in positions of real power and authority. Christina Lane, for example, praises the show as it "makes efforts to revise traditional power relations and reorient its male characters toward a valuation of female resilience and community."[69]

We, too, celebrate *TWW*'s depiction of strong women in powerful roles. At the same time, however, as a nationalistic text *TWW* maintains and reinforces traditional gender roles. The presidency is defined quite clearly in the show as a patriarchially dominated family. Women are routinely sexualized in ways that the men are not, and the messages that emanate from female characters routinely confirm powerful gender ideologies that are the bedrock of U.S. national identity. Our goal is to explore the ideological complexity of gender in *TWW*, noting how the text critiques and reinforces powerful gender stereotypes and challenges and preserves powerful gender norms and roles.

Our discussion of racial nationalism in chapter 3 also considers the intersectionality of race, gender, and romance. *TWW* premiered in the 1999–2000 television season, one in which the television industry faced considerable criticism for its failure to depict positive characters of color.[70] Indeed, the entire senior staff depicted in *TWW* is white. In response to challenges from the NAACP and others to include more people of color in its cast, *TWW* chose to have an African American actor play the personal assistant to the president—the president's "body man." *TWW*'s president appoints a Latino to the Supreme Court, has an African American woman as the national security advisor, and is regularly advised by an African American chair of the Joint Chiefs of Staff, evidencing the ways in which NBC responded to the call to diversify casting.

But the role that race plays in *TWW* is more complicated than the insertion of people of color into the cast. Chapter 3 explores the *TWW*'s manifestation of competing aspects of U.S. nationalism—a "civic nationalism" that upholds cherished American ideals of equality and justice and a "racialized nationalism" that is exclusionary and manifests a powerful whiteness in defining the U.S. nation.[71] We dispute the all-too-simple readings of race in *TWW* that consider the show to be either a space for the moral wisdom and voice of people of color or a hopelessly white vision of the U.S. presidency.[72] Again, as with gender, the messages emanating from *TWW* about race are complicated and polyvalent, presenting a complex vision of U.S. nationalism that still grapples with difficult issues of race.

In chapter 4 we examine the depiction of a militarized nationalism in *TWW* and again focus on intersectionality, paying attention to the relationship between *TWW*'s depictions of militarism and romance, gender, and race. In the process, we explore how nationalism perpetuates and reinscribes the power of the U.S. presidency in international affairs. The militarism of the show is ambivalent—Bartlet is identified as a president who has not served in the military and who wrestles with difficult military decisions. There is also ambivalence in the tension expressed between a realist orientation to foreign policy and a postrealist vision of the post–cold war world inhabited by the Bartlet administration. Despite that ambivalence, however, *TWW* recurrently invokes the military responsibilities of a white male president as well as his relationship with military leaders, particularly the chair of the Joint Chiefs. In this way *TWW* reestablishes the power of the president's romantic, commander-in-chief role, highlighting it as central, even dominant, in the wide scheme of presidential activity.

Of course, with such depictions *TWW* elevates threats from abroad and national security issues as a president's primary concerns. Because such issues, by definition, stress the commander-in-chief responsibilities of the presidency, they fit the show's focus on the executive branch and reinforce its depiction of a powerful and independent president acting unilaterally to achieve change and enact policy. This administration, furthermore, confronts realist challenges emanating from a proverbial adversary or representative of familiar geopolitical tensions (e.g., Russia) and postrealist problems indicative of post–cold war reality (e.g., global terrorism or civil war in Haiti). Using such issues as significant plot devices and drama frames, *TWW* positions the presidency as a focal point of all national activity, furthering a vision of U.S. nationalism that emphasizes the president as an embodiment of national identity. This militarized nationalism frames domestic concerns, especially in episodes depicting the president's reelection efforts.

Our analysis of *TWW* concludes with discussion of the program's predominant nationalistic messages, reflecting on the power of popular culture to imagine the American presidency, the U.S. nation, and a vision of U.S. nationalism that is romanticized, gendered, racialized, and militarized. In particular we discuss how each of these dimensions comes together in *TWW*'s direct response to the September 11, 2001, attacks on the World Trade Center and the Pentagon in the episode entitled "Isaac and Ishmael." Rarely has a prime-time television program responded to a national crisis with such immediacy and publicity. "Isaac and Ishmael" is unique not only for its direct response to the 9/11 terrorist attacks but also for its expression of a nationalism that is romantic, gendered, racialized, and militarized. In this way the episode represents the larger nationalistic message of *TWW,* and we explore the episode's meaning for understanding the power of the program's nationalistic vision of the presidency.

*TWW* offers viewers from around the world and in the United States a discourse about the American presidency that expresses the ambivalence of U.S. nationalism in the late twentieth and early twenty-first centuries. It is a presidentiality that taps into the institution's history, reacts to its context, and ideologically demarcates an image of the presidency for millions of viewers. Critically understanding *TWW* contributes to appreciating popular culture's political influence and the ability of such discourse to imagine a specific depiction of U.S. nationalism.

Our critical understanding of *TWW*'s nationalistic meanings and messages embraces a view of nationalism "not as the repository of a unitary, immutable, and essentialized identity," as Robert Burgoyne remarks, "but rather as the basis of critique, the basis for interrogating and exposing the relations of power that lie at the heart of the idea of nation."[73] This interrogation and critique exposes not only the relations of power characteristic of U.S. nationalism but also the dispute over what U.S. nationalism actually means—or what it means to be an American. In this way our analysis appreciates the influence of the "cultural nation" or ways in which nationalism emerges from the "folk, ethnic, and civic elements" of public life.[74] It also permits the space for making "audible the oppositional voices" that question dominant nationalisms and invite critique of hegemonic visions of the U.S. nation.[75]

# 1

## *The West Wing* as a Political Romance

Say they're smug and superior. Say their approach to public
policy makes you want to tear your hair out. Say they like high
taxes and spending your money. Say they want to take your
guns and open your borders. But don't call them worthless . . .
the people that I have met have been extraordinarily qualified—
their intent is good. Their commitment is true. They are
righteous and they are patriots.

—Ainsley Hayes, "In This White House"

IN 2001 the Council for Excellence in Government conducted a survey that asked Americans for their perceptions about government employees. The study discovered that elected officials had the "second most improved image" among all occupations, moving them ahead of business leaders and teachers in public esteem. The council attributed this rise in esteem to the positive portrayals of government officials on *The West Wing*. Because of the "depth of its [*TWW*'s] characters," the council concluded, and because of its focus on "real issues and sincere commitments" that reject the "cynical" vision of politics, *TWW* has done much to rehabilitate the image of government officials and political leaders.[1]

Such is the power of popular culture for public impressions of government, institutions, and individuals. Given this power, and given its role as a significant source of narratives about the presidency for vast audiences in the United States and abroad, popular culture ideologically shapes our understanding of this institution. Moreover, given the presidency's pivotal place in the government and as a representation of U.S. national identity, the narratives can function as significant rhetorics of nationalism. They construct a fusion between the fictional U.S. presidency and the values, the rhetorical markers, of U.S. nationalism.

Emergent public nationalisms are frequently defined via presidents who act as romantic heroes, protecting the nation, serving their country, and doing what is right. Even the most cursory examination of Hollywood presidents from the 1990s reveals a range of romantic heroes questing for justice and fighting for the American way.[2] Harrison Ford's President James Marshall in *Air Force One,* before saving his airplane, family, and staff from evil Russian terrorists, heroically proclaims before a ballroom of diplomats in Moscow, "Terror is not a legitimate system of government. And to those who commit the atrocities I say, we will no longer tolerate, we will no longer negotiate, and we will no longer be afraid. It's your turn to be afraid."[3] As aliens invade earth and threaten to destroy the planet in *Independence Day,* Bill Pullam's President Thomas Whitmore triumphantly declares, "From this day on, the fourth day of July will no longer be remembered as an American holiday but as the day that all of mankind declared we will not go quietly into the night. We will not vanish without a fight. We will live on. We will survive." He then boards his fighter jet to lead the human crusade against the invading aliens.[4] Morgan Freeman's President Tom Beck offers a final sense of closure after an asteroid hits earth and kills millions in *Deep Impact,* vowing to preserve the United States and its way of life. Michael Douglas's President Andrew Shepherd is the ultimate romantic hero in *The American President,* who not only chooses love before politics but also idealistically waxes eloquent about the genius of the American government.[5] Even a fake president, Kevin Kline's *Dave,* manages to engage the cabinet in a budget-cutting exercise to find enough money to save a homeless shelter. Indeed, with predictable regularity in films and television programs, presidents are often heroic figures, men (and they are always men) who do what is right and are noble, true, and committed to good causes and pure ends.

Romantic depictions of U.S. presidents, though, are not limited to popular culture. Michael Nelson remarks that one of the dominant modes for understanding effective or strong presidencies is a "savior model" of presidential leadership, where the president functions as the "chief guardian of the national interest, not only in foreign policy . . . but also in domestic affairs because of the pluralistic structure of government and society."[6] This romantic vision of the U.S. presidency exerts considerable influence on presidential behavior, contends Philip Abbott, because presidents seek to emulate their successful and strong predecessors. His theory of the "belated" president reveals that "without the creation of a poetic personage and the formulation of a narrative conveyed poetically, strong presidencies cannot be formed."[7] The conflation of romantic narrative in both popular television and presidential discourse is therefore not surprising. "Art cannot in essence be different from other cooperative social processes," Christopher Caudwell reveals.[8] Or, put differently by Northrop Frye, romance "is essentially a verbal imitation of ritual or symbolic human action."[9]

Whether in popular culture or on the news, romantic depictions of the presidency and individual presidents respond to their context and offer a resonant and hopeful vision of this institution. So, as media critic James Chesebro maintains, in the aftermath of the Vietnam War and Watergate, "Americans apparently found romantic conceptions increasingly satisfying and reliable" in their favorite television shows.[10] Similarly, Jimmy Carter's unsuccessful presidency created a context where the political culture craved a heroic, romantic president, and Ronald Reagan played that role well.[11] One of the tasks of a president, Woodrow Wilson concluded almost a century ago, was to make certain that "his position takes the imagination of the country."[12] A powerful way to achieve that goal is to become the nation's hero within a romantic narrative of the nation's history.

*TWW* responded to the uncertain state of the U.S. presidency in the late 1990s and early 2000s by offering a romantic vision of the office embodied by the person of President Jed Bartlet. Bartlet is a heroic figure on *TWW*, surrounded by other heroic individuals who are on a quest for a better America and a more humane world. Moreover, they confront a variety of villains and enemies attempting to thwart their work. But *TWW*'s romance challenges many of the conventions of the genre. In this way the show offers an ambivalent romance where the conventions of the narrative emplotment are complicated and interrogated within the plots and characterizations of the program.

For many romance narratives, the juxtaposition of the hero and the villain is an instrumental strategy, representing a glimpse into the hierarchy of the larger culture and its discourses. A conventional romance narrative, according to Mark Hunter, "plunges us into passion, conflict, triumph, and loss, then carries us back to the starting point, as though from out of a dream." Such a narrative "recounts a quest—for the truth and virtue that will rout the demons of the night, for a lost love or lost identity, for the paradise on earth where its heroes will regain happiness."[13] Frye argues that "in every age the ruling social or intellectual class tends to project its ideals in some form of romance, where the virtuous heroes and beautiful heroines represent the ideals and the villains the threats to their ascendancy."[14] The popularity of romance, maintains Frye, is grounded in the assumption that such a quest narrative "avoids the ambiguities of ordinary life, where everything is a mixture of good and bad, and where it is difficult to take sides or believe that people are consistent patterns of virtue or vice."[15]

Our vision of *TWW*'s romance should not be confused with the oppositional antinarratives that characterize much literature described as "postmodern." As some writers seek to "implode oppositions between high and low art, fantasy and reality, fiction and fact," they generate avant-garde texts that are unconventional and antagonistic.[16] *TWW* hardly qualifies as an avant-garde text. Our conception of its romance is somewhat narrower and refers to a romance that challenges traditional narrative frameworks where ambiguity is minimized and contingency ignored.

Instead of assuming the moral clarity of romance texts that Frye advances, we contend that contemporary romance discourse, like the political culture that produces it, can reflect deep-seated ideological dissonance, making the distinctions between good and evil more ambiguous in the postmodern age. "The stark good-versus-evil of romances often proves problematical for politics," notes Lewis.[17] John M. Murphy likewise reveals that in some contemporary campaign histories "the villain is not purely evil, nor [was] the hero purely good."[18]

These ideological complexities not only mirror cultural conflict but also authenticate the mimetic features of these romance texts. Such a presidential romance, which provides "for a freedom from tradition" and an "activation of difference," offers a complex presidentiality reflective of the ambiguity that characterizes the contemporary presidency.[19] This polyvalent image is trapped between a more progressive, community-based notion of inclusivity and an individualistic image that perpetuates the traditional, conservative vision of a hero (usually a white, male hero) embodying infinite power for righteous ends.

*TWW*'s romance can also be read from the perspective of nationalism, confirming the dependence of such nationalism on the narratives and rhetorics put forth to define contemporary national identity. The idea of the nation "as a form of narrative—textual strategies, metaphoric displacements, sub-texts and figurative stratagems" is rooted in a history that denies narrower and more rationalistic visions of the nation-state.[20] Moreover, the romance, according to literary scholar Doris Sommer, is a genre "which is itself a marriage of historical allegory and sentimentality" and that has worked vigorously to promote nationalisms around the world.[21] The genre is powerfully functional in the U.S. context. "That a romantic strain exists in American history and politics," contends Fisher, "is attested by the existence of American heroes, in particular, certain presidents."[22] Presidents are ideal romantic heroes in the U.S. context precisely because they are able to "connect a vision of the future with the mythic narratives of America's past."[23] Thus they express a vision of U.S. nationalism.

## Finding Order amid Chaos: Constructing the Presidential Hero on *The West Wing*

*The West Wing* was never supposed to be about the president. Working from his script notes for *The American President*, Aaron Sorkin envisioned a television drama about the inner workings of the White House staff, where the president would only appear occasionally. Sorkin was concerned that "if the President is a character, he's going to take up all the oxygen in the room." With the casting of Martin Sheen, and the realization of the importance of this character for the integrity of the drama, the original focus shifted, and the president became a pivotal, critical character on *TWW*.[24]

*TWW*'s construction of its presidential hero is unique, moreover, because it resists the usual dichotomies that typically occur in Hollywood presentations of the presidency. "Hollywood has cast its contemporary presidents," Roper contends, "either as personally corrupt and using government as a conspiracy intent on deception, or as straightforward action heroes whose exploits on celluloid may redress the inadequacies of their real counterparts in office."[25] *TWW*'s concept of the presidency is a vision of the office, and the individual who occupies it, as simultaneously heroic and human, romantic and flawed. In that sense *TWW* reaches beyond the Hollywood clichés to put forth a depiction of the presidency that is largely atypical of popular culture's representations of the office.

Central to the mimesis of *TWW* is its characterization of the presidency as primarily concerned with the management of chaos and uncertainty. In this sense *TWW* presents the requisite conflict required of the romance narrative.[26] Intriguingly, order and romance are inscribed on *TWW* by the manner in which the president and his staff manage external conflicts and challenges—fulfilling the "quest" dimensions of a romantic narrative—even as they experience internal questions and anxieties that interrogate the unified vision of the romantic hero in the narrative.

Indeed, from this perspective disorder represents an integral theme rather than a plot device to be resolved quickly at the end of each hour's episode, and such chaos reigned throughout the first eighteen of twenty-two episodes of the premiere season. Much of the first season of *TWW* highlights the inability of the Bartlet administration to fully control the nation's chaotic problems. Because the program centers on what Joshua Meyrowitz calls the "backstage" dimensions of the presidency, the personal anxieties of the president (and his staff) magnify and intensify the turmoil characteristic of the first season.[27] The result is a program that reveals the contingent nature of presidential action and emphasizes the anxiety of those who confront national problems. As such, *TWW* is a drama that both reaffirms and confronts the typical romantic conception of a presidential hero. At the same time, the show positions the president as a central figure in U.S. national life, putting forth via its presentation a sense of chaos and contingency. Such a version of U.S. nationalism sees the world as chaotic and in need of guidance from the president individually and from the United States more generally.

*TWW*'s pilot episode establishes the parameters of the Bartlet administration's chaotic presidency. It features a largely absent President Bartlet, who is missing from the White House as he recovers from a bicycle crash; it also reveals how little the staffers know about the various problems they confront. One plotline, for instance, concerns a Cuban boatlift headed toward Florida. Attempting to solicit information about its scope, Chief of Staff Leo McGarry realizes he has no information and asks his deputy, "True or false: If I were to stand on high ground in Key West with a good pair of binoculars, I'd be as informed as I am right now?" Later in the hour speechwriter Sam Seaborn summarizes the chaos of the pilot episode:

> I just found out the *Times* is publishing a poll that says a considerable portion of Americans feel the White House has lost energy and focus. A perception that's not likely to be altered by the video footage of the President riding his bicycle into a tree. As we speak, the Coast Guard is fishing Cubans out of the Atlantic Ocean while the Governor of Florida wants to blockade the Port of Miami. A good friend of mine's about to get fired for going on television and making sense, and it turns out I accidentally slept with a prostitute last night.[28]

Succeeding episodes exacerbate the uncertainty, chaos, and self-doubt that resonates throughout the first season of the Bartlet presidency as the staffers and the president confront crisis after crisis.

*TWW* arrays a cast of characters to tackle this chaos who are well-educated, honest, caring, and competent. The characters of the show routinely stride through the halls of the White House, speaking fluently, even eloquently, about national policy, philosophy, politics, and history. These political heroes demonstrate the "exceptional strength or ability" that is consistent with John Cawelti's construction of the "superhero" figure in adventure and romance narratives.[29] Moreover, in romance narratives, Chesebro writes, "romantic agents must be intellectually superior to others" and capable of "exercising superior control" over "their environment."[30] That dimension of *TWW*'s heroism is most clearly demonstrated by the intellectualism that is a vital part of President Bartlet's character.

*TWW*, generally, rejects a "common man" view of the presidency, offering instead an "intellectual" president as its romantic hero. In so doing, *TWW*'s president is somewhat unusual. David Burton maintains that the typical image of presidents is generally "devoid of intellectual distinction," even if the office was held in highest esteem when "American chief executives were republican variants of the philosopher-kings celebrated by the Enlightenment and scholarly witnesses to the very history they were working to make."[31] *TWW* offers a romantic hero who achieves heroic status not from military accomplishment or exemplary physical deeds but from a powerful—indeed, Nobel Prize–winning—intellect.

President Bartlet is rarely seen in situations or contexts on *TWW* during the first season that emphasize fealty with the people (e.g., shaking hands, seeking input from the public, and giving speeches). His intellectual capacities, however, are frequently displayed. Bartlet's intellectualism is firmly established in the second episode of the first season, "Post Hoc, Ergo Propter Hoc," when he quizzes his staff over the meaning of *post hoc, ergo propter hoc* and is credentialed by Josh as "Jed Bartlet, Nobel Laureate in Economics, three-term congressman, two-term Governor." In the same episode, a military officer tells Bartlet, "You have a once-in-a-generation mind, sir." Bartlet also frequently performs his intellectualism. In "A Proportional Response" he laments the inability of the United States to protect its citizens around the world:

> Did you know that two thousand years ago a Roman citizen could walk across the face of the known world free of the fear of molestation. He could walk across the earth unharmed, cloaked only in the words *Civis Romanis;* I am a Roman citizen. So real was the retribution of Rome, universally understood as certain, should any harm befall even one of its citizens. . . . Where is the retribution for the families and where is the warning to the rest of the world that Americans shall walk this earth unharmed, lest the clenched fist of the mightiest military force in the history of mankind comes crashing down on your house?

Both the Western-based historical allusion and the vocabulary of this statement reflect Bartlet's intellectualism and his ability to apply what he has learned to his official duties, molding him into the image of an intellectually heroic and elitist president.

Not only is Bartlet intellectually superior to the average voter but he is also surrounded by similarly intelligent people, many with advanced degrees and an extraordinary command of a range of topics and policies. We learn, for example, that Sam's law degree is from Duke, Josh's from Harvard, that C.J. is a graduate of University of California-Berkeley, and that Mandy has a Ph.D. in political science. With only some inconsistencies, the staff is highly informed on a variety of topics, and when they are not another staff member will routinely offer a crash course in the subject at hand. The president's aides understand and are competent in a remarkably large array of subjects and public policies. Together, these constructions of the president and his staff counter what Waterman, Wright, and St. Clair call "the common man image" of the presidency demonstrated by such presidents as Andrew Jackson, Abraham Lincoln, Harry Truman, and Jimmy Carter.[32] *TWW* constructs its president and his staff as the antithesis of the common person.

Alongside Bartlet's intellect is his role as a successor to a line of strong and secure presidents. *TWW* goes to considerable lengths to position the Bartlet presidency within the history of American presidents. "The notion that later presidents draw strength and support from their predecessors," Abbott concludes, "is at the core of a major ritual of American political culture." Indeed, Abbott says, presidents must engage in this "ritual task of emulation" in order to be successful.[33] *TWW* similarly displays its president within the context of U.S. history and the range of presidents that shaped that history. In the pilot episode, *TWW* visually places its characters firmly in the Oval Office, highlighting the Seal of the United States on the office's floor. Pictures of presidents past are everywhere in all episodes. What is more, such pictures are usually of easily recognized, strong presidents—George Washington, Abraham Lincoln, and Theodore Roosevelt. Although Bartlet occasionally invokes earlier presidents, *TWW* visually locates him within the trajectory of his strong predecessors, fulfilling the ritual task of emulation necessary for successful presidencies. Segues between scenes and out of commercials also frequently feature dramatic shots of the White House or other Washington, D.C., monuments and landmarks. With all of these techniques *TWW* reinforces the heroism of its protagonists as they carry on the legacy of great U.S. presidents in the venue of political power in the United States.

*TWW* constructs its presidential hero as confronting disorder and chaos armed with a powerful intellect and committed aides and supporters and emulating the strength of former presidents. Typically, though, romance narratives also develop through a specific "conflict between the hero and his enemy."[34] Certainly, the depiction by *TWW* of a chaotic political environment, with complex foreign challenges and complicated domestic problems, allows for the conventional construction of a presidential hero to confront such concerns and enemies. But on *TWW* this dialectic is also internalized as Bartlet tackles psychological enemies as well as more typical external foes. On *TWW*'s fifth episode, "The Crackpots and These Women," for example, the staff confronts numerous citizens who have fringe concerns that demand their attention. As the episode closes President Bartlet confides to Toby Ziegler his own internal insecurities, offering the ultimate in backstage understanding of presidential motives and anxieties:

> BARTLET: I know I disappoint you sometimes. I mean, I can sense your disappointment. And I only get mad because I know you're right a lot of the times. . . . The other night when we were playing basketball, did you mean what you said? My demons were shouting down the better angels in my brain?
>
> TOBY: Yes, sir. I did . . .
>
> BARTLET: I suppose you're right.
>
> TOBY: Tell you what though, sir. In a battle between a president's demons and his better angels, for the first time in a long while, I think we might just have ourselves a fair fight.

Put simply, *TWW*'s central heroic figure is not invincible. In Bartlet's vulnerability we see a challenge to the typical romantic narrative. This romantic ambivalence is enhanced further by the revelation in episode twelve ("He Shall from Time to Time") that President Bartlet is suffering from a form of recurring multiple sclerosis, information that has been hidden from the public. The president is even portrayed as weak by a Supreme Court justice who charges that he lacks the "guts" that the American people require of their president ("The Short List"). *TWW* presents viewers with a romantic hero who is humanized and flawed by the portrayal of his inner conflicts. Indeed, as Caren Deming concludes, characters constructed in this way are "heroic" because they "keep trying" in the face of adversity.[35]

These psychological and political struggles not only involve the president but also include other members of his staff. *TWW*'s narrative represents a collectivist notion of the institution, deviating from a stereotypical romantic hero-president who acts alone in a noble quest. Military decisions are portrayed, for example, as collective decision-making efforts involving the joint chiefs of staff, the president, and the president's chief of staff. In episode three of the first season, "A Proportional Response," this collectivity expands to include the backing of the "Western coalition" (e.g., Britain and Japan) in retaliation against the downing of a U.S. jet in the Middle East. As the president anxiously prepares to speak publicly about the retaliatory bombing all his staffers are present, busily assisting him during the chaotic scene. The episode ends on another note of collectivism when the president invites Charlie Young, an applicant for the job as personal assistant to the president, to "come help us out." Charlie's mother, as revealed earlier in the episode, was a District of Columbia police officer shot in the line of duty. Bartlet appeals to this event as he persuades Charlie to join the team in the effort to remove cop-killer bullets from the streets.

Later in the first season *TWW* provides a behind-the-scenes look into how the Bartlet administration engineered passage of a gun control bill (H.R. 802) through the collective efforts of Josh, Leo, and the vice president. Not only is the president uninvolved in securing the remaining five votes but also, during the bill's passage, he is asleep because of a backache that required medication ("Five Votes Down"). Such depictions disrupt the romantic notion of a heroic president as "the self-determining, autonomous individual."[36]

Presidential heroism is likewise problematized in these episodes. In the "Five Votes Down" installment, the president's disengagement is accented by his pain killer–induced interactions with his staff, leading him to nonsensically expound on Toby's "nice name," for example. Josh is portrayed as the one responsible for delivering four of the five swing votes, yet Josh wins over one recalcitrant congressional leader with political threats ("vote yes or you're not even going to be on the ballot two years from now"). Leo's "heroism" is notable because he convinces the vice president to deliver the remaining congressional leader's vote. That valor, however, is contextualized within the revelation of Leo's past drug and alcohol dependency and his wife's quest for a divorce because he paid more attention to his job than their marriage. The vice president is also presented as self-interested when he obtains the final vote for bill 802. He is, he declares, "going to be President of the United States one day." Thus, *TWW*'s presidentiality is predicated, in part, on a collective vision of leadership that destabilizes the heroes of the collective as well as the president's claims to valor.

In addressing the chaos that swirls around him during the first season of *TWW*, Bartlet's hesitant, tentative presidency comes to its apotheosis in the eighteenth episode, "Let Bartlet Be Bartlet." Facing conflicts over gays and lesbians in the military, low approval ratings in polls, an internal memo questioning the capacity of the administration to exert leadership, and a general malaise among the staff, President Bartlet and his chief of staff redirect the administration's focus. In the process, the episode articulates a presidentiality that is ideologically meaningful and characterized by a commitment to honesty, candor, and an unbridled pursuit of policy and ideals—all noble, romantic goals for the presidential hero to pursue. Such a vision emerges most powerfully in Bartlet and Leo's oddly therapeutic conversation at the end of the episode:

> BARTLET: I don't want to feel like this anymore.
> LEO: You don't have to.
> BARTLET: I don't want to go to sleep like this.
> LEO: You don't have to.
> BARTLET: I want to speak.
> LEO: Say it out loud. Say it to me.
> BARTLET: This is more important than reelection. I want to speak now.
> LEO: Say it again.
> BARTLET: This is more important than reelection. I want to speak now.
> LEO: Now we're in business!

The episode ends with Leo mobilizing the senior staff, who all assert loyalty to President Bartlet as they each proudly declare, "I serve at the pleasure of the president" ("Let Bartlet Be Bartlet").

In the concluding episodes of the first season a more decisively heroic president of the familiar archetypal romance emerges. At the end of episode twenty, "Mandatory Minimums," Bartlet is in bed as the entire senior staff, anxious over the events of the day, comes into his bedroom, one by one, seeking sage advice, solace, or forgiveness. The president calmly listens yet commands, "There'll be more meetings tomorrow. In the meantime, everybody calm down. Leo's got your engines fired like you're running Daytona. That's fine, keep them there. Guess what. Mistakes are going to be made. Minimize them, fix them, move on. . . . Listen to me. I have never lost an election in my life. If we do this right, people are going to respond." At the end of the episode the president confides to Leo, "I'm sleeping better. And when I sleep, I dream about a great discussion with experts and ideas and diction and energy and honesty. And when I wake up, I think, I can sell that." Although the notion of the collective is still present in *TWW*'s romance, individualism is more prominent. The president ends the day by himself in his bedroom, preparing to dream of greatness as the lone romantic leader of the United States.

*TWW*'s first season ultimately resolves both the internal and external disorders confronting the Bartlet presidency by firmly establishing the character of the presidential hero. Much of the first season is devoted to character development and establishing plot, setting, and drama. Within this developing framework the president emerges as a heroic figure—an individual who fights the good fight, questing for justice and honorable ends. The primary villain this presidential hero faces is the chaos of national and international affairs. Other villains—whether Republicans, Christian conservatives, or nuclear weapons–wielding governments in South Asia—each underscore the disorder facing Bartlet and his aides as they work for order guided by principle. But in the end it is the intellectually gifted, committed, honest presidential hero who can tame the chaos and restore an order rooted in the ideals of the nation.

*TWW*'s first season was dominated by a central tension—between the quest for order and the internal interrogations of the president and his staff—and that tension is most starkly presented in an episode from the first season, "The State Dinner." Facing a state visit from an uncooperative Indonesian president, the president also confronts two drama frames—a major hurricane off the Atlantic Coast and an impending national trucking strike. At the conclusion of the episode First Lady Abigail Bartlet says to her husband, "You have a big brain, a good heart, and an ego the size of Montana. . . . You don't have the power to fix everything, but I do like watching you try." With that one line *TWW* captures the romantic appeal of its presidential character and the collective heroism of his White House—watching them try to fix everything, pursuing their quest for justice, as they face the extraordinary challenges of contemporary life and the internal doubts that face us all.

## Suppressing the Internal Demons: Deconstructing Presidential Heroism in *The West Wing*

Disorder and chaos appear in almost every episode of *TWW*. After all, as a drama about presidential politics *TWW*'s mimetic hopes rest on viewers perceiving that it is capturing the contingencies and unexpectedness of contemporary life in a fictional White House. The show works in the realm of what historian Hayden White has termed "figural realism," or the sense that fiction and reality exist on the same "ontological order."[37] Yet within the "realistic" chaos of *TWW*'s political domain is the reaffirmation of presidential heroism, especially as established in the latter episodes of the show's first season. Shunning the popular denigration of politicians as fake or insincere, *TWW* articulates a presidential heroism grounded in authenticity such that the program's heroic figure emerges when freed from the pressures of re-election and is allowed to speak openly and honestly. Only through such candor and authenticity, *TWW* suggests, can the president and his heroic staff strive to manage the chaos they confront.

At the end of the first season, *TWW* artfully crafts a suspenseful cliffhanger designed to peak viewer interest and maintain viewer involvement with the show over the rerun-laden summer months. Coming as it did at the end of a season that establishes the romantic heroism of Jed Bartlet as president of the United States, "What Kind of Day Has It Been" furthers that heroism. Most of the episode reinforces the "Let Bartlet Be Bartlet" theme as the president engages young citizens in Rosslyn, Virginia, in a stimulating discussion about national issues while his staff successfully manages a series of chaotic events. Following this townhall meeting Bartlet is shaking hands with voters when gunfire rings out and chaos, again, ensues. The episode and season end with no sense of who was shot. In one powerful episode, *TWW* not only reifies the heroism of its central character and leaves viewers in suspense but also begins the symbolic deconstruction of presidential heroism that will occupy much of the second season's plotline.

*TWW*'s second season begins with the immediate aftermath of the assassination attempt, where we learn that President Bartlet has been wounded and that the gunmen seriously injured Josh Lyman. All events of the second season's opener occur "In the Shadow of Two Gunmen." Viewers see the consequences of the assassination attempt on the president and his staff and acquire background information about the characters, which is offered through a series of flashbacks recounting the campaign that resulted in Bartlet's election. From this episode come two moments where the heroism of the president and the romance of *TWW* is problematized as they reveal the "internal demons" of Jed Bartlet.

"In the Shadow of Two Gunmen" explains how the team of Bartlet advisers joined the presidential campaign and catapulted their candidate to the White House. A clever device, these flashbacks demonstrate the ambivalence that Bartlet experienced during the early days of his presidential campaign. As staffers join the campaign, they confront a candidate who is surly, indifferent to their advice, and unpleasant; Bartlet is even unable to remember the names of his most important campaign advisors. The construction of the candidate's internal uncertainties culminates in an exchange during the decisive Illinois primary as Josh remarks to Abigail Bartlet, "Your husband is a real son-of-a-bitch, Mrs. Bartlet." She replies, "He's not ready yet, Josh. He's terrified." At various points throughout the flashbacks of the second season's opener, *TWW* introduces this internal demon confronting candidate Bartlet—terrified uncertainty about becoming president. It is only at the conclusion of the episode that Bartlet decides he is, in fact, ready to be president. Rather than the confident and assured president of "Let Bartlet Be Bartlet," this vision of presidential character questions the heroic image constructed at the end of *TWW*'s first season.

The deconstruction of presidential heroism at the outset of *TWW*'s second season is consistent with, and also challenges, long-standing presidential imagery. Bartlet becomes a reluctant candidate pressed into service against his will for the good of the country. Barry Schwartz, in his study of the eulogies for George Washington at the turn of the nineteenth century, concludes that Washington was offered as a "heroic prototype" for his embodiment of specific virtuous characteristics, including self-sacrifice, disinterestedness, authenticity, and piety.[38] Washington was the classic Cincinnatus or Moses—a reluctant leader called to service by the needs of the people and the community and moved to such service by a higher power or calling.

*TWW* offers a similar vision of Jed Bartlet. In a flashback scene from "In the Shadow of Two Gunmen," Bartlet asks Leo why he is working to promote a Bartlet candidacy. Leo's reply is instructive: "Because I'm tired of it, year after year after year after year. Of having to choose between the lesser of who cares. Of trying to get myself excited about a candidate who can't speak in complete sentences. Of setting the bar so low I can hardly look at it. They say a good man can't get elected president. I don't believe that, do you?" Leo utters this speech after he has fired all the hired political consultants, whose preoccupation has been whether Bartlet should use his opponent's name in stump speeches. Politics as usual, represented by the consultants, is the villain in this romantic vision. Politics as usual has produced candidates who do not rise to the level of presidential hero, according to Leo's formulation, and *TWW* offers such a candidate in the person of Jed Bartlet. His quest, his purpose, is to lead the nation away from the mediocrity and malfeasance of politics as usual, a theme that is demonstrated throughout the second season of *TWW*.

That heroism is challenged, and the image interrogated, because of the fear—indeed, the terror—that grips Bartlet in the flashback sequences from "In the Shadow of Two Gunmen." Part of what establishes presidential heroism is an interpersonal distance between presidents and voters, a distance eroded by the dominance of television in U.S. politics, where, as political communication critic Roderick Hart has argued, voters are fed an illusion of intimacy about political leadership.[39] *TWW* further feeds that illusion, breaking down the distance between president and citizen by bringing viewers deeply into the emotional and personal dimensions of presidential life. As such, viewers are privy to Bartlet's reluctance to run for president. They learn that he does not simply long for the quiet life in New Hampshire, or seek to remain close to his family—typical Cincinnatus reactions. Instead, Bartlet is depicted as uncertain, afraid, about his capacity to perform the duties of the office. At the conclusion of Leo's speech about the need for a "real" candidate, Bartlet queries, "Doesn't it matter that I'm not as sure?" *TWW* offers a unique glimpse of presidential psychology with the repeated portrayals of Bartlet's anxiety, deconstructing his heroism as a president and reinforcing the intimacy of televisual presidential politics.

Politics emerges as a barrier to honest, moral leadership in *TWW*'s presidentiality, and several episodes of the show's second season reinforce this construction of politics as a villain to be overcome by presidential heroism. In "The Midterms," for example, Bartlet is forced to watch the election of his political nemesis to the Manchester, New Hampshire, school board. In the same episode Sam recruits a law school classmate to run for Congress only to withdraw White House support after it is revealed that the candidate prefers all-white juries when trying criminal cases. Both plots demonstrate the unpleasantness of politics; the wrong people win elections, and otherwise good people are treated badly by the system.

Much of the nastiness of politics and the villainy of *TWW*'s romance is found in Congress. The Senate, for instance, refuses to pass a necessary nuclear test ban treaty in "The Lame Duck Congress" because of a shift in political power as a result of midterm elections. In "Shibboleth" the president's desire to appoint Leo's highly qualified sister to a Department of Education post is stopped because Republicans in Congress have photographs of her preventing student prayers at a public school event. Demonstrating nonpartisan disdain in "The Lame Duck Congress," Leo quips, "Look, even when they're here in session, trying to get a hundred senators in a line is still like trying to get cats to walk in a parade."

The White House and Congress spar dramatically in "The Leadership Breakfast," an episode that epitomizes *TWW*'s construction of the presidency as heroic and noble and Congress as base and political. Members of Congress and their aides only seek political power, according to this romance, and are not striving for the public good or fulfilling the public trust. After a day of political sparring, the episode features the chief of staff to the new Republican majority leader playing power politics when she says to Toby, "We're in the majority and things are going to have to look it, and by the way, don't ever walk into my office without an appointment." Bartlet's White House quests for justice, seeking to do what is right (in "The Leadership Breakfast" they are fighting for a patients' bill of rights and an increase in the minimum wage) even as they must sometimes reluctantly play politics and confront an overly political, often obstructionist, Congress to achieve their noble goals. Such constructions of the balance of power confirm many political observers' worries over the growing power of the rhetorical presidency that mitigated congressional suasive and political force throughout much of the twentieth century.[40]

Of course, the fact that Bartlet resolves his anxieties about being president of the United States, wins his first election, and is usually able to better the malevolent politicians on Capitol Hill solidifies *TWW*'s heroism. In addition, this depiction of the presidency can be read as a marker of U.S. nationalism. It promotes a political system dominated by a presidency pursuing noble ends. A nationalistic reading of *TWW* sees the United States as a nation where a good man can be elected president despite the perils of politics as usual, low expectations do not dominate, and honesty and authenticity prevail. Thus, even as *TWW* questions the political and reveals the inner demons plaguing its hero it still elevates the president to a level of genuine heroism. In so doing it reinforces a rosy image of politics in the United States and the goodness of the nation. *TWW*'s first season evolution to the "Let Bartlet Be Bartlet" apotheosis represents just how, in Fisher's terms, "the emergence of hero is a dynamic process, a negotiated meaning generated among the people over time."[41] By introducing Bartlet's anxieties about being president, his inner demons of worry and ambivalence, *TWW* further negotiates the meaning of this heroic figure.

Even as *TWW* establishes Bartlet's psychological readiness for leadership, "In the Shadow of Two Gunmen" also reintroduces a plot element that was prominent during the show's second season and offers additional insights into the romantic nationalism put forth by *TWW*. As the doctors prepare for surgery on the wounded President Bartlet, his wife, who, viewers learned in the first season, is a medical doctor, asks to speak to the anesthesiologist. She tells him, "There are fourteen people in the world who know this, including the vice president, the chief of staff, and the chairman of the Joint Chiefs. You're going to be the fifteenth. Seven years ago, my husband was diagnosed with a relapsing, remitting course of MS. When all this is over, tell the press, don't tell the press, it's entirely up to you." Another internal demon strikes at this president—this one physical rather than psychological—and it comes to threaten the essence of his administration even as the ultimate disposition of this plotline reinforces the romantic heroism of *TWW.*

In the United States, notes Anne Norton, "physical prowess has figured prominently in the mythology of leadership."[42] Americans are preoccupied with the physicality of their presidents, and presidents go to significant lengths to demonstrate their health or conceal their illnesses. This makes sense, of course, given the centrality of the president to the nation's sense of self-identity; if the president is a marker of U.S. nationalism, an ill president represents an ill nation. When *TWW* gave its president MS in the first season it directly challenged the mythology of presidential leadership as it also complicated the romantic heroism of its own nationalism. Those complications continue and are developed more fully in the second season as the president and his aides confronted the disease itself and the political consequences of concealing it from the public.[43]

At the conclusion of "The Leadership Breakfast," Leo and Toby are discussing the role of political parties in the United States and the likelihood that Bartlet will seek a second term. Their conversation concludes with Leo saying, "Shake my hand. We just formed it . . . the committee to re-elect the president." Midway through the second season *TWW* introduces the political plotline of a reelection campaign complicated by the president's reluctance (a simmering problem for Bartlet) and recurrent health problems. It is reelection politics, therefore, that frame the discussion of MS and come to define how this presidential malady affects the romantic image of the presidency articulated in the show.

Seeing Bartlet's MS as an opportunity to engage the "ethical and practical considerations of a zone of privacy for presidents," Staci Beavers highlights the specific contextual framework of the inner demon that plagues Jed Bartlet.[44] A persistent concern at the end of the Clinton presidency was the level of privacy to which presidents and their families are entitled, and this particular plot engages that issue in a manner that avoided the salacious prurience of the Monica Lewinsky scandal. The ethical lapse in this case is similar—lying, or not being wholly truthful with the American public—although the object of the presidential mendacity is less sensational. Both scandals, though, work to deconstruct presidential heroism, inviting a symbolic reassessment of presidential heroism. As John B. Thompson concludes, political scandals are ultimately "struggles over symbolic power in which reputation and trust are at stake" with the capacity to destroy both reputation and trust for political leaders.[45] In this way, *TWW*'s scandal of the president's MS directly addresses such questions, highlighting the general cultural anxiety about political reputation and trust emergent from the Clinton presidency. Moreover, *TWW*'s resolution to the plotline reconstructs presidential heroism, affirming again the persistent *TWW* theme of letting Bartlet be Bartlet.

Bartlet's MS is a largely dormant plotline until midway through the second season. Occasionally mentioned, the plot does not dominate or control the action of *TWW*, and the characters rarely discuss the affliction. That changes in "The War at Home," in which "wars" between the United States and Colombian drug lords, between Congress and the White House, and between the president and the First Lady all frame the drama and create a tension-filled episode. The First Lady, realizing that her husband intends to seek reelection, challenges him, asking, "Do you get that you have MS? . . . Do you get that your own immune system is shredding your brain and I can't tell you why? Do you have any idea how good a doctor I am and I can't tell you why?" She continues by detailing the symptoms of "secondary, progressive MS," which he will possibly face in two years: "Fatigue, an inability to get through the day . . . memory lapses, a loss of cognitive functions, failure to reason, failure to think clearly." The exchange dramatically expresses the physical challenges confronting the presidential hero, trials that threaten his viability as president. The plot disrupts *TWW*'s romance because it assaults the competent heroism of the presidency as constructed in the show.

As with the first season, the chaos, the disorder, that threatens the Bartlet presidency and interrupts the romance of *TWW* comes at the end of the season and invites resolution before the season cliffhanger. The MS plotline culminates in the episode entitled "Seventeen People," where the president finally begins to tell his staff about his affliction. Toby has realized that someone is keeping a secret, and he confronts the president and Leo with his suspicions. Described as the conscience of *TWW*, Toby is the show's moral compass.[46] He voices a range of concerns that arise from the fact that the president has MS and articulates the most pessimistic view of the situation. The nationalism of the episode is also evident in the tension when Toby's moralism interrogates the president, who is the embodiment of the nation-state. Toby's arguments all concern the impact of Bartlet's disease, and his secrecy about it, on the institution of the presidency; when read nationalistically, his fears reaffirm the power and importance of the presidency for the United States. Toby argues that decision-making occurred in an extra-constitutional manner when the president suffered an MS attack during the crisis between India and Pakistan and again during the assassination attempt (both instances that occurred in the first season):

The Commander-in-Chief had just been attacked, he was under general anesthetic. A fugitive was at large, the manhunt included every Federal, state and local law enforcement agency. The Virginia, Maryland, New Jersey, Pennsylvania, and Delaware National Guard units were federalized. The KH-10s showed Republican Guard movement in Southern Iraq and twelve hours earlier an F-117 was shot down in the no-fly. And the Vice-President's authority was murky at best. The National Security Advisor and the Secretary of State didn't know who they were taking their orders from. I wasn't in the Situation Room that night, but I'll bet all the money in my pockets against all the money in your pockets that it was Leo. Who no one elected. For ninety minutes that night there was a coup d'etat in this country.

Toby's arguments are exclusively about the institutional ramifications of Bartlet's illness. His concern is that proper constitutional procedure was ignored and decisions were made to avoid scrutiny of the president's health. Toby's concerns are bigger than Bartlet; Toby's worries are about the credibility and stability of the institution and the nation.

*TWW*, though, was not content to only complicate its narrative via Bartlet's MS with dialogue about the constitutional consequences of his affliction. Murray Edelman reminds us that "history is biography and that political leaders shape the fortunes of peoples and nations."[47] *TWW* recognizes this essential dynamic in U.S. politics, and the MS plotline moves swiftly away from Toby's institutional concerns back to the character of Jed Bartlet. After Toby's speech, Bartlet angrily responds, "I feel fine, by the way, thanks for asking. . . . Are you pissed 'cause I didn't say anything or are you pissed 'cause there were fifteen people who knew before you did? I feel fine by the way, thanks for asking."

The focus shifts with Bartlet's response, and this particular president is again the emphasis of the show. Later, the president says, "I have no intention of apologizing to you, Toby." Toby asks why not, and Bartlet again stresses the personal dimensions to his disease: "'Cause you're not the one with MS, a wife, three kids, and airports to close. Not every part of me belongs to you. This was personal. I'm not willing to relinquish that right." All the concerns Toby articulates about the Constitution and the illegal transfer of power, are obliterated as the president makes the MS plot all about himself and his personal and unique response to the situation. With this move *TWW* reestablishes the focus of the plot, and by extension the show, back to the romantic hero president who fights for his privacy while also being concerned about the consequences of his actions. The institution of the presidency is not what matters in this presidentiality. What matters most is the rise and fall of an individual, heroic president.

Bartlet's MS, with all of its political consequences and potential ramifications for his presidency, dominates the action of the final episodes in the second season. In "The Fall's Gonna Kill You" it is clear that other members of the staff have learned about the disease, and the episode features numerous interactions between the principals of the show and the White House counsel, Oliver Babish. In addition, the drama frames of the episode include news of a Chinese satellite's impending crash to earth and the difficulties facing the Justice Department as it prosecutes lawsuits against big tobacco for perpetrating "a fraud against the public." Josh even expresses some anxiety that tobacco's fraud is not dissimilar from White House deceptions about the president's health. "We are not big tobacco," Leo assures him. By the next episode, "18th and Potomac," the administration commissions a poll (about a fictional governor of Michigan who contracts a debilitating disease and then does not publicly disclose his affliction) to measure public reaction about the potential revelation of the president's MS. The poll reveals the likelihood of strong public disapproval for Bartlet's subterfuge. In addition, the installment ends with the death of Delores Landingham, the president's personal secretary who often provided a moral voice. The drama frame is obvious. A source of moral guidance and direction is eliminated at the very moment when the morality of the administration is most at peril.

Each of these installments of *TWW* leads to the final, histrionic second season's finale, "Two Cathedrals." Using the narrative device of a strange May tropical storm moving up the East Coast, the episode highlights the tumult that confronts the romantic heroic president and his staff, culminating with a dramatic presidential monologue in which Bartlet confronts God in the National Cathedral after Mrs. Landingham's funeral. The president asks Leo to seal off the cathedral and then, against the spectacular backdrop of America's national church, he engages in a compelling conversation with God that begins with the rather startling line: "You're a sonofabitch, you know that?" The monologue works in contradistinction to a typical "priestly" role for presidents where they "represent the people before God and in so doing celebrate and comfort the citizenry."[48] Here, and in a decidedly unpriestly manner, the president challenges God with Mrs. Landingham's death and the shooting of Josh in the assassination attempt: "That was my son. What did I ever do to yours but praise His glory and praise His name?" Ultimately, the diatribe morphs into a confessional as the president admits, "Yes, I lied, it was a sin. I've committed many sins, have I displeased you, you feckless thug?" He recites some Latin phrases, translated as "am I really to believe that these are the acts of a loving God? A just God? A wise God? To hell with your punishments.

I was your servant here on Earth. And I spread your word and I did your work. To hell with your punishments. To hell with you."[49] He concludes by announcing, "You get Hoynes." Part confessional, part attack, and part concession, the monologue is fascinating for its manifestation of *TWW*'s presidential vision as it opposes long-standing images of presidents as arbiters and manifestations of America's spiritual and civil religions. In its multifarious character the monologue further complicates the romantic heroism of its main character.

In a compelling way the confrontation reinforces Bartlet's heroism while simultaneously deconstructing it. The president is heroic as he battles for what he believes to be right even as he interrogates the religiosity conventionally associated with presidential heroism. Furthermore, the dramatic monologue engages the inherent relationships that exist between religion and political scandal, a relationship where, as Thompson notes, political scandal becomes a "secularized form of sin."[50]

Derived etymologically from the Greek word *skandalon,* the contemporary word *scandal* was "first used in a religious context in the . . . Greek version of the Old Testament" and referred to a trap or obstacle that led people to question their faith, to doubt God, or to lose their way.[51] *TWW* plays out this ancient meaning of the idea of scandal and uses the plot as a device to display the internal psychological dynamics of the presidential hero as Bartlet questions his faith and relationship with God and loses a sense of his purpose or motivation for remaining in the White House. Furthermore, the plot emphasizes and interrogates Bartlet's religious persona as carefully constructed throughout the first two seasons. At various points in *TWW* Bartlet is depicted as a deeply religious individual, fluent in classical Latin, at ease quoting the Bible, and quick to consult religious advice when faced with moral issues like the death penalty. This religiosity works on several levels as it enhances the president's intellect, tempers his liberalism, and elevates his moral character. As such, when the show taps into the latent religious meanings of scandal *TWW* deconstructs its presidential hero in a dramatic and climactic fashion. Indeed, for much of the "Two Cathedrals" season finale the audience is led to suspect that Bartlet will not seek reelection as a result of his religious and political anxieties.

Of course *TWW* could not end its season with a thoroughly deconstructed heroic figure. To have the president concede that Hoynes will succeed him would leave the show with little or no future. Instead, "Two Cathedrals" reconstitutes its presidential hero with the mystical assistance of the ghost of Mrs. Landingham. Bartlet is in the Oval Office, preparing to announce his decision at a press conference, when the specter of Mrs. Landingham appears and reorders the president's priorities away from his personal problems to the problems of the nation. The president then goes to the press conference, and it is clear by the end of the episode, and the second season, that he will seek reelection. Rather than indulge his personal anxieties, rather than surrender to his anger at God or the difficulties he has encountered, the heroic president stays to fight for those who are less fortunate and need his leadership. Once again *TWW*'s nationalism is evident as the presidency is reconstructed as an institution where the nation's concerns are predominant.

*TWW* is never content, however, to completely deconstruct its presidential hero. Even though this president faces difficulties and challenges that most fictional presidents do not and that most citizens do not see (a debilitating disease, significant personal insecurities about his leadership ability, an assassination attempt, and religious uncertainty) he nonetheless is continually brought back to his real purpose, his heroic quest: to better the lives of those less fortunate and protect and serve the United States. In this quest the president is aided by a group of dedicated staffers who never waver in their allegiance, even when they learn that they, too, were deceived about the president's health.

Through it all, the persistent tension between the presidency as an institution and the individually embodied presidency plays itself out week after week. That tension is another dimension to *TWW*'s nationalism, moreover, because it speaks to the inherent conflict between the individual president and the presidency as a manifestation of the American nation. As such, *TWW*'s presidentiality is both unconventional because it allows viewers to see the internal unease, the almost paralyzing fretfulness, of its presidential hero and traditional because it depicts that hero as institutionally dedicated to the pursuit of justice and unwavering in his commitment to quest for right. As he confronts these extraordinary challenges, bringing order to the chaos and fighting internal apprehensions and physical malady, he is still heroically dedicated to fighting the good fight.

## Fighting External Threats: Presidential Heroism, Terrorism, and the End of Politics as Usual

Even before *TWW* could begin its third season, the nature of the presidency changed again in the United States in the wake of the dramatic 2000 election and the attacks on the World Trade Center and the Pentagon on September 11, 2001. Both events affected the presidency as depicted in *TWW*.[52] The construction of presidential heroism, the romance of the show, shifted in the third and fourth seasons. The plots that dominated those seasons involved external dangers from terrorism and from the mundane, mendacious "politics as usual" mentality of U.S. presidential elections. *TWW* did not surrender the depictions of political chaos or the indulgence of its haunted presidential hero confronting personal anxieties but shifted its focus toward a more typical, romantic rendition of presidential heroism. Given the dramatic events of 2000 and 2001, it is hardly surprising that the fictional presidential hero of *TWW* turned his attention to fighting external enemies. In so doing, *TWW* reinscribed its romantic heroism in a way that elevated the institution and the individual character above the dangers confronting the nation's political culture.

Military images, metaphors, and narratives frequently dominate politics in the United States.[53] The word *campaign* is synonymous with attempts to secure electoral dominance and military victory. Our election language is replete with discussions of campaign "strategy," "battleground states," and "war rooms."[54] And emergent from the presidential election campaign is the heroic victor, poised to lead the nation even as he has just survived the difficulties of political "battle." The 2000 election called this sense of presidential campaigns into question as common military language dominated discussions of the campaign. After weeks of wrangling in the swamps of Florida election law, the "victory" of George W. Bush did not put to rest the anxieties the election occasioned, nor did he emerge as a victorious leader ready to guide the nation. It was only in the immediate aftermath of 9/11 that George W. Bush achieved the typical level of presidential leadership that would normally adhere to the victor of a presidential campaign. All of this—the uncertainty of the 2000 election and the quest for leadership in the wake of 9/11—created a context for *TWW*'s presidentiality to shift. Its depiction of Bartlet's reelection campaign reestablishes the presidential hero and constructs a presidency predicated on intelligence and moral vision while depicting the dangers of foreign terrorism for the United States.

As *TWW*'s third season began the lingering questions about the president's willingness to seek reelection were gone, although uncertainty about the disposition of his MS disclosure remained. The third season's premiere, a two-part episode entitled "Manchester," primarily focuses on the formation and announcement of the reelection campaign. In the process the episodes also grapple with persistent feelings of guilt and uncertainty about the president's affliction. A distinct focus of the plot in these opening episodes is the tension between politics and governing, between the consultants brought in to assist with the reelection effort and the heroic staffers who are the regulars of the show. "Politics as usual" becomes the enemy, the external threat, as the two staffs struggle to define Bartlet's reelection message.

Edelman observes that political enemies are regularly depicted as "aloof and clannish and they insist on entering social circles where they are not welcome."[55] Such a construction is evident in "Manchester," where consultants are portrayed as interlopers who constantly struggle with White House staffers and are routinely distracted by the symbolic and the political rather than the more noble policy ends that concern the heroic staff. This depiction is reinforced through a drama frame in the teaser for the second part of "Manchester." Sam and Toby are arguing with the consultants in the barn of the Bartlet farm when C.J. spots a snake. The snake in the hay is a rather obvious metaphor that connotes the threats to the staff's authority and their efforts to enact strong public policy. And the threat is not insignificant. Josh remarks at one point, "Seriously, that's a pretty big snake."

"Manchester," though, establishes the lines of authority in the campaign and also reinscribes the presidential heroism of *TWW*'s romance. When Bruno Gianelli, a top-flight political consultant, is negotiating his position with the 2002 Bartlet reelection campaign, he demands "unfettered access to the president." Leo rejects this condition, and Bruno argues that it is a "deal breaker," threatening to take the matter to Bartlet. When Bruno negotiates with the president Bartlet reestablishes Leo's important role: "I'm sorry, Bruno, Leo runs the show." What matters to this White House, and this president, is governing and policy. Politics only intervenes as a stage in the process. Keeping consultants distant from "real power" reinforces the authority of the president and his staff and reins in the political. Given the persistent perception that politicians and presidents are governed almost exclusively by political considerations, polls, and strategy, *TWW*'s alternative offers a more heroic and dedicated vision of governance guided by right and integrity.[56]

As "politics as usual" is marginalized and the consultants are deemphasized in Bartlet's quest for reelection, *TWW* clearly delineates the purpose of the election, which markedly conforms to the presidential heroism constructed in the show's romantic vision. The reelection campaign is dedicated to pursuing sound policy to help the unfortunate and downtrodden: "For all the new jobs we've created," Bartlet tells C.J., "there are single mothers working two of them at minimum wage. There are school districts where less than half the students graduate and a kid born in Harlem is more likely to go to prison than a four-year college. They're bringing guns to school." In another remark to the staff Bartlet proclaims, "It's not our job to appeal to the lowest common denominator. . . . It's our job to raise it. If you're going to be the education president, it'd be nice not to hide that you have an education." The ghost of Mrs. Landingham from the end of the second season lingers as the president articulates a rationale for reelection based on a type of heroism that tries to reclaim the "moral highground" for the presidency.[57] Much as Jimmy Carter fought to bring a sense of moral purpose to the White House, so, too, does Bartlet's heroism stem from his dedication to a morality of purpose and direction. In this sense Bartlet enacts a powerful "visionary" role of the presidency, where, as Mary Stuckey and Shannon Wabshall note, "Presidents dream for us. They tell us where we are headed, they enunciate our national goals."[58]

Bartlet's presidential heroism, though, is not simply about pursuing sound public policy. Instead, the goals and purposes of the reelection are also understood within the context of the MS revelation and the ensuing scandal. The visionary policymaker role of Bartlet's heroic presidency meets, within this plot, another important role that all presidents portray. Presidents must, according to Stuckey and Wabshall, "exemplify the best that is in us, not the worst. He is therefore charged with the task of representing us while being superior—but not too superior—to any individual citizen."[59] The MS plotline provided Sorkin and the other creators of *TWW* with an opportunity to manifest that "national symbol/role model" position of the presidency.

In "Manchester" the president begins the process of confronting the MS issue by apologizing to his staff: "It occurs to me that I've never said I'm sorry. I am—for the lawyers, for the press, for the mess, for the fear. Bruno, Doug, Connie, these guys are good. They want to win. So do we. The only thing we want more is to be right. I wonder if you can't do both. There's a new book and we're going to write it. You can win if you run a smart, disciplined campaign. . . . We're going to write the book right here, right now, at this very moment today."

Bartlet's apology works alongside his vision of the reelection campaign to manifest, again, his principled presidential heroism. His apology is fused with his desire to do the "right" thing, to pursue the "right" policies. Politics as usual is overwhelmed by the larger purpose. Read against the cultural angst over the presidency at the end of the Clinton years in the aftermath of the 2000 election and in the wake of 9/11, the vision is a noble one that makes the institution, and the fictional people who populate it in *TWW*, heroic and soothing.

Bartlet's MS affliction and his attempts to hide his disease from the public occupy considerable plot time in the early episodes of the third season and culminate in a manner that both disposes of the plot and offers a powerful commentary on the cultural angst about the institution in the aftermath of the Clinton scandals. As usual, the MS plot is understood as a romantic tale where the heroes are the president and his staff and the villains are those who oppose them. In this instance, as is so often the case in *TWW*, the villain is Congress. At one point early in the first season Josh says, "I'm so sick of Congress I could vomit" ("Five Votes Down"). As *TWW*'s plots develop, Congress comes to represent the "politics of personal destruction" *topoi* of contemporary Clintonian politics as it commences a series of investigations about the president's actions regarding his MS. Their primary target is Leo, and the plot comes also to implicate his alcoholism and deep friendship with the president.

In an episode entitled "Ways and Means" the White House staff attempts to manipulate the investigation of the president to their advantage, especially because the appointed independent prosecutor is seen as fair and balanced. As C.J. tells Leo, "We need to be investigated by someone who wants to kill us just to watch us die. We need someone perceived by the American people to be irresponsible, untrustworthy, partisan, ambitious, and thirsty for the limelight. Am I crazy, or is this not a job for the House of Representatives?" With Leo's permission, C.J. manipulates the process by enticing the congressional Republicans, who take the bait and begin aggressive hearings investigating the MS disclosure.

This construction of the American government, with the presidency under siege and Congress acting inquisitorially, preserves the romantic vision of the presidency in *TWW* by positioning the White House as the aggrieved party fighting for justice. However messy politics is, however vindictive and prosecutorial Congress becomes, the heroic presidency will still fight hard for the national good, and that is precisely *TWW*'s vision of the presidency in the aftermath of the Clinton impeachment and the election debacle in Florida after the 2000 campaign.

As if to emphasize its romantic theme, "Ways and Means" also presents other plots that work as drama frames for the MS scandal and investigation. The president and Leo are dealing with a fire raging through Yellowstone National Park and decide, on the advice of experts, to allow the blaze to burn out naturally despite protests from the governor of Wyoming. At the same time, Sam is dealing with a recalcitrant California politico who seeks assurances from the White House for political payoffs in trade for public support in the president's reelection bid. Each plot frames the larger issue of the president's MS as they highlight the risks and uncertainties of political decision making. In each plot, of course, the strategy works. C.J. manages to motivate a hostile Republican to begin investigations in Congress, the fire ultimately recedes, and Sam secures the support of the California union leader. Once again the heroic White House prevails, fighting for the right ends but opposed every step of the way by politics as usual.

The MS plotline comes to a meaningful and ideologically reassuring conclusion in two episodes midway through the third season: "Bartlet for America" and "H.Con. 172." Using the flashback strategy again, "Bartlet for America" emphasizes the personal costs of the president's actions during the MS cover-up on those he cares about most, fusing again the institutional with the personal in *TWW*'s romantic depiction of the presidency. Leo is to testify before Congress, and the testimony will likely reveal his alcoholism and previous misuse of prescription drugs. At the same time, the hearings are also inquiring into Abby Bartlet's role in the decision not to reveal the president's disease. "Abby's about to get spanked," he worries. "Guys, the things we do to women. My wife's a first-class scientist." The hearings are contextualized through flashbacks that demonstrate how Leo persuaded Bartlet to run for the presidency and how the First Lady assured her husband that a physical would reveal nothing about his MS. By "H.Con. 172" the resolution to the plotline is complete, and the president accepts responsibility for his decision by agreeing to a congressional censure resolution. In a speech that reveals much about the state of the presidency following Bill Clinton, Bartlet says, "I was wrong. I was. I was wrong. C'mon, we know that . . . I may not have had sinister intent at the outset but there were plenty of opportunities for me to make it right. No one in government takes responsibility for anything anymore. . . . We obfuscate, we rationalize. 'Everybody does it,' that's what we say . . . I am to blame. I was wrong."

In almost perfect counterpoint to Bill Clinton's repeated prevarications during the Lewinsky scandal, the heroic president, Jed Bartlet, stops the investigations, comes clean, and restores honor and dignity to the office in the process. As Pamela Ezell notes, the scene "demonstrates a Capraesque notion of honesty as the best policy, and celebrates the common man for his wisdom and tolerance, while turning away from the establishment elite."[60] In the process "Bartlet for America" and "H.Con. 172" resolve the MS plotline in a manner that maintains the president's heroism, offers a telling commentary on the state of the contemporary presidency, and presents a romantic presidency as a necessary corrective to the excesses of the Clinton years. The enemy—"politics as usual" as represented textually by Congress and intertextually by the memories of Bill Clinton—is defeated, and the heroism of the presidency is restored.

Bartlet's quest for reelection occurs simultaneously with an emergent plot about the dangers of international terrorism, and both plots work as commentary on each other. Moreover, *TWW*'s decision to construct its presidentiality around the threat of terrorism reflects the anxieties emergent from the post–9/11 context in the United States. For *TWW* to be a viable mimesis of the contemporary presidency it almost had to create a terrorism plot. The show has always presented international tensions, but the more overt focus on terrorism is telling given the events of 9/11, and they reveal again the importance of presidential heroism in times of national emergency or crisis. When such crises occur, Thomas Cronin and Michael Genovese observe, "We instinctively turn to the president [who is] asked during a time of crisis to provide not only political and executive leadership but also the appearance of confidence, responsible control, the show of a steady hand at the helm."[61]

Romantic heroes are strongest when they confront unambiguous enemies "characterized by an inherent trait or set of traits that mark them as evil, immoral, warped, or pathological and therefore a continuing threat."[62] *TWW*'s romance depends upon ambiguity and contingency. As the Bartlet administration confronts international terrorism, the contingent nature of the show's romance challenges larger cultural notions of terrorism as unequivocally evil. For *TWW*, terrorism is a problem sponsored and located primarily in a fictional country called Qumar. Qumar, allied with the United States in *TWW*, is strongly criticized in an early episode of the third season, "The Women of Qumar," when C.J. crusades on behalf of oppressed women in that country, efforts that echo many complaints issued against Saudi Arabia's treatment of women. Her arguments are rebuffed, trumped by the need to preserve the U.S. alliance with Qumar in the unstable Middle East. The relationship with Qumar changes, however, as *TWW*'s third season progresses.

During times of crisis presidential leadership takes on added urgency and acquires a greater sense of morality and gravity.[63] As *TWW* grappled with the problem of international terrorism at the same historical moment that the United States was launching a war against the same foe, the show commented on its context and offered a vision of terrorism, an alternative to the enemy articulated by the Bush administration. At times, *TWW*'s Bartlet sounded much like President Bush. In "100,000 Airplanes," Bartlet says in a State of the Union address: "Today we are faced with a new challenge. Now, in a new century, when we meet and master new forms of aggression and hatred, ignorance and evil, our vigilance in the face of oppression and global terror will be unequaled by any moment in human history." Bartlet even articulates the same sense of mission, of almost reckless abandon, in committing to the pursuit of terrorists: "And to the enemies of freedom, the enemies of democracy, the enemies of America, the enemies of humanity itself, we say here tonight with one voice, 'There is no corner of this earth so remote, no cave so dark, that you will not be found and brought to light, and ended.'"

Like Bush after the 9/11 attacks, Bartlet is transformed into a wartime president, a transformation that reaffirms the heroic posture of *TWW*'s romance. Whenever a president becomes a wartime commander-in-chief, according to Sandra Silberstein, he "is exercising extraordinary powers, powers that are comfortably granted in a democracy only in the context of a very strong consensus."[64] Echoing Bush's rhetorical response to 9/11 allows Bartlet to become more heroic, to assume a persona of a romantic president fighting an unseen, dangerous enemy in order to preserve freedom and democracy. Furthermore, the transformation reinforces the show's nationalism, positioning the president again at the center of national activity and public life.

Qumar and terrorism in general recede as plots for *TWW* when the reelection campaign resurfaces to become the show's dominant focus. Bartlet faces a former governor of Florida, Robert Ritchie, in the election, and the campaign becomes a contest between Bartlet's intellectualism and Ritchie's anti-intellectualism. In a not-so-veiled comparison with George W. Bush, the Republican Ritchie is portrayed as likeable but limited in his understanding of domestic and foreign policy. Of course, this tension functions as a commentary on terrorism as well. The implication is that intelligence and knowledge are necessary to confront the dangers of international terrorists. "Knowledge is valued most insofar as it is immediately useful in getting things done," concludes presidential historian David Burton.[65] In a president, such utility in the post–9/11 world must concern international terrorism. Seen in that way, Bartlet's staffers shape their campaign strategy around the president's intelligence. As Toby tells the president in "Hartsfield's Landing," "Then make the election about smart and not. Make it about engaged and not. Qualified and not. Make it about heavyweight. You're a heavyweight and you've been holding me up for too many rounds." In a world where the enemies and the dangers are powerful, *TWW* suggests, an intellectual, engaged president is essential for effective leadership.

*TWW*'s confrontation with terrorism reaches its apex with the conclusion of the third season. Bartlet is presented with conclusive evidence that the defense minister of Qumar, although an ally of the United States, is also a terrorist and supports an al-Qaeda–like organization with funds and other means. Drawing from previous plots and character definitions, *TWW* portrays Bartlet as tormented by a plan to assassinate the Qumari defense minister. The certainty and moral purpose evident from Bartlet's State of the

Union address in "100,000 Airplanes," is gone, and the parallel between his response to terrorism and the Bush administration's is complicated. Faced with a clear plan to eliminate a known terrorist, Bartlet ponders the morality of the decision, questioning its ethical consequences and implications for U.S. foreign policy. In "Posse Comitatus," the third season's finale, Bartlet is presented with the plan to assassinate and forced to make a decision. He approves the assassination plan despite his moral objections.

What emerges is a contingent understanding of international terrorism, a complicated vision of how a presidential hero confronts this persistent, powerfully relevant, problem. The brash certainty that Bartlet displayed earlier in the third season, and the parallel bravado of the Bush administration, are modified when Bartlet voices more intense and complicated moral questions about confronting international terrorists. Again, as with so much of *TWW*'s construction of the presidential hero, there is a broad sense of complication and introspection to Jed Bartlet. He is an intellectual who sees the world and its problems for their complexity as he strives to do what is right, just, and moral. Moreover, in the context of the reelection campaign such heroism is positioned against the uninformed, intellectually incurious opponent.

At bottom, *TWW* constructs powerful enemies as opponents for the presidential hero—external threats that work alongside the internal demons and physical maladies to challenge President Bartlet and complicate his heroism. Bartlet, as a presidential hero and stand-in for the larger nation-state, must confront the agents of "politics as usual" in the guise of Congress, political consultants, and incompetent opponents who seek the presidency. As Bartlet and his staff oppose these enemies they articulate their quest for policy and action that preserve the moral and right and help the less fortunate. In many ways Bartlet becomes the antipolitical president despite his obvious political strengths and abilities. At the same time, the Bartlet administration confronts the dangers of international terrorism, and their efforts to oppose terrorists are wracked by similar insecurities and internal interrogations that define the presidential hero of *TWW*. As *TWW* articulates Bartlet's self-doubts and moral concerns about fighting terrorism, the program offers an alternative to the moral certainty of the Bush administration and complicates its romantic depiction of the American presidency.

## Romantic Presidentiality and *TWW*'s Nationalism

Reflecting on the nature of presidential leadership, Stuckey and Wabshall delineate the various roles that presidents play in the national imaginary: "The

president is our father figure; he protects and guides us. He is our visionary; he dreams for us. He is our head of government; he acts for us. He is our
policymaker; he legislates for us. He is the architect of our national identity; he defines us. He is our national role model; he exemplifies us."[66]

All of these roles, many of them heroic, are depicted in *TWW*'s characterization of its presidential hero. Even as he confronts chaos in the nation and
the larger world, as he battles against internal insecurities and physical maladies, and as he challenges the presumptions of "politics as usual" and fights
against the dangers of international terrorism, President Jed Bartlet maintains
his focus. He reflects a compelling heroic identity that fits well within the program's overall romantic narrative.

*TWW*'s romance, its vision of nobler, better U.S. politics, is a dominant
message communicated overtly and implicitly to viewers. In this way *TWW*
is successful as a romantic depiction of U.S. national identity and articulates
a version of that identity that viewers grasp. One need only glance at a few
of the dozens of Web sites devoted to the show to see the power of their overall theme. Bartlet4america.org, for instance, identifies the president as "directly descended from one of the signers of the Declaration of Independence,
New Hampshire Democrat Bartlet exudes a folksy charisma that often ob-
scures his brilliance, but not his devotion to doing what's right for the country." One fan (sammyjoe1984) posted the following on a message board devoted to every facet of *TWW*, making a comment that nicely reflects the
romantic power of the show's depiction of the president:

> martin sheen is amazing as the president. there is this one episode in the thrd
> [*sic*] season when cj wants to quit cause she messed up and thinks that she can't
> do her job . . . cj and the pres get into a fight and the pres has this big speech.
> cj is so much taller than the pres (he's no longer martin sheen . . . he's the pres-
> ident of the united states) . . . she towers ovr [*sic*] him . . . but martin sheen
> is amazing as the president that when he talks he demands respect . . . and the
> way he acts u [*sic*] have to give it to him . . . u [*sic*] want to give it to him. i've
> always thought that martin sheen is great as the pres and nobody can do it
> bettr [*sic*] (not even bush jr.) . . . but aftr [*sic*] that scene i just had to say WOW!
> that's all that could describe it. plus because of his character and the way he
> acts . . . i'd pick him ovr [*sic*] michael douglas any day![67]

A self-described Chinese immigrant living in Australia (han_yang) indicated his love of *TWW*, saying, "To me, the West Wing show is emblematic
of the America I desperately wish to believe in."[68] Moreover, "whiteotter"
from Florida reveals the polyvalent nature of the show's text: "Some might
think that only jingoistic supernationalists enjoy the West Wing, but nei-

ther of those words describe me. I feel very comfortable questioning the decision my government makes, and I appreciate how the West Wing has broadened my understanding of how it operates."[69]

Gauging audience reactions to mass-mediated texts is always a difficult task, and such comments are in no way exclusive of the commentary to address *TWW*. The program has supporters as well as detractors. Regardless of their predisposition toward *TWW*, viewers produce meanings that are negotiated and reflect their engagement with the text as thinking, active agents. Simultaneously, though, viewers are not presented with limitless ranges of meanings. As John Sloop notes in his discussion of how large audiences agree on meanings, "The meanings presented in mass mediated texts are ones that place 'governing' interests at the center, making visible the meanings that most clearly fit the interests of those in the strongest positions of power." This view is not a consistent dominant ideology thesis, Sloop notes, but a recognition that such texts are "biased toward certain interests and that those interests have the advantage of making visible certain ideas and images, critiquing and disciplining all cases that work against that vision."[70]

*TWW*'s romantic portrayal of its presidential hero is one that responds to compelling nationalistic needs in the United States. As Fisher notes, "America needs heroes and rituals, presidents and elections, to signify her whole meaning—moralistic and materialistic; she requires symbols her citizens can identify with and can gain sanction from for what they are as individuals and what they represent as a nation."[71] The heroism of *TWW* fulfills this need, offering Bartlet as a character who is both superior and similar to the citizens he is supposed to represent. Moreover, as it positions the presidency at the center of U.S. national identity *TWW* offers a presidential hero who mirrors the complexity and contingency of the larger U.S. community and puts forth a complicated narrative of nationalism that amplifies the anxieties and uncertainties of the contemporary United States.

It is *TWW*'s romance that makes the presidential hero less remote and more believable in the show's mimetic depiction of U.S. political culture. *TWW* does not fall prey to the fabulism of other romances about the presidency. Bartlet is not larger than life. He is a decidedly human hero, filled with insecurity, plagued by disease and self-doubt, and forced to confront difficult, challenging foes. In this way *TWW* avoids the "expectation of miracles and the fear that wells within us when miracles do not occur" that characterize so many heroic narratives about the presidency.[72] Its presidentiality is more genuine, more mimetic, as it imagines a presidency that faces the difficult contingencies of the contemporary world.

As a compelling romance, *TWW* powerfully responds to the prevailing context about the presidency in the Clinton and Bush years. In a historical moment where the president is diminished by the end of the cold war and citizens know more and more about their presidents because of the invasive power of television, the U.S. presidency is a demythologized institution, and the sources of its heroism are more complicated.[73] *TWW* recognizes this shift in presidential heroism and depicts its presidential character accordingly. In addition, Bartlet's heroism responds to the various characteristics of both Clinton and Bush. Bartlet is intelligent and astute, Bartlet is moral and committed to his family, Bartlet is repentant and guilty when he makes a mistake, and Bartlet is sensitive to the complicated moralities he confronts as president. As with many of the individual plotlines, the mimesis of *TWW* is manifest in the heroism, the romance, when a fictional president confronts real problems and deals with them in ways that are humanly heroic, thus demonstrating a contingent and sensitive presidency. Yet within this same humane, contingent depiction is the intellectual, white, male, militarized presidency/president. Our analysis now turns to the ways in which the romantic rendition of the presidency in *TWW* interfaces with its complicated ideological commentary.

# 2

# Gendered Nationalism and
# *The West Wing*

The things we do to women.

—President Josiah Bartlet, "Bartlet for America"

FOR MANY SCHOLARS the concepts of nationalism and gender are inextricable. As Jean Pickering and Suzanne Kehde argue, "Nationalism is the field over which gender differences are played out, making possible what otherwise seems an irrational if common disposition of putative gender differences."[1] Conceptions of gender and nationalism transform over time, indicating the legacies of past ideological commitments. Nationalism and its ideological components are historically grounded and simultaneously connected to on-going political discussions, the emergence of new ideological trends, and overall cultural shifting in ideological battles over intransigence and change in public conceptions of national identity.[2] In order to understand the ways that U.S. nationalism and gender play out on *The West Wing*, a brief history of such ideological commitments must first be traced, beginning with the constructed relationship between conceptions of nation and family.

Even from the beginnings of contemporary nationalism, depictions of "nation" were framed or aligned with discursive constructions of "family." George L. Mosse maintains that the "triumph of the nuclear family . . . coincided with the rise of nationalism . . . in . . . eighteenth century" Europe.[3] Such national and familial conflations are rooted in the rhetoric of the French Revolution, and these family images represented "a timeless and global unity of loyalty" that "served as a guarantee for the continuation of traditional bonds between individuals as the process of nation building widened the understanding of loyalty to include the national community."[4]

England, of course, conceived of itself as the mother country to the children of the American colonies before the American Revolution. Politicians such as George Washington, John Adams, Thomas Jefferson, and James Madison have historically been described as the nation's Founding Fathers. Many early presidents (e.g., James Madison and Andrew Jackson) also conceived of Native Americans as America's "red children," reinscribing similar symbolic and oppressive constructions that the British imposed on its colonies. Rogan Kersh expands the familial concept beyond particular groups, maintaining that the early part of the nineteenth century witnessed "repeated assertions of interdependence among different classes, regions, and interest groups" that "routinely drew parallels to the union of wife and husband." The metaphor of "sexual union" represented the implicit, sometimes explicit, symbolic foundation that underlay many nationalist constructs.[5]

Conceiving of the nation as a family influenced the power dynamics within the nation, and family metaphors offered "a 'natural' figure for sanctioning national hierarchy within a putative organic unity of interests." More specifically, "Hierarchies within the nation could be depicted in familial terms to guarantee social difference as a category of nature," because, as Anne McClintock asserts, "the subordination of woman to man and child to adult was deemed a natural fact."[6] Conceiving of the nation as a family, Nira Yuval-Davis contends, "can determine more or less the structure and power relations in the state and civil society."[7]

A key focus then and now was the patriarchal power that extended from family to nation and back to family. Such power influenced and was affected by the cultural understandings of masculinity and femininity and the relationship of women and men to the nation-state. Like many historical and contemporary families, most nations have long been considered as patriarchal sites of power. Tamar Mayer points out that "nation remains . . . emphatically, historically, and globally—the property of men," which reinscribes "patriarchal hierarchies and norms" that "enable men and nation to achieve superiority over women and a different Other by controlling them."[8]

The historical conceptions and practices of masculinities in Western cultures offer insight into ways that men were socialized to participate in the national experiment. Grounding such patriarchal principles in "classical republicanism," Carroll Smith-Rosenberg observes that the "eighteen-century Anglo-American republican political body was always emphatically male."[9] Indeed, in eighteenth-century European culture, "Women were certainly regarded as different from men, but different in the sense of being incomplete or inferior examples of the same character," which were assumptions that "accompanied the bourgeois ideology of 'separate spheres' in the nineteenth century."[10] Nineteenth-century schools also participated in the national project, John Beynon suggests, instituting a curriculum that trained elite white males in first-world cultures to exhibit "grit, self-reliance, determination, leadership and initiative." These qualities were "acquired in male company from exposure to the 'great outdoors' far removed from the domestic and the feminine." Such conceptions were grounded in Christian principles symbolized in "muscular and manly" terms and embodied by Jesus. Athletics also represented an important means for socializing male children for public participation. Beynon maintains that "a direct link [was] made between all-male games and sport . . . and patriotism and Empire-building."[11] That helped inspirit feelings of "national superiority."[12]

"Fatherland" served as the "force behind government."[13] The nation's mothers were expected to fulfill their own unique national roles as well.[14] Nations were constructed as families, requiring both masculinity and femininity to sustain them.[15] Such matriarchal roles, though, emphasized different attributes associated commonly with women. "Classical republicanism had . . . banished women from the political arena," Smith-Rosenberg asserts, because they were seemingly void of the necessary "physical strength and martial skills [needed] to defend their nation's . . . honour" as well as the "economic independence that made manly civic virtue possible."[16]

Women's national roles, though, were important in their own right, as exemplified by the ideology of "Republican Motherhood." Mothers of the Revolutionary Era and beyond were expected to commit themselves to promulgating civic virtue. A republican mother was thus imbued with the power to prepare her children, particularly those who were male, for citizenship.[17] Although women's political acts were centered in the private-domestic sphere, the republican mother's purview of activity expanded to include nongovernmental volunteer spaces. The "Benevolence Empire" represented a late eighteenth-century Christian force that elite and middle-class women "extend their maternal and domestic expertise to those of the community less able to care for themselves."[18] Such expectations are still evident; first ladies in particular continue to commit themselves to issues linked "to social welfare activities, especially those involving children and women." Although these are laudable activities, the historical legacy that their authority is still vested "in non-governmental" affairs still influences women in political life.[19]

Men's and women's responsibilities to the nation represent, in many ways, oppositional constructions that have differing implications. Whereas men serve as the "protectors" of the nation, women are often conceived as "protectors of the integrity of the family and its individual members."[20] Men "defend the national image," but women are conceived as the nation's "biological and symbolic reproducers" and the "bearers of national traditions."[21] Whereas the male physique "is connotative of power and strength," women's bodies represent sites of control as "variations of struggles for power by new or would-be guardians of the nation are . . . played out over the feminine body; over the feminine space of the nation."[22]

Such maternal constructs are often perceived more positively within the nation-state, even as they promote women's disempowerment and subordination.[23] Even less appealing images, however, are linked to women's sexuality—images of threats to the established order and national unity.[24] As Eley and Suny explain, "Women are not exactly absent from the scene of nationalist grandiosity but figure as important supporting players—as 'conquerors' mistresses, wartime rape victims, military prostitutes . . . pin-up models on patriotic calendars' and, of course, as workers, wives, girlfriends, and daughters waiting dutifully at home."[25] The more disempowered constructs and narratives of threat help inspire enhanced measures of national control.[26]

Gendered nationalism thus represents a site of ideological contestation. From the colonial period through the end of the nineteenth century, Kersh observes, "American national-union ideas [were] a focus of continual debate, [their] meaning and purposes contested by successive generations of elites, their followers, and people on the margins of the civic culture."[27] Today, however, "nationalist identities are more ambiguously gendered" than they perhaps once were in U.S. history.[28] And some, like Eley and Suny, see nationalism as a site not only to "resist the uncontrollable transformations of our time" but also as a place of "'cultural recovery' that could potentially lead . . . to acceptance, even celebration, of difference."[29]

## The Masculine and Sexualized Contexts of *The West Wing*

*The West Wing*'s gendered nationalism must be situated within a complex web of historical and ideological dissonance. Like its larger national and ideological environment, Sorkin's fictionalized presidency on *TWW* is located within a masculine, nationalist context framed by familial metaphor. Not surprisingly, President Bartlet functions as the father figure whose republican mother—his personal secretary, Mrs. Delores Landingham—has shaped his psyche. This depiction thus historicizes and collapses notions of family, nation, and the presidency. Abigail Bartlet also plays out the drama of a republican mother and is forced to negotiate the postfeminist terrain and contestation of a career woman in a more traditional role.[30] The position of the "first sons" is portrayed specifically by Josh and Sam, yet several staffers' relationships with their own fathers are accentuated at various moments in the show's progression and normalize the powerful role that fathers play in the nation-family.

Within this hierarchical and familial context, romance flourishes between the White House staff and those who are irregularly featured as supporting cast on *TWW*, sexualizing the show's political context. In the end, true romance imbued with passion, respect, and commitment is reserved for the president, the embodiment of the nation; love of the president, and thus the nation, must transcend other competing romances. Within this sexualized context the women of the West Wing are filled with power and influence yet delegitimized as political actors. Women's issues are also construed as falling outside the scope of the male political context, reifying men's control over the nation-state, marginalizing women on *TWW*, and reinscribing the mythos of presidency as the key ideological site of U.S. nationalism. In the end, the president represents the father to whom all commit, evidencing the lasting, loving, and loyal relationship between citizens and their president and, by extension, the nation.

## The Presidential Family

The conception of *TWW*'s national family is evident in several scripts, some more explicit than others. The "War Crimes" episode of season three exhibits the use of what we have termed a drama frame. In that episode, a verse of the Bible frames the relationship of husband to wife and then of president to vice president, connoting a hierarchical union within both familial and political roles. Upon leaving a church service, the Bartlets debate the contested meaning of Ephesians 5:21 in the company of Charlie. After the president notes that the church service "sucked," the First Lady recounts scripture, "'Husbands love your wives as Christ loved the Church and gave himself up for her.'" Directing his comment to Charlie in his wife's presence, the president retorts, "Yeah, she's skipping over the part that says 'wives, be subject to your husbands as to the Lord for the husband is the head of the wife as Christ is the head of the church.'" He later elaborates that the scripture was really not about husbands and wives but about "all of us" as he continues his recitation, "'be subject to one another out of reverence to Christ.'"

That theme ("'be subject to one another'") frames the remainder of the episode. Within this plotline Bartlet tries to convince the vice president to attend the funeral of shooting victims in Texas at the same time the National

Conference of State Legislatures meets there. The president asks Hoynes, an anti-gun-control Texan, to give a gun-control speech even though the vice president argues, "We're not going to get anywhere by treating gun owners like psychopaths . . . particularly in the South." The episode portrays the president as beholden to the vice president because, Toby remarks, "If the president wins reelection, it will be on the vice president's coattails." Bartlet and Hoynes reinforce the symbiotic subjectivity inherent in the presidential and vice presidential relationship:

> PRESIDENT: The only way you're going to get the nomination, you know that don't you, is if I win.
> VICE PRESIDENT: And the only way that you're going to win is if I'm on the ticket, you know that, don't you sir?

Ultimately, Hoynes goes to Texas at the president's request even though he believes that "going down there is suicide," communicating that the vice president is, in the end, subject to the president. The mutual subjectivity, likewise evidenced in the conversation between the Bartlets, also establishes the hierarchy of power. The president is the final decision-maker in the administration. Abigail Bartlet's presence in the series is at best intermittent, emphasizing the centrality of the president's role and the more marginalized status of a First Lady in the nationalist context. In addition, the president's evocation of the Bible, particularly the figure of Christ, reinscribes a patriarchal dynamic of power between husband and wife. As Kersh explains, "The roots of union talk run deep in Protestant Christianity."[31] So do the lingering values of true womanhood that construct women as submissive to their husbands and naturally more religious—a power dynamic rooted in the Bible, a text Bartlet often references.[32]

Using scripture about the union of men and women to frame the relationship between the president and vice president insinuates a familial relationship in the national political context. Family tropes are rearticulated in other ways as well. When expressing his views on the conflict inherent between Congress and the presidency, Toby discloses to Leo: "That is what my ex-wife [a member of Congress from Maryland] and I did for years. We had these rules that we could talk about anything but why we couldn't live with each other." Leo responds with a story about a senior Democrat mentoring a newcomer to the House of Representatives. The "freshman Democrat" wanted to "'meet the enemy—the Republicans.'" The "senior Democrat said, 'the Republicans aren't the enemy, they're the opposition. The Senate is the enemy.'" After relaying the story Leo returns to the drama frame of marriages:

"Toby—Jenny and I wouldn't talk about it either. You know why? . . . because we loved each other and it was awful and we knew it was never going to change, ever" ("The Leadership Breakfast"). Such drama-framing once again conflates politics and family. The institution of marriage is used to frame politics, naturalizing the conflict between the Democrats and Republicans, House and the Senate, presidency and Congress, and husbands and wives.

A similar family-politics conflation is articulated in the episode entitled "The Stackhouse Filibuster." C.J. writes to her father that she cannot attend his seventieth birthday because of a senator's filibuster of the Family Wellness Act. Sam is likewise writing to his father to confront him about a conflict first revealed in a previous episode ("Somebody's Going to Emergency, Somebody's Going to Jail") regarding a revelation that Sam's father had a clandestine relationship with another woman for twenty-eight years. Although everyone is angry with Senator Stackhouse for his filibuster, they help ensure that the senator is successful in adding an autism provision to the bill because his grandson suffers from that condition. As the president explains the protectionist role of grandfathers to C.J., "We'll make enemies, we'll break laws, we'll break bones. But you will not mess with the grandchildren." In the end, C.J. equates grandfathers with all that is good about politics and tells her father, "Tonight, I've seen a man with no legs stay standing . . . and a guy with no voice keep shouting and if politics brings out the worst in people, maybe people bring out the best because I'm looking at the TV right now and damn if twenty-eight U.S. Senators haven't just walked on the floor to help . . . grandfathers all." Josh writes to his mother because of his father's recent death (even as he mentions his late father prominently in the e-mail), but the remainder of the episode focuses on grandfathers and fathers, emphasizing the patriarchal centrality in such constructions to family, politics, and nation.

Within *TWW*'s national family the president acts as the key father figure. Early in the show's creation, Aaron Sorkin reports, Martin Sheen "was pushing for sons for the President" because Bartlet has three daughters in the show's narrative. "No, no, no," Sorkin said, "these guys are your sons," and Sheen concluded that "Bartlet really is a strong father figure."[33] When watching the show it becomes apparent that the president is a father figure and mentor for at least two characters, Josh and Sam, albeit in different ways.

During a flashback scene of the opening episodes of season two ("In the Shadow of Two Gunmen, Part 2") Bartlet consoles Josh after his father dies, visiting Josh unexpectedly at Chicago's O'Hare Airport before returning to a primary election victory celebration. Josh shares that his father "would have liked tonight. . . . He would have been proud." The president reassures Josh in fatherly terms, "Trust me Josh, I'm a father. He was already." In the finale of the same season ("Two Cathedrals") the president yells at God from the National Cathedral in Washington immediately following Mrs. Landingham's funeral. Season two began with the aftermath of an attack by gunmen on the presidential entourage, seriously injuring Josh and wounding the president. Emphasizing his role as father and the patriarchal symbolism of Christianity, the president shouts, "I think you're just vindictive. What was Josh Lyman, a warning shot? That was my son. What did I ever do to yours but praise His glory and praise His name?" The season ends with viewers not knowing whether the president will seek a second term. Closing scenes take place to the backdrop music of Dire Straights' "Brothers in Arms," furthering the masculine political context in which father-son bonds and male-centered relationships form the familial basis of the nation's political institutions.

In the third season the president guides Sam in a game of chess and helps him discern the appropriate move in a conflict between China and Taiwan ("Hartsfield's Landing"). Bartlet leads Sam through the chess match and the conflict with China and encourages him to "see the whole board." In the end Sam deduces the president's strategy on China and is awed by his mentor's cunning capabilities. The president responds, "You're going to run for president one day. Don't be scared. You can do it. I believe in you. That's checkmate."

"Hartsfield's Landing" continues the themes articulated in previous episodes in which the concept of father functions in another way to frame interactions with Sam as well as offer insight into the personal and presidential psyche. In season three, Toby pressures the president to speak out on the issue of affirmative action in response to a Republican opponent's critique of its influence on university enrollment decisions. In an extended and heated exchange with the president Toby speculates that the reason for his reluctance to weigh in on controversial issues is that the president's "father never liked him . . . he [the president] was too smart." Toby also suggests that the president's father hit him, which explains Bartlet thinking that if he can just "win one more election . . . maybe your father. . . ." The president becomes angry and orders Toby out of the Oval Office before he finishes the thought that Bartlet is still trying to be the kind of man his father would respect and love. As Toby leaves we see the image of a tortured president, head in hands and haunted by the ghosts of fathers past. Throughout the exchange a lit portrait of George Washington shines in the background, communicating that Bartlet lives not only in the shadow of his deceased father, whose expectations he could never meet, but also with the knowledge that the mythic stature of past presidents is likewise beyond contemporary attainment.[34] The Founding Father's legacy, and his father's expectations, are emblematic of hegemonic masculinity that upholds expectations for men that are "more often than not . . . impossible to live up to." What results is a "terrible sense of failure."[35]

The authority and presence of the father is furthered in the following episode as the president plays chess with not only Sam but also Toby after he presents them with chess sets given to him by India's prime minister. As Toby and the president continue their conversation about the president's reluctance to speak out on controversial matters the president assures Toby that his disinclination is not "because of my father." After Toby calls Bartlet's father "an idiot," the president demands, "Please, can we talk about my father with some respect? The man's gone. . . . He's my father."

In reasserting the authority of the father figure, even those who abuse their sons, the masculine nature of politics is likewise reasserted. The symbolism of father frames the issue of the presidential campaign while the president is shown preparing his White House son (Sam, who later leaves to run his own congressional campaign) to perpetuate the masculine quality of the nation. The president ultimately acts in the capacity of a moral father for Sam, whose own father's morality was questioned in the revelation of marital infidelity. Sam, who functions as the son the president never had, represents a way for Bartlet to counter his own father's foibles and parent a son in a moralistic, appropriately mentoring way. Such extended mentoring is not part of Bartlet's relationship with his daughters. The strong father-son bond of socializing boys to men is reserved for the sanctity of male-male relationships. The West Wing is thus a male preserve where national and personal issues are played out and resolved. As McClintock asserts, white men's role in the nation-state is to "embody the forward-thrusting agency of national progress."[36]

*TWW* offers a masculine-based political context, but women serve important roles. Delores Landingham in particular embodies many values of republican motherhood and offsets the moral inequities of the president's father. As the president prepares for Mrs. Landingham's funeral ("Two Cathedrals"), several flashback scenes explain the relationship between the president and his long-time administrative assistant. Mrs. Landingham and Jed Bartlet first met at the latter's prep school, where Mrs. Landingham worked as secretary for Bartlet's father, the headmaster. She also represented the women on staff who were seeking higher wages. Rather than take their case to Bartlet's father she asks the teenaged son to function as the women's advocate. She supplies him with the necessary data on wage discrepancies, and in response Jed says, "I'm not a woman and I don't work here." "The women who do are afraid for their jobs . . . what is it you are afraid of?" she scolds, reflecting the civic virtue of republican mothers. After they banter back and forth she concludes, "Look at you, you are a boy king. You're a foot smarter than the smartest kids in the class. You're blessed with inspiration . . . look, if you think we're wrong . . . then I respect that. But if you think we're right and you won't speak up because you can't be bothered, then, God, Jed, I don't even want to know ya."

The scene reinforces the notion that men engage in political activity; women work behind the scenes and men function as their political voices. It is a formative moment in the political education of Jed Bartlet. Mrs. Landingham inspired him to represent the women, serving as a moral yet "chauvinistic" leader in the process. As Murray Edelman notes, even when leaders exhibit "compassion" and are involved in "helping others," "sexism and chauvinism are [still] implicated."[37]

The flashback scene, though, functions as the drama frame for the president's decision to seek reelection. As he agonizes over the momentous decision the ghost of Mrs. Landingham appears in the Oval Office. The two have a similar exchange to the one that occurred some thirty to forty years earlier:

PRESIDENT: The party's not going to want me to run.
MRS. LANDINGHAM: The party will come back. You'll get them back.
PRESIDENT: I got a secret for you, Mrs. Landingham, I've never been the most popular guy in the Democratic Party.
MRS. LANDINGHAM: I've got a secret for you Mr. President. Your father was a prick who could never get over the fact he wasn't as smart as his brothers. Are you in a tough spot? Yes. Do I feel sorry for you? I do not. Why? Because there are people way worse off than you.

Before she departs and the president resolves to fight for a second term, Mrs. Landingham concludes, "You know, if you don't want to run again, I respect that. But if you don't run because you think it's going to be too hard or you think you're going to lose, well, God, Jed, I don't even want to know ya."

The two scenes are instructive because Delores Landingham is portrayed as the one who helped shape the president's political values associated with a selfless search for morality and justice. Her role, though, is very much limited to behind-the-scenes status. She inspires the governor-turned-president from the role as secretary rather than as a visible actor in the political sphere.

Mrs. Landingham functions as the ideal republican mother in other ways as well. Her two sons were killed in Vietnam, and she spends the remainder of her life aiding public servants, using her moral sensibilities to shape the political values of the man who would become president. As Floya Anthias and Nira Yuval-Davis contend, images of the "nation as a loved woman in danger or as a mother who lost her sons in battle is a frequent part of the particular nationalist discourse in national liberation struggles or other forms of national conflicts when men are called to fight 'for the sake of our women and children' or to 'defend their honor.'"[38] Jed Bartlet stands up to his abusive father on behalf of women and seeks reelection to help defend the honor of all Americans. Delores Landingham embodies the ideals of republican motherhood, preparing the adolescent-turned-governor-turned-president for his participation in the public sphere and sacrificing her biological sons for the sake of the nation.

Even though Jed Bartlet's biological mother is seemingly still alive in *TWW*'s narrative, she receives no character development and is noticeably absent from the story's plotlines, evidencing the lack of mythos surrounding mothers and politics. The one bit of information offered about Bartlet's mother is that she, as good republican mothers do, passed down her religion (i.e., Catholicism) to her son, an action spoken of with derision by the president's father, who expresses anti-Catholic sentiments in a flashback moment ("Two Cathedrals").

Abby Bartlet likewise exhibits republican motherhood values that have frequently had formative influence on the role of First Lady from the eighteenth century forward.[39] In many ways the president's wife on *TWW* exhibits some of these same traditional republican motherhood commitments; in other ways, however, she reflects the routinized entrance of women into the public sphere at the end of the twentieth century. Her sphere of influence centers on issues of health. Although she is identified as a thoracic surgeon, an adjunct professor of thoracic surgery at Harvard Medical School, and a doctor on the staff at Boston Mercy Hospital and Columbia Presbyterian Hospital ("The Fall's Gonna Kill You"), she is also especially concerned about children's health, a common theme for republican mothers. Despite her impressive credentials, most of her expertise on the show centers on the president's health or the health of their children. In the opening episode of season two, Abby Bartlet takes charge in the hospital after her husband is shot, ensuring that the other doctors answer to her ("In the Shadow of Two Gunmen"). She also immediately rushes to his side at any hint of illness ("He Shall, from Time to Time"). On the one hand, Abby Bartlet is portrayed as a very successful doctor, which defies conventional constructions of women's roles within the nation-state. On the other hand, such connections between first ladies and health issues reflect the legacy of republican motherhood as women translate their concern with the health of the family to the health of the na-tion.[40] Because Abby Bartlet is the president's doctor her role as caretaker of the nation's commander-in-chief is likewise advanced.

Apart from issues involving her husband's health, when Abby Bartlet does speak out she is often silenced. In "The White House Pro-Am" of season one she becomes involved in a legislative dispute when she pressures a female member of the House to drop a child labor amendment from pending legis-lation. The culminating dispute with the president marginalizes and dimin-ishes her. During their Oval Office confrontation Bartlet reveals frustration about the perception that his wife is handling him on issues related to the child labor amendment, and he reins her in after it becomes clear that her staff is leaking information that goes against the presidentially backed legislation. In the end, Abby admits her errors and is humorously chastened by the pres-ident:

> FIRST LADY: I concede I was wrong about the thing.
> PRESIDENT: Good.
> FIRST LADY: However . . .
> PRESIDENT: No, "however." Just be wrong. Just stand there in your wrongness and be wrong. And get used to it.

Despite the humorous tone of the interaction, the First Lady is still re-minded of her role within the masculine-controlled context. As Benedict An-derson explains this dynamic of the contemporary, postmodern nation: "Ac-cess to nationhood and citizenship has undermined the control of individual male household heads over 'their' women, who are no longer excluded from the public sphere; but it has also encouraged the newer subordination of women, and the appropriation of their labour, by a male-dominated national collective."[41]

Abby Bartlet is much more contentious than Mrs. Landingham, the ideal republican mother, and demonstrates professional and personal mistakes and the ambiguities of women and work in the postfeminist age. Not only is she complicit in hiding the president's illness but she also breaks laws and per-jures herself on behalf of his health. This depiction of the First Lady questions her morality as a doctor and as the nation's republican mother. During the second season episode entitled "18th and Potomac" we learn that Abby wrote illegal prescriptions for her husband's medication and then had them shipped to various locations during the campaign. Oliver Babish, the White House counsel, tells her, "You violated the medical ethic rules of three state boards: New Hampshire, Arizona, and Missouri." In further identifying her professional errors Babish charges, "The AMA's code of ethics pretty well spells out the egregiousness of treating your own family members." The First Lady's only defense is "we do it anyway." She also falsifies her daughter's Georgetown University health application, which becomes a central issue of concern in the precongressional investigation period.

Abby Bartlet pays the price for her husband's cover-up. In a revealing third-season episode, "Dead Irish Writers," she calls together the women of the West Wing (Donna and C.J.) and Amy Gardner (Josh's girlfriend and a well-known women's activist) to discuss her fate over multiple bottles of wine during her birthday celebration. This community of women, which includes the show's personifications of feminism (Amy and C.J.), convinces Abby to give up her medical license for a year in the face of threatened medical board sanctions:

> AMY: Mrs. Bartlet . . . well if the most that they can give you is a whole year's suspension, is it . . .
>
> FIRST LADY [interrupting Amy]: Is it that big of deal? . . . Yes, I'm a doctor. It's not like changing your major. You of all people . . . women talk about their husbands overshadowing their careers. Mine got eaten.
>
> C.J.: Your husband got eaten? . . . You've got a husband and children, a home, and a life and we're talking about one year and your not having a medical license.

In the end, Abby Bartlet voluntarily gives up her medical license for the remainder of the time her husband is in office. It is not the men of the program who request that she make the sacrifice but the strong and progressive women. As Vavrus reveals in her discussion of postfeminism, one characteristic of postfeminism and media is "the shift from a vision of collective politics for social change to an individualistic focus; successes and failures are attributed to individual women rather than to a complex formula of individual work, group efforts, and structural influences."[42] *TWW*'s depiction of Abby Bartlet and the role of the other women in securing her contrition during the MS plot indicate this postfeminist tendency. The women assume responsibility for persuading Abby to accept the sanction; they are the ones who do the dirty work of politics. Although various men question the First Lady about her role in the MS plot it is the women on *TWW* who move her to perform the ritualized sacrifice of surrendering her medical license (and professional identity) for the greater national good. Although the president is mindful of the sacrifices his wife is making, he accepts her decision without protest, telling her, "I love you very much." "I love you too," Abby responds, reaffirming her love for the patriarch of the family and the nation.

*TWW*'s portrayal of Abby Bartlet thus reflects the contentiousness of professional women in the public sphere. Although hugely successful, she demonstrates very questionable judgment in her role as the president's doctor and removes herself from medical work voluntarily. As Imelda Whelehan explains a common narrative inherent in postfeminist discourse reflective of such gendered constructions, "The media at once pronounce the official equality of women, and then go on to catalogue the ills that this brings—the stresses and strains that 'prove' women are biologically incapable of fully entering a man's world."[43] Abby Bartlet not only displays a lack of professionalism in her public/career role but she also, as the nation's republican mother caring for her family's health, suggests the complications of republican mothers assuming too many responsibilities outside the domestic or volunteer spheres. The women on *TWW*, her "feminist" advisors, resolve the dissonance over Abby Bartlet's complicity in the cover-up and motivate her decision to give up her medical license. Such a ritualized sacrifice is warranted, Donna suggests, because, after all, "Mrs. Bartlet . . . you were also a doctor when your husband said, 'give me the drugs and don't tell anybody' and you said 'ok.'" ("Dead Irish Writers"). It is the women who reinforce the importance of marriage and family over career in this masculine context and offer up Abigail Bartlet as the scapegoat. In the aftermath of national exigencies, Kenneth Burke notes, cultures often restore order by sacrificing the scapegoat, who "performs the role of vicarious atonement," completing the necessary redemption cycle.[44] In the end, she loses her job as doctor whereas the president retains his as president.

Family functions as a central frame for the nation and the political life of *TWW*. Janice Doane and Devon Hodges observe that "as the family is subjected to such modern processes as urbanization and industrialization, family values, norms, and concepts undergo changes. This does not mean . . . that all premodern forms of ideation simply disappear; . . . these traditional structures of consciousness may survive long into the modern period."[45] *TWW*'s family, not surprisingly, is patriarchal although it has also adapted to the legacy of second-wave feminism and the introduction of women into the political sphere.[46] Abigail Bartlet's connection to the nation is also "submerged as a *social* relation to a man through marriage."[47] In the end, the family, although progressive in that the women in it have entered the work force, still reflects what Bernadette Casey et al. predict is "television's influence . . . [on] maintaining social and ideological systems" rather "than changing them."[48]

*The Sexual Context of* TWW

The family trope frames *TWW*'s depiction of the presidency, but the show is also imbued with a strong sense of sexuality. The Bartlets' relationship, for example, is often sexually charged. Many women (and to a lesser extent the men) who visit the Bartlet White House are likewise sexualized and represent possible sexual partners, and potentially threatening encounters, for the men and women of the show. The presence of a decidedly male gaze further sexualizes women who venture in and out of the national experiment. As Julie Mostov maintains, "In the politics of national identity the nation becomes a lover and mother to men—demanding of loyalty and sacrifice, comforting, yet vulnerable, needing protection and requiring revenge."[49] Women on the program are framed by a male gaze and often distract the men from the stress of the nation's complex issues.

In the sense that *TWW* depicts its characters as part of a metaphorical family, most men and women on the show avoid the suggestion of "incest" by becoming sexually engaged with those outside of the "family's" inner circle. Josh and Donna's interactions, however, evidence a tension surrounding the concept of eros in the nation's family. Although the staff pursues many sexual opportunities, the ultimate love affair is reserved for the president, the personification of nationalism. As such, *TWW* manifests James Jasinski's conclusion that "our experience of a narrative can recall, if we engage it in its fullness, a sense of politics as an ongoing project of communal (re)constitution: a continual process of shaping and reshaping our possibilities for collective action."[50]

In only the fifth episode of the first season the show's writers establish the masculine context by accentuating the male gaze. During "The Crackpots and These Women" President Bartlet offers an encomium to the women gathered in the White House for a celebration. He, Leo, and Josh are oddly positioned in the scene, giving them the ability to gaze and comment upon the various women around them surreptitiously. Their comments, although praiseworthy, are highly gendered and othering and illustrate *TWW*'s overt masculinity:

> BARTLET: We were talking about these women.
> JOSH: Yeah?
> LEO: We can't get over these women.
> BARTLET: Look at C.J. She's like a fifties movie star, so capable, so loving and energetic.

LEO: Look at Mandy over there. Going punch for punch with Toby in a world that tells women to sit down and shut up. Mandy's already won her battle with the president. The games over, but she's not done. She wants Toby.

BARTLET: Mrs. Landingham. Did you guys know she lost two sons in Vietnam? What would make her want to serve her country is beyond me, but in fourteen years, she's not missed a day's work, not one.

All the women are valued and praised but in gendered ways. C.J. is noticed for her energy and appearance and Mrs. Landingham for her faithless dedication to national duty. Even when Mandy is admired for perseverance and commitment, those traits are contextualized as a gender role reversal. And despite the men's exaltations, what the scene reinforces most clearly is the dominance of male perspective on *TWW*. That the episode's writers saw the need to engage in this epideictic exercise separates male from female, othering females as objects of gaze and comment and further demarcating *TWW*'s masculine presidency. As Laura Mulvey notes, "The male protagonist is free to command the stage, a stage of spatial illusion in which he articulates the look and creates the action." To the extent that the "man controls the film fantasy . . . [he] also emerges as the representative of power."[51]

Women as the subjects of the gaze are furthered sexualized on *TWW*. The First Lady is sexualized by her husband and also by a male visitor to the White House. In one scene the president also constructs the other republican mother as another possible receptacle for his robust sexual appetite. During the second season, in an episode entitled "And It's Surely to Their Credit," the president is portrayed as starved for sex. Abby is depicted as "randy" as he orders her to "take your clothes off . . . get them off." He warns that she has two minutes to disrobe "or I swear to God I'm going to get Mrs. Landingham drunk." The president's nickname for the First Lady is often "hot pants" or "sweet knees" ("And It's Surely to Their Credit"), whereas she calls him "jackass" ("Twenty Hours in America"). More revealing, she is also sexualized by Lord John Marbury, British ambassador to the United States: "Abigail . . . your breasts are magnificent," he says as he begins to dance with the First Lady at her birthday party. He asks the president if he was initially attracted to "her magnificent breasts." The president displays considerable displeasure, noting, "You know John, there are places in the world where it might be considered rude to talk about the physical attributes of another man's wife." Marbury later inquires as his hands move toward Abby's body, "May I grasp your breasts?" She responds, "You may kiss my cheek" ("Dead Irish Writers").

The president's objection is not about the sexualization of women but rather the sexualization of his wife. The gaze throughout the scene is clearly centered on the First Lady's body, particularly her breasts. Elizabeth Grosz writes that the "coding of femininity with corporeality" often encourages the idea that men can "satisfy their . . . need for corporeal contact through their access to women's bodies and services," ultimately "contain[ing] women" in the process.[52] Both the president and the ambassador play out such assumptions over the body of the First Lady.

Zoey, the Bartlets' youngest daughter, is likewise sexualized in season one and beyond as the president works to protect her chastity. In her first appearance on the show, he notes that his "beautiful daughter" is "starting Georgetown in the spring—this prior to medical school and a life of celibacy" ("The Crackpots and These Women"). Although the president functions as Zoey's sexual protector he also humorously offers any one of his daughters as a reward for the individual who helped resolve a stand-off in Iowa with the young men who bombed the athletic facility at the fictional Kennison State University. "Mike," the president jokingly asserts, "pick yourself out a daughter. My oldest is married but I can have it annulled. The Pope said he'd do it, I swear to God" ("The Red Mass"). Also in the fourth season, the president comments to Charlie and Josh on different occasions, "Boy, Zoey's growing up nicely, isn't she?" When they both separately respond in suggestive ways, with Charlie noting, "Yes, she is," and Josh asserting, "Man, I'll say," the president expresses displeasure visually ("Guns Not Butter"). Without the men's visibly expressive nonverbal reactions the sexual content of the conversation is less apparent. Yet as Michael Griffin asserts, visual discourses "symbolize socially shared concepts." In this scene the "socially shared concept" is the sexualization of the president's daughter, a *topoi* of male discourse that normalizes sexuality in a nationalist setting.[53]

C.J. and Ainsley Hayes, associate White House counsel, are likewise sexualized through a male-centered gaze. In a second-season episode both women are portrayed as being at work in the White House but not wearing pants. When C.J. appears on the show *Capitol Beat*, which is covering the State of the Union address from the White House, its host introduces her as the "very lovely, the very talented—Claudia Jean Cregg." At the commercial break he announces to everyone in the room that because she sat in paint, "C.J.'s not wearing any pants . . . no pants whatsoever." While C.J. walks around in only a coat, Ainsley is attired in a bathrobe during certain White House appearances because she, too, sat in paint. Also in the episode, Sam tries to orchestrate a meeting between Ainsley and the president, instructing him to say, "A lot of people assumed you were hired because you're a blonde Republican sex kitten. They were obviously wrong and keep up the good work." When the president ventures to Ainsley's basement office she is dancing in her bathrobe, trying to entice Sam to join her. She screams when the president unexpectedly walks in. As everyone's gaze is fixed on Ainsley the president states, "What's up? . . . I never knew we had a night club down here. . . . A lot of people assumed you were hired because you were a blonde Republican sex kitten and well, they're obviously wrong. Keep up the good work." This "sex kitten" status, which appears oddly situated in the White House workplace, is suddenly naturalized by Ainsley's actions and appearance and the presidentially directed gaze ("Bartlet's Third State of the Union"). In a separate episode C.J. is further sexualized by Bruno Gianelli, Bartlet's reelection campaign director, who tells her, "Man, you've got a killer body, you know that?" ("Ways and Means"). The masculine gaze thus centers on women's bodies that on *TWW* are often sexualized for comic effect. "When nation, gender and sexuality intersect," Mayer contends, "the [woman's] body becomes an important marker" in the "national" and "masculine project."[54] Not only are the bodies sexualized in the nation-state but the comedic roles that such sexualized bodies play also undermine the seriousness of women in politics.

Relationships are common between staffers and nonpermanent cast members, exacerbating the sexualized context of *TWW*'s nationalism, complete with threatening overtones. Sam and Mallory O'Brien, Leo's daughter, a teacher, have an off-and-on-again relationship that spans at least three seasons. Although attracted to one another, the couple often engages in competitive banter that is sometimes sexual, as when Mallory tells Sam that she is having "a lot of great sex" with her professional hockey playing boyfriend ("*Galileo*"). Sam and Ainsley also engage in flirtatious behavior as she begs him to dance with her when she is attired in her bathrobe ("Bartlet's Third State of the Union").

As Ainsley is sexualized she likewise threatens Sam's masculinity. Even though before their first encounter on a news show Sam calls her a "young, blonde, leggy, Republican" who apparently "didn't know anything," she decisively wins the spin battle as Josh watches. "Come quick," he instructs Toby. "Sam's getting his ass kicked by a girl" ("In This White House"). Even when interacting with his father over e-mail, Sam relays being "spanked" by a nineteen-year-old intern over issues of governmental waste. The intern was not of sexual interest, yet she is spoken of in sexual and demasculinizing (and thus threatening) terms ("The Stackhouse Filibuster").

As the show attends to the complex issues of the nation viewers are constantly reminded that the characters, especially the women, are still fundamentally sexual beings. Anne Norton talks of "representation" as a means of creating "ourselves in a new world order." When representing sexuality, this "'natural drive'" "becomes a matter of writing, a literary act" that at once reinscribes traditionally hierarchical relationships between men and women and layers them with warnings of destabilization. Norton expresses that feminine power (embodied on *TWW* in characters such as Ainsley Hayes and Abby Bartlet) "is associated with a threat not only to particular husbands but to patriarchy, not only to men but to those qualities the culture marks as male."[55]

Other encounters are likewise sexualized between women and men, yet such relationships are marginalized distractions in the staff's work for the president. Leo's primary love interest after his divorce is with Jordon Kendall, his lawyer during congressional hearings over the president's cover-up of multiple sclerosis. In "Bartlet for America," a third-season episode, Jordon sits passively beside Leo, who is speaking on his cell phone with the president prior to testifying before Congress:

> PRESIDENT: How does she [Jordan] look?
> LEO: Who?
> PRESIDENT: Her.
> LEO: She looks good.
> PRESIDENT: What is she wearing? . . .
> LEO: Spandex

Throughout his testimony and during breaks, Leo repeatedly asks Jordan out to dinner. Over time, the relationship develops, and the two are later shown dancing outside the Oval Office. She also defends the president and Leo in an international dispute in future episodes.

C.J. has two notable relationships with the men she encounters as part of her work environment. One in particular offers critical insight into the intersectionality between gender and nation. Danny Concannon represents an occasional love interest for C.J. throughout the first two seasons. Although he disappears for many episodes, Danny returns in the fourth season to create unresolved expectations for reigniting the relationship. More significantly, however, in season three C.J. becomes romantically attracted to her bodyguard when an e-mail stalker threatens her. The threatening messages begin arriving after C.J. is critical of Saudi Arabia's treatment of women ("Enemies Foreign and Domestic"). Recognizing that she should not have been so aggressive in her remarks, she considers "apologizing," a move that demonstrates the guilt she feels in confronting the patriarchal hierarchy. Ron Butterfield, head of the president's Secret Service detail, assures C.J. that the threats have nothing "to do with that . . . Muslim extremists don't get personal . . . They don't want to kill one person, they want dozens or hundreds."

The stalker plot carries through the remainder of season three and culminates in its concluding episode. Initially, C.J. acts as the rebellious woman, refusing protection and engaged in acts of resistance to the "hegemonic projects."[56] Although she informs the president that the act of protection "might be an overreaction," he performs his fatherly duties and insists, "You're part of my family and this thing is happening and I simply won't permit it." He tells C.J. to "sign the piece of paper" that authorizes Secret Service protection for her ("Enemies Foreign and Domestic"), reifying notions of women as "prized and revered objects of protection."[57] She acquiesces but continues her rebellious acts and hostility against Simon Donovan, her white male protector: "Here's my rules and regulations. I'm getting in my baby blue '65 Mustang convertible and I'm going to feel the wind in my hair and any place else I want. You can look at my tail lights . . . I will see you at home." Demonstrating that "no doesn't mean no," Simon confidently awaits her return. He has removed the spark plugs and other parts of her car's engine.

In time, C.J., the representation of the vulnerable nation-state, predictably falls in love with her protector, who refuses her advances until his duty to his nation is fulfilled. C.J.'s admiration for Simon is most apparent once she watches him fire a gun in the Secret Service firing range. After she falls to the ground when she fires a gun herself, and after Simon hits his target dead center, C.J. softens her demeanor. He looks at her and says, "Well?" "Yes," she responds. "Yes. I like that you're tall." The reply puzzles Simon ("You do?"). Romantic music plays in the background as C.J. admits, "It makes me feel more feminine. I'm going to go change" ("We Killed Yamamoto"). In the season finale we learn that C.J.'s stalker has been caught. In celebration she and Simon plan to meet at the end of the Broadway play they are attending with the president. Before that can happen, Simon enters a convenience store, interrupts a robbery, and is gunned down. C.J. is devastated when her romantic protector is brutally killed only hours before they are free to openly pursue their relationship ("Posse Comitatus").

The romance between C.J. and Simon Donovan is shattered in this narrative. The strong, independent woman/nation-state is forced into a protective state by the fatherly president. The protector, a strong and handsome white male hero figure, dies, giving his life because of his service to that nation-state.[58] As Mayer argues, "Because women's bodies represent the 'purity' of the nation and thus are guarded heavily by men, an attack on these bodies becomes an attack on the nation's men."[59] Masculinity is defined via the defense of the feminine, and the female figure may frequently function metaphorically as the larger nation.[60]

Marilyn French offers a different perspective to the fairy-tale ending gone bad, suggesting, "If the author does not grant a virtuous female character eternal felicity, either she doesn't deserve it or the male bar [of justice] is not just. Because in a patriarchal world the latter is unthinkable, her virtue must be deceptive."[61] Although nearing a conventionally romantic ending, C.J. is prevented from living out the romantic illusion with another white male protagonist. Given that the story line began with and is thus framed by her diatribe against patriarchy, and because she resisted the protective role of the hero only to fall in love with him, one could view such events as potential punishment for being outspoken. Also important, though, is the presumed monogamy between the staff and the president and between the nation and the president. Within this story line another West Wing relationship fails. In season four, C.J. recovers from her loss and devotes full attention to reelecting the president—the worthiest, most faithful, and presumed exclusive receptacle for the romantic emotions of *TWW* staff.

Other serial yet unsuccessful relationships are evident. In season one, Charlie and Zoey become romantically involved only to break up after the presidential assassination attempt that targets Charlie. In another instance, Toby's former wife is impregnated with sperm he donated when they were married. Toby spends part of seasons three and four trying to convince her to remarry him so as to create a traditional nuclear family. By the end of Bartlet's first term these relationships, although sexualizing the people of *TWW*, have yet to culminate in a successful relationship, whether a long-standing love affair or stable monogamy.

Josh has the most complex, on-going relationship struggles on *TWW*. He and Mandy are colleagues when the show begins, even though they had recently ended a romantic relationship. Their encounters are still sexually charged and played out in power battles similar to those of Sam and Ainsley in later episodes. "You answer to me and you answer to Toby," he declares. "In your dreams, in your little dreams" is her retort ("Post Hoc, Ergo Propter Hoc"). Mandy leaves the show after the first season, and the love affair is not rekindled. The next love interest for Josh is his secretary, Donna, a relationship that exhibits the hierarchy that often exists between a boss and an assistant. In many scenes Josh and Donna walk hurriedly through the halls of the West Wing. With few exceptions she follows him, almost jogging to keep up with his brisk stride. Even though Donna is occasionally shown as progressive and insightful, she frequently talks to Josh's back as she follows him to get his coffee and then back to his office. Her repeated placement behind Josh visually reinforces the hierarchy of the relationship, as does Josh continual yelling "Donna" whenever he needs her attention and other scenes, such as in the "Manchester" episode, where she is left to carry their suitcases.

Their relationship, although hierarchical, is sexually charged yet taboo. Josh is compelled to seek sexual encounters with women who reside and work outside the West Wing family. In an exchange during the second season he tells Donna to arrange an accidental meeting between the president and the Ukrainian parliament leader. As he encourages her "to set up the meeting and knock 'em dead," he pulls her close, grabbing her waist and swatting her behind ("The Lame Duck Congress"). It is unusual office conduct that would most likely not be part of a man's interaction with another male colleague. Sexual tension, though, is more explicitly played out during season two, when Josh shows interest in Joey Lucas, a freelance pollster. Donna's response is to give Josh dating advice, telling him, "You should ask her out," or "You have to ask a girl out on a date" ("Bartlet's Third State of the Union"). During the following episode, "The War at Home," she explains women to Josh, "We like to be wooed . . . she wants you to ask her out Josh. . . . You missed the signs." Although Josh seems interested in Joey he is perplexed by Donna's insistence. "You wouldn't think she'd be jealous?" he asks Sam. He also admits that he usually does "everything within my considerable capabilities to sabotage" Donna's dates. In the end, Joey, observing Donna and Josh's relationship, explains to Josh: "She likes you and she knows it's beginning to show and she needs to cover herself with misdirection."

During "Seventeen People," an episode of the same season, the relationship is further explicated even though it is one that can never be consummated. Josh gives Donna flowers on the "anniversary" of the moment that they resumed working together after Donna left to return to her boyfriend. She is angry, though, because the flowers remind her that she left Josh's employ to reunite with her boyfriend, only to come back after she left him a second time. She notes to Josh, "You took me back when you had absolutely no reason to trust me." She also admits, "Yes, you are better than my old boyfriend," who stopped at a bar on the way to pick her up from the hospital after she was in a car accident. In a touching moment, Josh responds, "If you were in an accident, I wouldn't stop for a beer." "If you were in an accident, I wouldn't stop for red lights," she replies. "Thanks for taking me back."

The unconsummated romantic relationship between Donna and Josh functions as a drama frame for the relationship between citizens and nation, conflating a discourse of sexuality and romance embedded within notions of nationalism. Although their "relationship" is very public—even Amy asks Josh the following season, "Are you dating your assistant?"—it cannot be sexually acted upon because Josh definitively suggests that he is "not" dating Donna ("The Women of Qumar"). In his analysis of political and personal intimacy in the film *The Big Chill,* Jasinski draws on Hannah Arendt's work and notes, "Intimacy . . . cannot sustain political action or political community through time."[62] What is required instead is a relationship that reflects "a form of relating-together through things held in common," as Ronald Beiner explains.[63] Such an appropriate political environment avoids the "consequence" that intimacy provokes, where "critical communal tasks like judging moral character or selecting courses of action on grounds other than instrumental reasoning become impossible."[64] In a political context founded upon familial conceptions, sexual unions among staff members are threatening to the nation-state; even sustained relationships with others outside the family are problematized because they distract attention from the nation's business.

*TWW*'s context is thus sexualized even though serious passion for the nation's business takes precedence over the complexities of sexual relationships. Leo sacrifices his marriage for the president in season one, telling his wife, "This is the most important thing I'll ever do, Jenny. I have to do it well." Jenny queries, "It's not more important than your marriage?" He is silent for a moment and then utters, "It is more important than my marriage right now, these few years while I'm doing this, yes it's more important than my marriage." He then watches his wife of decades leave as he commits his life to the president ("Five Votes Down"). C.J.'s relationship with Danny, the *Washington Post* journalist, also falls victim to her relationship with the president. In a first season episode, "Lord John Marbury," important information is kept from C.J. regarding troop movements in Kashmir. When she briefs the press she denies rumors of such movement only to be embarrassed by having to go back and explain the military crisis. Toby apologizes to C.J. for keeping her uninformed, explaining the decision on the grounds that "people see you with Danny." As Toby elaborates, "We sent you in there uninformed because we thought there was a chance you couldn't" lie to the press. Later in the same season C.J. is also blamed for leaking to Danny a memo of Mandy's criticizing the Bartlet presidency ("Lies, Damn Lies and Statistics"). In the end, the relationship does not develop because, as she says, "It would hurt my reputation" ("In Excelsis Deo"). C.J. is part of the West Wing family, yet her potential sexual liaison with a member of the press raises questions about her loyalty to the president, conjuring up images of "woman-as-traitor."[65]

The ultimate and sacrificing emotions are reserved for the president, who is the recipient of compassion, commitment, and respect. During the first season, in the episode entitled "Let Bartlet Be Bartlet," Leo assures the beleaguered Bartlet that his staff will "walk into fire for you." The team reaffirms Leo's sentiments as they step forward one by one, pledging, "I serve at the pleasure of the president." As John Breuilly points out, "Political identity and political loyalty are, first and foremost, with and to the nation."[66] This loyalty and soldierlike commitment to the commander-in-chief is reaffirmed visually in the first season's holiday episode, "In Excelsis Deo." As a choir of children sings "The Little Drummer Boy" in the White House, the last scenes of the episode cut back and forth between the president's staff and a funeral at Arlington National Cemetery for a homeless Korean War veteran, complete with full honor guard. We see soldiers marching in perfect order as they carry the casket; we see the profiles of *TWW* staff, who, one by one, join a line with the president as they watch the children sing. We see soldiers saluting their superior officers; we see the staff's profiles as they stand at attention, the president first in line. All the staffers join the line, smiles on their faces, as they express their joy of service and commitment. The patriotism from both acts of subjectivity reifies the hierarchical relationship in the discourse of nationalism; the honor guard funeral frames the staffs' relationship to the president, complete with the common assumptions of military service, duty, honor, country. As Gunther Kress and Theo van Leeuwen assert, "For participants to be put together in a syntagm which establishes a classification means they were judged to be members of the same class and are to be read as such. As in language, naturalization is not natural. The picture itself constitutes the relation."[67]

The only successful long-term relationship on *TWW* likewise involves the president as he and the First Lady are allowed to engage in an appropriate sexual union, preserving the committed heterosexuality of the presidency and the nation-state. As Connell explains, "Gayness, in patriarchal ideology, is the repository of whatever is symbolically expelled from hegemonic masculinity," which helps guarantee "the dominant position of men and the subordination of women" and gay men.[68]

The president, who embodies nationalism, becomes, in an ideal romantic sense, a receptacle for the citizens' admiration, love, and romance. Such devotion happens in *TWW* despite the president's acknowledged foibles and insecurities, a construction that reaffirms the hierarchy common in nationalist discourse. As Robert Burgoyne notes in his analysis of films about U.S. history from the 1980s and 1990s, "The concept of civic nationalism" represents a "powerful and resonant appeal . . . in a period when ethnic and racial [and gender] conflict in the United States has again forced a reevaluation of the meaning of national belonging."[69] The political roles women play, as well as issues aligned with women, offer insight into *TWW*'s gendered nationalism.

## The Women of Politics and the Politics of Women

Women assume important roles in the Bartlet administration and the larger political culture. The press secretary (C.J.), the national security advisor (Nancy), a political advisor (Mandy), a political pollster (Joey), a Secret Service agent (Gina), and a member of the White House Counsel's Office (Ainsley) are all women. In addition, women serve as lobbyists, members of Congress, political operatives, and pollsters on *TWW*. In certain ways they are shown as very competent and strong political operatives. In other ways their political acumen is often challenged, especially during time of considerable crisis when their emotions overtake their rationality in the complicated and competitive terrain of political Washington, reifying age-old stereotypes of male rationality and female emotiveness. In the process, women's issues are often marginalized for the "real" business of politics in a male political preserve.

C.J. represents an important site, where gender and politics play out. She is an integral member of the president's inner circle, and her authority is established early in the first season. In an interaction with Sam, C.J. asserts her status after learning that Sam accidentally slept with a prostitute: "I'm your first phone call . . . before, now, in the future. . . . Anytime you're into something and you don't know what, you don't keep it from me. I'm your first phone call. I'm your first line of defense. You have to let me protect you, and you have to let me protect the President." At the conclusion of a heated exchange C.J. says, "We're done talking now, you can go" ("A Proportional Response"). Assuming such an assertive and protective role with her male colleagues disrupts more traditional lines of authority in which men are generally portrayed as the "protectors" of women.[70]

In the second season C.J. confronts a retiring general determined to embarrass the president publicly by questioning his military authority. Because of her careful background work C.J. thwarts General Barrie's decision to conduct a television interview. He calls her "kitten" and suggests he will be telling his "story to Tim Russert." She retorts, "No I don't think you will General . . .

I noticed among your many decorations is the distinguished combat service medal. . . . You won it while on temporary duty with the Navy's USS *Brook*. . . . The thing is the *Brook* was never fired on and it never shot its guns. Right now . . . you're wearing a medal you never won. How does that usually go over with the boys?" The general objects, returning the conversation to Bartlet: "He never served in uniform, not once and he presumes." C.J. interrupts, concluding as the scene comes to closure, "Is there anything else, sir?" ("And It's Surely to Their Credit"). In "The Leadership Breakfast" episode C.J. is again portrayed as more politically astute than Toby, who respectfully commands that a joint presidential-congressional press conference be held on Capitol Hill rather than in the White House. C.J. refuses to attend the press conference, and, as she anticipates, a member of Congress uses the event to criticize the president, describing him as saying "one thing to our face and another thing to us through the media . . . ambushing us with ultimatums and threats." In the end, Josh tells C.J., "You had a lot of opportunities today to say, 'I told you so,' . . . You're a class act." What such depictions of C.J. suggest is a disruption of traditional feminine characterizations, at least in part, which typically represent a "romantic sentiment" of "dependence and goodwill that gives the masculine principle its romantic validity and its admiring applause," as Susan Brownmiller asserts.[71]

Although depicted as politically astute in many episodes, C.J.'s political credibility is likewise challenged in many others. In season one, she makes a public statement that inaccurately describes how the president is required to nominate a Democrat and a Republican to the Federal Election Commission. Leo, in response, calls C.J.'s error "a dumb mistake" ("Mandatory Minimums"). In the same season she is portrayed as someone who needs to be educated about the most basic of governmental functions. She seeks instruction from Sam, for example, about census sampling; despite being a high-ranking White House functionary, she does not grasp the fundamentals of the U.S. census ("Mr. Willis of Ohio"). In another first-season episode she announces her lack of economic aptitude, proclaiming, "I really don't understand anything" ("The White House Pro-Am"). C.J.'s competence and apparent feminist persona are neutralized from time to time, often through humor, and work within a television grammar that frequently seeks to "contain the threat that powerful women" pose, as Bonnie J. Dow asserts.[72] The implication is that there is still much work to be done to integrate women fully into the male world of politics.

In stereotypical fashion C.J. is depicted as being highly emotional, especially on issues pertaining to violence against women, again questioning women's role and full participation in the political sphere. As the public face and voice of the Bartlet administration she seems unable to handle the pressure when the news breaks over the president's cover-up of multiple sclerosis in the opening episode of season three. During one of the first press conferences after the public disclosure, and only a short time after she learned of the president's affliction, C.J. visibly struggles to answer questions, beginning statements only to stop, retract, or rephrase. Ultimately, she errs by suggesting that the "president's relieved to be focusing on something that matters," when referring to the newest crisis in Haiti. After the mistake Toby storms out of the press conference area and says, "I don't believe it." Sam, equally angry, questions, "He's relieved he might have to send troops into battle . . . and kill Haitian civilians because it takes his mind off having lied to the electorate?" When C.J. passes Toby and Sam she yells, "Just don't say anything . . . damn it" as she walks away, shouting and crying ("Manchester, Part 1").

In the following episode ("Manchester, Part 2") Abby even suggests to the president that he "think about sitting her down for a few days . . . at least on Haiti," an assignment eventually shifted to Nancy McNally, the National Security advisor who briefs the press at the president's request. C.J. offers her resignation, but the president convinces her to remain and acknowledges that it was a "mistake benching you for that last press conference." He concludes, "I need you too." By the subsequent episode C.J.'s political credibility is reaffirmed as she works the press conference in such a way that inspires the Republican Congress to investigate the president—a strategy they believe will divert negative attention away from the president and on to the Republicans. Oliver Babish tells C.J., "You took a beating the last few months . . . and I was wondering if you're trying to get back in the game with one swing?" ("Ways and Means"). In the end C.J. is vindicated, which suggests that she has become a valuable, competent political actor in the West Wing.[73]

C.J.'s emotiveness, though, occasionally overpowers any sense of rationality, which is a historically rooted assumption that if women enter the male political sphere "the feminine disease of hysteria may be transposed to the social body which would result in *political* hysteria."[74] Such a depiction is evident when another woman urges the president to "sit her down"—to remove C.J., that is, from the public sphere—during the crisis in Haiti.

In a third-season episode entitled "The Women of Qumar," C.J. personifies the overly emotional political woman, and the story line likewise reveals the ancillary role that women's issues play in presidential politics. She is outraged by a recent disclosure that the United States will negotiate an arms package with Qumar so the U.S. military can renew an air base lease in the small mideastern country. "Listen," C.J. tells Leo, "three weeks ago a woman in Qumar was executed for adultery. She didn't need a lawyer because there wasn't a trial. It was her husband's word against her's. . . . Later today I'm going to announce that we're selling them tanks and guns?" "Yeah" is his response. C.J. walks away, a look of anger and determination on her face, but does not let the issue drop. As she later informs Josh, "In Qumar, when a woman gets raped, she'll generally get beaten by her husband and sons as a punishment. So at some point, we should talk about how to spend the $1.5 billion they're giving us" for the arms sale. Her emotions become so extreme that she vents her anger on an unsuspecting group of World War II veterans protesting a Smithsonian exhibit that portrays a "vengeful America." With Toby present C.J. derides the elderly veterans, saying, "You're protesting because you think the Smithsonian isn't paying proper respect to what you and the soldiers of the 10th Armored, Third Army risked and lost your lives for six decades ago. How would you feel . . . if I told you that at my press briefing at the end of the day, I was announcing that we were selling tanks, missiles, and fighter jets to the Nazis?" At this point Toby tells C.J. to "step outside." Before he can reprimand her, she retorts, "You know if I was living in Qumar, I wouldn't be allowed to say 'shove it up your ass Toby,' but since I'm not, shove it up your ass Toby." The scene ends.

Despite repeated efforts, C.J.'s concern about Qumar attracts minimal attention from her colleagues. They are sidetracked by a more important crisis—mad cow disease. In the end, Nancy McNally confronts C.J. directly and declares, "This is the real world and we can't isolate our enemies." C.J. keeps repeating, "They're beating the women, Nancy." The national security advisor eventually departs, noting once again, "It's a big world, C.J., and everybody has guns and I'm doing the best I can." C.J. eventually suppresses her anger and does not raise the human rights issue in the press briefing. Instead, she relegates women's rights, as human rights, to the private sphere at the request of another female authority figure.

The issue reinforces women's emotionality on women's concerns and suggests that the real issues are those that affect the food chain and military tactics—violence against women is not part of "real-world" politics. As Fran P. Hosken notes, physical violence against women is carried out "with an astonishing consensus among men in the world."[75] Part of the difficulty with such violence against women is the long-held belief that the "public/private dichotomy . . . leads to the assumption that the rights bearer is the head of a household and that an important one of 'his' rights is the right to privacy in his personal and family life." Such assumptions place "serious obstacles in the way of protecting the rights of women and children."[76] Such depictions of third-world women in particular reinforce the powerlessness of this group because geopolitical conflicts often play out over the bodies of women. As Chandra Talpade Mohanty asserts, "Defining women as archetypal victims freezes them into 'objects-who-defend themselves,' men into 'subjects-who-perpetrate violence,' and (every) society into powerless (read: women) and powerful (read: men) groups of people."[77] Not only are women reified as victims but such issues are also dismissed as ones the United States cannot address in the political world. It is curious that the episode's drama frame is mad cow disease. Although not explicitly linked to issues about women the crisis in the episode is associated with the disease, not the abuses against women.

Yet another international and domestic woman's issue plays out in the same episode as the First Lady demands that Josh meet with Amy Gardner of the Women's Leadership Coalition to talk about problems with the word *forced* being used in a U.N. treaty to modify the word *prostitution*. Josh expresses fear about meeting with Amy, whose outer office is decorated with pictures of strong women. "The art around here scares the hell out of me," he tells her, reinforcing the idea that feminists are to be feared.[78] Amy explains the violence enacted upon women and girls: "The worst case scenario was five days ago when four thirteen-year-old Thai girls were found having hanged themselves in an abandoned house . . . in Bethesda [Maryland] . . . not half way around the world, Bethesda. There were sheets over the windows, triple locks on the doors, no phones. . . . Their parents had sold them to work as babysitters."

"How is that not forced prostitution?" Josh, whose fear is nonverbally apparent by the lack of eye contact with this women he knew in college, cautiously inquires. Amy complains that inserting the word *forced* into the treaty will make it hard to "prosecute" such cases. She eventually plays the political card: "The woman's vote isn't just half of your constituency. It's the entire margin of victory." Josh, as he does repeatedly, serves as the voice of establishment politics: "Who else are you going to vote for?" In a later interaction between the two, Josh uses a discourse of choice that has become the hallmark of postfeminism: "How am I not supposed to call you a hypocrite when you say that the government shouldn't tell women what to do with their bodies?" "Prostitution," Amy responds, "is about the subjugation of women by men for profit."

In many ways Josh and Amy's debate accentuates the complications of this timeless and ongoing issue. The debate likewise exhibits important markers in the status of women's rights in the postfeminist television age. On the one

hand, Amy offers an assertive and compelling argument that forces the Bartlet administration to attend to an issue on the international stage. On the
other hand, her feminism is neutralized in subtle ways. She is portrayed as
being a "lipstick feminist" who is quite attractive and wears fashionable, conventionally feminine clothing. As Norton observes, "Woman's body becomes
a 'figure of speech' . . . to alter the meaning of words."[79] To assure Josh and
the audience that she is not one of those second-wave "radical" feminists,
Amy declares, "I didn't burn my bras J., in fact I like my bras." Their banter
over the issue of forced prostitution eventually is sidetracked by Josh's inquiry
into Amy's feeble attempts to make animal balloons for her nephews, an as-
surance that she likes children, particularly boys. The discussion is further de-
railed by Amy's inquisition over Josh's relationships with Donna and Joey. As
Josh departs from the second encounter in Amy's office she throws a water
balloon animal at him from the window, several stories above the street. He
responds, "What are you, fifteen years old, you almost hit me in the head?" In
addition to juvenilizing Amy, the focus on women's right to choose a life of
prostitution furthers the postfeminist discourse that women's rights concern
individual decisions, even those that lead to potential violence and degradation. As Dow contends, postfeminist discourse circulating in popular culture accentuates the values of family and rugged individualism: "patriarchy
is gone and has been replaced by choice."[80]

In *TWW*, antipatriarchal forces are given voice by strong women characters such as C.J. and Amy. Yet the strength of their arguments is neutralized
by C.J.'s mistakes and Amy's movement back and forth from the seriousness
of the issue and her thoughts of romance and flirtation with Josh. Josh also
uses the language of "choice" to justify nonintervention, which raises doubt
about the issue's importance on the national and international stage. In the
end, he declares, "Forget for a second that it's a woman's issue. The law isn't
a deterrent. Prostitutes advertise in the yellow pages." Amy has no retort and
changes the topic to Josh's decision to visit her in person rather than call. The
remainder of the conversation switches to Josh's relational status and balloon
animals.

The issue of marriage incentives represents another site where *TWW* plays
out feminist cultural politics. This political dispute begins in the third-season
episode entitled "We Killed Yamamoto." By this point Josh and Amy's relationship has progressed, and they are spending nights together. Amy, cooking for Josh, notes, "Well spiced, just like myself." Josh replies, "This is going
to be a good night. My woman, a fine stew, and a Mets game on national TV."
This particular romantic and traditionally domestic interlude is interrupted

however by Josh's disclosure that in order to get the Working Toward Independence welfare bill through Congress it was necessary to incorporate "marriage incentives" as an enticement for certain conservatives. The argument begins immediately and centers on the rightness of marriage incentives versus the pragmatics of politics. Amy, who represents the voice of idealism as well as the voice for progressive women, asks, "Does my government really believe that the law can create a family? . . . Do these old fat-assed men really believe that if they just pay people to act like *Leave it to Beaver,* everything will be fine? Did you really think the person in my job is going to sit . . . this is about collecting votes from white men." Josh becomes the voice of realism, as he did during the previous argument over forced prostitution, "Amy, if we don't get elected, I promise you, President Ritchie is going to have a lot less sympathy for your agenda." "This bill isn't going to pass" she threatens. The dispute plays out over multiple episodes and extends into season four.

The complication of the issue and the political dispute stands to influence both Josh's and Amy's careers, demonstrating the messiness of politics, particularly politics related to women. Leo and the president are angry with Josh because his girlfriend is the one who instigated the opposition. "Is there nothing you can do to tame that woman?" Leo inquires, normalizing women's potential for threat within the nation-state. The president also chastises Josh, asking, "True or false, Josh, my life would be better right now if you and your girlfriend swapped jobs? . . . Why is it for every good thing you do around here, we've got to endure three screw-ups? . . . Win the damn vote." In the end Josh reestablishes his masculinity and wins the vote despite Amy's best efforts to mobilize opposition. Josh wins, though, because, as he explains, "I bought her [Amy's] boss."

Not only does Amy lose the vote but she also loses her job. As they meet at the end of the day Josh rearticulates the need for mobilization on such issues: "Every serious Democrat is going to unite behind this Democrat." "Every serious Democrat should be thinking about leading and not following" she responds ("Posse Comitatus"). At last Amy becomes a follower. After working briefly for progressive Senator Stackhouse's limited bid for the presidency she finally helps the Bartlet administration address issues for women during the presidential debate. She justifies her eventual cooptation by arguing, "[I'm] voting for the president . . . [because] I'm crazy about the president . . . and I'll keep poking him with a stick. That's how I show my love. But as a woman's issue, it's a no-brainer. The next justice can overturn *Roe* and you don't screw around with that" ("The Red Mass").

The evolution of this issue is instructive because it portrays gender politics in a nationalist, postfeminist context. Josh, the seasoned political actor, is shown to be much more politically savvy than Amy, whose feminist perspective prevents her from seeing the larger political landscape. It is Josh who mentors her around political landmines and helps her understand the need to work within the white male system. After all, it is a woman, Amy's boss, who is rendered as untrustworthy because she turns against Amy. Josh helps save Amy from this impractical world of women's political organizations and serves as her primary connection to the male political world.

Enloe says that "controlling girls and women becomes a man's way of protecting or reviving the nation. Not a few nationalist women have assisted in those efforts by policing other women."[81] *TWW* clearly integrates women, and issues associated with women, into the nationalist narrative even though the women are supporting players in such rhetorics.[82] In the political world of *TWW,* women often operate as the only female voice in any conversation because men usually far outnumber them in the program's scenes, further normalizing the male dominance of politics. As Connell maintains, "Hegemony . . . does not mean total control. It is not automatic, and may be disrupted—or even disrupt itself."[83]

This othering process is exacerbated by the construction of women's issues as distractions that disrupt the real world of male politics. The de-centered world of *TWW,* though, is recentered in this romantic nationalist narrative because feminism is rightly co-opted, and women come to symbolize the "fruits" of male political victory. Yuval-Davis notes that it is common for women to "retain an object rather than a subject position" in the "body politic."[84] That similarly shifts women's political issues—and the women who champion them—to the margins of the political sphere. Loretta Stec likewise suggests that in nationalist projects, women often have "their identities constructed for, and agendas subordinated to, the needs of the 'nation.'"[85]

Bruno Gianelli, the president's campaign manager, further reveals this marginalization of women's issues when he confidently declares, "The biggest nonsense issue in the campaign will belong to the women." C.J. disagrees with Bruno, noting that a focus on Abby Bartlet's comment that she is now "just" a wife and mother after her decision to give up her medical license "is not a woman's issue. It's a dumb woman's issue." Bruno concludes, "I think anybody whose got a five-point majority and still doesn't control the agenda might be spending a little too much time reading about how to get a man over his fear of commitment" ("Twenty Hours in America").

Although Bruno is othered in this political narrative because of his sexist acts and comments, his political prowess is revered on election night when C.J.

declares, "In a poll taken three days after the MS announcement, the president lost to Ritchie by nine points. He won by eleven. You did it." Even though Bruno tells C.J., "It's time for watermelon" because carloads of women are "unloading" at the White House "from the Women's Leadership Coalition" and "Women's Action Network" to celebrate the president's victory, she effuses, "You are entitled to the status you earned. . . . We owe you Bruno" ("Process Stories").

In the end, Amy's love and loyalty are finally and properly directed toward the president as the embodiment of nationalism, demonstrating how even the most strident and oppositional political actors know right from wrong when appropriately enlightened. Norton identifies the "President's role as a sign" that "enables the President . . . to embody individuality, subjectivity, and national unity" and "to present an image of the people to itself: singular, united, and with common material form and a single will."[86] Amy is even invited into the presidential family by the end of the fourth season, serving on Abby Bartlet's staff rather than the president's, which allows for the romance with Josh and the president to continue.

The other feminist characters are likewise sexualized as women from members of the feminist organizations who arrive at the White House to celebrate the president's victory. The visitors' sexy evening attire cements their status as sexual objects of the successful male political actors who run to the door to greet them. The relationship between nationalism and gender is an integral one in *TWW* and in the nation-state in which it was produced. As Yuval-Davis asserts, "In this culturalized discourse, gendered bodies and sexuality play pivotal roles as territories, markers and reproducers of narratives of nations and other collectives."[87] The conflation of family and nation, Blom suggests, "facilitated the construction of national identities and national loyalties."[88]

Such visions of gender are not isolated, however, to offer a rhetoric of nationalism. They intersect with other powerful nationalistic discourses in *TWW* to articulate a compelling presidentiality that is rooted in a specific vision of the U.S. nation-state.

# 3

## Racialized Nationalism and
## *The West Wing*

Now that we've abolished discrimination from our laws,
we need to abolish it in our hearts and minds.

—President Josiah Bartlet, "The Two Bartlets"

FROM ITS VERY constitutional beginning, race and citizenship were contested issues for the United States. In Article 1, section 2 of the Constitution, significantly, the measure of taxation was calculated "by adding the whole Number of free Persons, including those bound to Service for a Term of Years, and excluding Indians not taxed, three fifths of all other Persons." Indeed, the authors of many of the nation's founding documents wrestled with the persistent conundrum of slavery. Further conflating whiteness and citizenship, the Naturalization Law of 1790 mandated that "any alien, being a free white person, who shall have resided within the limits and under the jurisdiction of the United States for two terms, may be admitted to become a citizen thereof."[1]

Over the next two centuries and beyond, deliberations over race and nation occupied the attention of U.S. presidents, congressional leaders, and Supreme Court justices. Moreover, for most of U.S. history, white identity has been the basis for a series of exclusionary policies and the overall cultural and political hegemony of the community. Much of the conflict surrounding issues of nationalism challenged and/or reified assumptions that power was rightly held by white men.[2] As Ian F. Haney López explains, "The existence of Whites depends on the identification of cultures and societies, particular human traits, groups and individuals as non-White. Whites thus stand at the powerful vortex of race in the United States; whiteness is the source and maintaining force of the systems of meaning that position some as superior and others as subordinate."[3]

As with gender, the history of U.S. nationalism cannot be separated from matters of race and ethnicity. As Anthony W. Marx argues, "Not only did states reinforce race to unify the nation, but race also made nation-states" into these symbiotically "linked processes."[4] Recall that there are, we believe, two influential and opposed ideals at work throughout U.S. history. One is grounded in what Gerstle calls "civic nationalism," which promotes "the fundamental equality of all human beings"; the other, termed "racialized nationalism," posits the nation in "ethnoracial terms."[5] On matters of race, European heritage, especially from Northern and Western Europe, was equated with "natural white superiority," a "color line" that seems to be "drawn by God or biology." Elaborating further, Marx contends that "slavery, proscriptions against miscegenation, colonialism, imperialism, manifest destiny, racially exclusive forms of citizenship or nationalism, and exploitation were all justified by whites as preordained in nature."[6]

Such assumptions were foundational to many policies affecting the treatment of African Americans in U.S. culture. The commitment to federalist principles in the United States helped southerners repeatedly turn to states' rights to justify the continued enslavement of African Americans.[7] Even northerners who abhorred slavery did not conceive of blacks in citizenship terms. Paul Goodman writes that "so unprepared were whites for black citizenship that the suffrage laws enacted during the Revolutionary era failed to specify whites only until a wave of black voting triggered a wave of exclusions, in Maryland in 1783 . . . in Connecticut in 1814 . . . in New York in 1821 . . . in Pennsylvania in 1838." Many northern states (e.g., Massachusetts) discouraged free blacks from settling. Other, newer states such as Ohio attempted to ban blacks—a prohibition that, although ineffective, inspired many free blacks to flee to Canada.[8] As the idea of abolition gained political power, presidents such as Andrew Jackson and Martin Van Buren sought to silence abolitionists, characterizing them as "antislavery radicals."[9]

In order to deal with free blacks, the American Colonization Society (ACS) formed in 1817 to recolonize blacks in Africa or the western regions of the United States, a plan that attracted the support of southerners as well as Thomas Jefferson, James Madison, John Quincy Adams, Henry Clay, and Abraham Lincoln. The United States followed Great Britain and abolished the slave trade, legislation that took effect in 1808. Just as Great Britain created Sierra Leone to help halt the slave trade, so, too, did the United States establish Liberia, a colony in Africa, and relocated some thirteen thousand free blacks there.[10]

Southerners supported colonization because of fears that free blacks would incite a slave revolt. Others assumed that deliberations over colonization could delay the inevitable battle over slavery. Until the issue of colonization was resolved, many reasoned, there could be no decision over the continued practice of slavery in the United States. Although it attracted considerable attention from the 1820s through the 1850s and beyond, the ASC, which often held its initial meetings in the House of Representatives, failed in its mission, in part because southerners like Andrew Jackson feared that a national policy on colonization could lead to a national policy on slavery.

The impact of the ACS, though, outlived the organization's energy. David Zarefsky notes that Lincoln supported Henry Clay's "policy of colonization . . . as late as 1862."[11] The issue of colonization also entered the debate over the U.S. annexation of Texas, another potential relocation site for free blacks.[12] Addressing the ideological legacies of the colonization movement, Goodman asserts that "by dwelling unceasingly on the degradation of the African race in America, the ACS functioned as a defamation society that fed, reinforced, and gave elite respectability to popular prejudice."[13] Such acts of slavery were often viewed benevolently as a means to "Christianize" the genetically "inferior" Africans.[14]

The treatment of Native Americans in eighteenth- and early-nineteenth-century America likewise reified ethnocultural commitments to U.S. nationalism. The colonization movement gained force as the U.S. government simultaneously worked to relocate Native Americans in remote regions of the Territories. Although early political leaders often expressed guilt over Native American removal, Rogan Kersh suggests that by 1820, "'an era of removal'" emerged that "featured little of the discomfort expressed by revolutionaries and constitutional framers at excluding longtime residents from national membership."[15] President Washington kept a "rhetorical distance" and treated Native Americans as "foreigners to be courted with treaties"; Jefferson viewed them "as the subject for an interesting social experiment" wherein whites could attempt to mentor the "savages," potentially making strides "forward to a civilized state."[16] President Jackson, however, grew impatient with the experiments and championed the Indian Removal Act, which Congress passed in 1830. Even many who opposed removal did not envision Native Americans as part of the "circle of national unity." As the Republic attended to questions of slavery and relocation, immigration was on the rise, and the nation's territory was expanding. Kersh describes how these forces and changes magnified the "notions of national union limited to a divinely chosen, homogeneous white American 'race.'"[17]

The Civil War and Emancipation Proclamation brought renewed hope for African American equality. Yet even Lincoln, an ardent opponent of slavery and proponent of African American civil rights, was still ambiguous about matters of equality. What he called for, Zarefsky notes, was an "economic equality of the races" rather than a political and social equality.[18] Lincoln only promoted suffrage for African American men in the last speech he gave.[19] Despite Radical Republican overtures to punish the South after the end of the Civil War, Lincoln sought to appease Southerners, conciliation activities that President Andrew Johnson strengthened after Lincoln's assassination.

Even Northerners eventually lost their resolve to enforce Reconstruction amendments once an economic downturn hit in the 1870s. Marx contends that "the price of . . . reconciliation was to be paid by African Americans" because the "old tradition of regional compromise and constitutional division of power was restored to encourage nation-state consolidation" as the Fourteenth and Fifteenth Amendments were all but disregarded by the late 1870s. The Civil Rights Act of 1875 was overturned in 1883, and by 1896 *Plessy v. Ferguson* set legal precedent for the next fifty years and more, declaring that "laws permitting, and even requiring," the "separation [of the races] in places where they are liable to be brought into contact do not necessarily imply the inferiority of either race to the other, and have been generally, if not universally, recognized as within the competency of the state legislátures in the exercise of their police power."[20] Ruth Roach Pierson explains that nineteenth-century nationalist narratives "played themselves out in a world increasingly organized according to the discourses of 'race,'" which by the turn of the twentieth century "join[ed] with evolutionary theory and social Darwinism to give shape to a discourse of civilization that ranked nations and hierarchized and excluded social groups within nations."[21]

As Jim Crow retaliations and nationalist narratives restricted the rights of African Americans, a host of anti-immigration laws were passed between the 1880s and the 1950s. Among the more notorious was the Chinese Exclusion Act of 1882, the first "statutory restrictions since the short-lived Alien Acts of 1798" that "suspended" the immigration of "Chinese laborers" on the grounds that such migration patterns endangered "the good order of certain localities."[22] Kersh blames this "xenophobic surge" in part on "economic uncertainty" as well as the immigrant flow from 1881 to 1890, when approximately 5.25 million arrived in the United States. It was "a total greater than all combined immigration from 1781–1860."[23]

Such exclusionary efforts, though, were only in their infant stages. The 1907 Immigration Act excluded "idiots, imbeciles, feebleminded persons, epileptics, insane persons" and "anarchists" in addition to "physically defective" individuals.[24] The Immigration Act of 1917 and the Immigration Restriction Act of 1924 sought to exclude Asians and specified Europeans, particularly those from Southern and Eastern Europe, who were more likely to be Jewish and Catholic. More specifically, the act created the "Asiatic Barred Zone" that covered most of East and South Asia except for Japan and segments of China. During this same period, Congress voted on a bill to exclude blacks from the United States, but the NAACP helped kill the bill in the House of Representatives after considerable debate.

By the time of the Great Depression, immigration attention turned more toward Mexico, culminating in Operation Wetback of the 1950s, when more than a million individuals were deported in 1954 alone.[25] López explains that such "racial restrictions on immigration were not significantly dismantled until 1965, when Congress in a major overhaul of immigration law abolished both the national origin system and the Asiatic Barred Zone."[26]

Throughout the period of heightened immigration restriction, certain presidents used the bully pulpit to champion assimilation. In his *American Ideals* (1903), Theodore Roosevelt talked of "Americanizing . . . the newcomers to our shores" and explained the process of "Americanism": "We must Americanize them in every way, in speech, in political ideas and principles, and in their way of looking at the relations between Church and State. We welcome the German or the Irishman who becomes an American. We have no use for the German or Irishman who remains such. . . . We have no room in any healthy American community for a German-American vote or an Irish-American vote."[27] For Roosevelt, "U.S. citizenship was an all-or-nothing proposition, one in which devotion to the American flag not only came first but also was singular."[28]

Gerstle charges that Roosevelt's nationalism, as refined in his postpresidential "New Nationalist" campaign, helped define U.S. nationalism until the mid-1960s. On the one hand, the proponents of Roosevelt's new nationalism articulated "political and social equality for all," yet simultaneously and with contradiction they "subscribed to the racial notion that America, despite its civic creed, ought to maximize the opportunities for its 'racial superiors' and limit those of its 'racial detractors.'" Political leaders were also prepared to "discipline immigrants . . . and others who were thought to imperil the nation's welfare."[29]

Woodrow Wilson also addressed the issue of "Americanism and the Foreign Born." During an address on May 10, 1915, he asserted, "You cannot dedicate yourself to America unless you become in every respect and with every purpose of your will thorough Americans."[30] "Loyalty for Americans, then," James R. Andrews summarizes, "was tested by one's ability to rise above one's national origin and pledge allegiance, instead, to this new land of new people," integrating the "many into one" as "an updated feature of traditional American exceptionalism."[31]

The presidency, however, became a site of civil rights advancement in the latter part of the twentieth century. Harry S Truman, of course, offered the rhetorical leadership that helped desegregate the Armed Forces, Dwight D. Eisenhower supported the Civil Rights Acts of 1957 and 1960, and John F. Kennedy eventually used his office to champion civil rights. Most significantly, Lyndon B. Johnson publicly supported the Civil Rights Act of 1964 and Voting Rights Act of 1965, and he helped create the rhetorical foundation for affirmative action, which was codified under Richard Nixon. Jimmy Carter championed human rights and equal opportunity, and William Jefferson Clinton is well remembered for his initiatives on race.[32] As Garth E. Pauley concludes, "For all of the shortcomings of their rhetorical leadership on civil rights, modern presidents often moved the nation toward overcoming its racial problems through their discourse on race."[33]

In spite of such leadership on civil rights policies, contemporary presidents have demonstrated considerable ambivalence on matters of race, as did Abraham Lincoln a century earlier. Russell L. Riley asserts that the "American presidency is an institution that under ordinary circumstances is not well suited to addressing the grievances of racial minorities. Indeed, careful study of the history of the institution reveals that the presidency has typically been used in ways hostile to minority interests, especially with respect to African Americans."[34] Kenneth O'Reilly is similarly ambivalent regarding civil rights and the presidency: "Of the forty-two presidents of the United States only Lincoln and Lyndon Johnson stand out for what they ultimately did on the matter of civil rights for all." That said, O'Reilly suggests that they, too, "brought baggage to their great accomplishments: Lincoln with his white supremacist caveats . . . and Johnson with his . . . Vietnam draft boards (that always came first for the people at the bottom he otherwise seemed so intent on helping)."[35]

Because of the political quandaries that surround most issues concerning race and politics, many presidents have offered more nuanced positions. As Fields points out, "It was much more 'presidential' to address the end of the African slave trade, prohibited by Congress . . . after 1807, than to confront the divisive issue of human bondage within our own borders."[36] Bill Clinton tried to have it both ways on questions of race when he "expressed the angst and hope of race in America," regularly returning to "questions of race and racial harmony" while he also simultaneously accentuated the image of a "white southerner—the presidential candidate who, in 1992, vigorously attacked Sister Souljah and . . . shunned Jesse Jackson."[37]

Such advancements on race have thus been accomplished in spite of—and in some cases because of—presidential discourse and actions. Marx reminds us that "gradual expansion of citizenship is . . . gained through protracted contestation," often enacted by those outside of the government. Despite such advances, the legacies of exclusion are not only evident but also still exist. Marx writes, "Unmaking racial domination does not unmake the prejudice upon which domination was built and then reinforced, nor dissolve a now-consolidated racial identity."[38]

White racial identity has also strengthened since the 1980s, and there is a serious possibility of growth and increased influence throughout the U.S. European population.[39] As such ideological battles continue it is important to note how the power of civic nationalism that neutralizes matters of race is symbiotically joined with a racialized or ethnic nationalism. Robert Fine contends that "civic and ethnic forms of nationalism are not so alien from one another as they at first sight might appear: there is a kinship between a politics based on patriotism" and the "'politics of difference,'" accentuating the "equivocation which runs through nationalism itself."[40]

Not surprisingly, *The West Wing* depicts the power structure and racial ambivalence that permeates U.S. history. It accentuates presidential whiteness. Bartlet's aristocratic ways are biologically linked to the Founders, accentuating presidential romanticism while normalizing the whiteness of the position. Although the show features persons of color in powerful roles, such performances, particularly those involving the military, reinscribe the hierarchy of a white male president in command of black military leaders, ensuring the containment of black power and advancement. The whiteness of the presidency is juxtaposed against portrayals of marginalized others who seem less fit to govern than their white counterparts. In this contested environment identity politics is equated with group self-interest and political predicaments to be avoided or dealt with outside the media spotlight. The world of other is cast as an environment of violence and chaos. The white male president must manage that environment so as to reestablish global order or ignore as historical and irresolvable disputes beyond human control.

## Presidential Whiteness

Increased attention has developed on recognizing and destabilizing whiteness as a racial category and power structure even as scholars are clearly mindful that "the word itself may tend to essentialize and homogenize the phenomenon in a way that runs counter" to such decentering moves.[41] The first task of whiteness projects is to isolate and unpack discourses of power. Kalpana Seshadri-Crooks conceives of whiteness as a "master signifier . . . that establishes a structure of relations, a signifying chain that through a process of inclusions and exclusions constitutes a pattern for organizing human difference."[42] Whiteness for John Fiske "comprises the construction and occupation of a centralized space from which to view the world," normalizing that which is associated with whiteness while "abnormalizing" that which is not, resulting in "strategic deployment[s] of power."[43]

Such conceptions of whiteness are grounded in assumptions that race represents a social construction that has material consequences. López, like many race scholars, has acknowledged the complexities of whiteness: "Whether one is White depends in part on other elements of identity . . . [and] is highly contingent, specific to times, places, and institutions." People become white, López concludes, by virtue of the social context in which one finds oneself but also by virtue of the choices one makes.[44]

*TWW* appeared on the NBC schedule at the same time that the major broadcast networks were facing criticism for the predominantly white casting of their programming. When the 1999–2000 fall schedule was announced, many were quick to notice the lack of diversity in casts, and some groups held hearings and threatened boycotts to protest this homogeneous programming. *TWW*, like many other shows, diversified its cast. How it did so is revealing of how the show addresses questions of race.

Rather than create a role for a person of color among its senior staff, *TWW* executives diversified the cast by hiring Dulé Hill to play Charlie Young—an early-twenty-something African American who is President Bartlet's personal assistant, his "body man." Charlie is responsible for keeping the president on schedule, waking him in the morning, and handling personal matters. Of course, having an African American serving a white president invoked racial concerns and issues, which *TWW* addressed in the text of the show. In the first season's episode, "A Proportional Response," Josh speaks with Leo about the racial implications of hiring Charlie for this position. Leo then consults the chair of the Joint Chiefs of Staff, Admiral Percy "Fitz" Fitzwallace (John Amos) about whether the hire has racial implications. Fitzwallace is African American so asking him about the matter highlights the otherness of African Americans in *TWW*. His response is also instructive and reveals an ideological orientation toward racial matters in *TWW*:

> LEO: The president's personal aide, they're looking at a kid. Do you have any problem with a young black man waiting on the president?

FITZWALLACE: I'm an old black man and I wait on the president.
LEO: The kid's gotta carry his bags.
FITZWALLACE: You gonna pay him a decent wage?
LEO: Yeah.
FITZWALLACE: You gonna treat him with respect in the workplace?
LEO: Yeah.
FITZWALLACE: Then why the hell should I care?
LEO: That's what I thought.
FITZWALLACE: I've got some real honest to God battles to fight, Leo.
  I don't have time for the cosmetic ones.

Fitzwallace's comments accomplish ideological dismissal of racial questions and concerns in White House hiring practices. Such questions are discharged as being cosmetic and of no concern or import. They also hold out the normative consequences of whiteness, stressing that more important questions about wages and respect should overcome the tedious and cosmetic concerns with race. Read in the context of protests against network casting prejudices, *TWW* further denigrates racial concerns, suggesting implicitly at least that just as Leo's questions about Charlie's race are cosmetic, so, too, are concerns about network casting decisions.

The exchange between Leo and Fitzwallace likewise establishes the hierarchy of Bartlet's administration. Fitzwallace, although not pictured in the credits, continues in seasons two, three, and four to play a more significant role in *TWW* as chair of the Joint Chiefs of Staff. In the second season the producers bring in Dr. Nancy McNally (Anna Deavere Smith) as national security advisor ("Somebody's Going to Emergency, Somebody's Going to Jail"), another person of color given a recurring role.

Although both Fitzwallace and McNally are placed in positions with significant power and influence, the structural order that Fitzwallace acknowledges ("I'm an old black man and I wait on the president") clarifies the presidential hierarchy. Gerstle suggests that integration often occurs first in the military rather than the culture at large because of "the control that its leaders [are] able to exercise over its [military's] composition and behavior." To that end, integration in the military acts as "controlled assimilation" that relies "on military hierarchy and its regulatory power."[45] In an explicit discussion of the ways in which whiteness plays out in primetime television, Herman Gray concludes, "As with images of black success in television news and talk shows, this exceptional blackness has to be harnessed and ultimately placed in the service of good."[46]

Even as Fitzwallace and McNally are integral to military decision making, the racialized hierarchy of *TWW* is further reinforced early in the show. In the second episode, "Post Hoc, Ergo Propter Hoc," President Bartlet talks openly with a military aide (an African American male) about his insecurities related to the military. When a group of Syrians later shoots down the aide's military aircraft, killing him, Bartlet becomes so upset that he threatens to "blow them [the terrorists] off the face of the earth with the fury of God's own thunder."

In the next episode, "A Proportional Response," a similarly emotional Bartlet challenges his military leaders on the validity of proportional responses to terrorism. Toby Ziegler characterizes the president's tension level when describing a dinner from the previous evening: "The president was up from the table every five minutes teeing off on Cashmen and Berryhill. He's barking at the Secretary of State, he's scaring the hell out of Fitzwallace, which I didn't think was possible. He's snapping at the First Lady. He's talking about blowing up half of North Africa." Later in the episode Bartlet accedes to a proportional response, but only after railing at assembled military leaders about the weaknesses of such a response. He offers an alternative: "The disproportional response. Let the word ring forth from this time and this place, you kill an American, any American, we don't come back with a proportional response, we come back [bangs fist on table] with total disaster!"

Although Bartlet expresses ambivalence about his commander-in-chief status and is eager to seek out the views of his military commanders, he is situated in the ultimate position of power by virtue of being president and also by his performance of that office. And though *TWW* evidences a genuine move toward an integrated military, the constitutionally dictated hierarchy establishing the president as commander-and-chief situates such assimilationist practices within a context of empowered whiteness. The Constitution stipulates a balance of powers, but *TWW* imbues the presidency with the ultimate power on national and international matters—a role performed through whiteness and force. Even the chair of the Joint Chiefs of Staff fears the president's wrath.

White presidential power is reinforced most blatantly in the first season ("Celestial Navigation") when Leo McGarry and Deborah O'Leary—the African American secretary of housing and urban development—discuss her testimony on Capitol Hill. Conflict erupts when she suggests that her congressional inquisitor, and all Republicans by extension, are racists. Rather than support his appointee, the president, via the chief of staff, forces her to apologize:

O'LEARY: The man's a racist.

LEO: Maybe so—

O'LEARY: Maybe!

LEO: Debbie.

O'LEARY: He's using his government authority to spit at poor people and minorities, which in his mind are the same thing.

LEO: Look . . .

O'LEARY: He's doing it because he can. He's doing it because he can score points with his narrow-minded constituents.

LEO: His narrow-minded constituents are also *our* narrow-minded constituents.

O'LEARY: Oh, for crying out loud, Leo. When're you guys gonna stop running for president?

LEO: When angels dance on pinheads, Debbie. We need their votes on any number of issues, including, by the way, the budget for the Department of Housing and Urban Development.

O'LEARY: Attacking HUD is code for attacking blacks.

LEO: Thanks. Having been born yesterday on a turnip truck . . .

O'LEARY: Do you not think it is my role as the highest-ranking African American woman in government to point out that . . . ?

LEO: I think, Debbie, your role first and foremost is to serve the president—a task today at which you failed spectacularly. . . . You're gonna apologize.

O'LEARY: I'm sorry.

LEO: Not to me, Debbie.

O'LEARY: Look, I called it like I saw it.

LEO: Well, now you're gonna apologize for it.

O'LEARY: I can't.

LEO: You can.

O'LEARY: I won't.

LEO: You will.

O'LEARY: Is that an order?

LEO: You're doing great work, Deb. President's nuts about ya, always has been. He'll cry for three minutes after he fires your ass and then he'll say, "What's next?"

O'LEARY: Leo, if I've gotta go and ask Wooden for forgiveness, he's gonna lord it over me from now until the end of time.

LEO: It's the cost of doing business.

O'LEARY: Done.

This exchange is highly instructive, revealing how *TWW* subverts questions of race and racism beneath the grammar of cynical politics. Ideologically, the scene reinforces the power of whiteness (and masculinity) such that the white member of Congress is aided by the chief of staff, who is also white, to compel the indignant African American woman to apologize for expressing her beliefs and ideas. Her power and voice are silenced, and the whiteness of the presidency is reinscribed. Not coincidentally, perhaps, in this same episode the white West Wing staffers compel the Latino Supreme Court nominee to ignore the indignity of racial profiling for the sake of the political goal of securing appointment to the High Court.

bell hooks has said that "one of the tragic ironies of contemporary black life is that individuals succeed in acquiring material privilege often by sacrificing their positive connection to black culture and black experience," just as Debbie O'Leary was compelled to do in order to keep her job.[47] Placing people of color in inherently subordinate positions, where they are expected to enact their subordination, only reinforces the power of whiteness even as such media moments suggest more progressive images of assimilation and multicultural normativity. Fiske observes that "whiteness survives only because of its ability to define, monitor, and police the boundary between itself and its others and to control any movement across it."[48] The white power structure of *TWW*, however, is further naturalized through the construction of the president's mythic ancestry.

## Whiteness, Presidentiality, and Representative Government

A fraternity of white male exceptionalism is powerfully affixed to *TWW*'s ideology. This exceptionality exempts Dana Nelson's arguments about America's national manhood: "White male exceptionality is experienced through the imagined reconstruction of white fraternity. It offers us a usefully simplified instance of the model linking representative citizenship to the abstract identity of white manhood, and of the psychic transfers entailed in national manhood's embrace of representative democracy."[49] *TWW*'s pervasive visual encomium to white presidential heroes is mimetic and legitimates the whiteness of this fictional president. The backdrop of all episodes is replete with pictorial representations of romantic heroes such as George Washington, Abraham Lincoln, Theodore Roosevelt, and Franklin D. Roosevelt; the historical markers promote the individualism of *TWW*'s presidency and embody the country's historical and on-going commitment to whiteness in this ultimate position of power.

Such collective memories of romantized presidents persist not only in popular culture but also in presidential oratory. Fields discusses the power that the Founding Fathers and the earliest presidents held for their successors. In speaking of Van Buren's presidency, Fields notes, "In addition to the genuine respect expressed for their fathers, there is also regret, an apology for having been born too late and the practical recognition that Van Buren, unlike those who were 'there' could not trade on a personal connection to the heroic past." Similarly, Fields writes that Franklin Pierce felt pressured by the mythic legacies of the earliest presidents. Many mid-nineteenth-century presidents feared they were "not living up to expectations established by their predecessors," political actors whose greatness is repeatedly invoked in contemporary presidential oratory and establishes a living mythic memory of presidents past.[50]

Contemporary presidents construct visions that link themselves ideologically and politically to the Founders, but *TWW* goes a step further toward naturalizing presidential whiteness by conjoining Bartlet biologically with them. During the first season ("What Kind of Day Has it Been"), we learn that Bartlet's great grandfather's great grandfather, Dr. Josiah Bartlett (a different spelling), signed the Declaration of Independence, an ancestral lineage reemphasized in season three ("The Two Bartlets"). Like *TWW*'s president, Josiah Bartlett also served as the governor of New Hampshire—indeed, the first governor of that state. President Bartlet connects his family further to other revolutionary heroes, noting that Paul Revere was a "friend" of the family ("Shibboleth"). In describing the Americanism of the nineteenth century, Leroy G. Dorsey and Rachel M. Harlow note how Theodore Roosevelt, in "retelling of world history" through *The Winning of the West*, emphasized that "success could depend, at least in part, on having the *right* bloodline." European immigrants were thus constructed "as providing the *right* blood for the American body."[51] To that end, the fact that Bartlet's is a privileged bloodline perpetuates the notion of a white presidential lineage that assumes historically and biologically rooted notions of white superiority on matters of political governance.

Even though Martin Sheen, who plays President Bartlet, claims a familial ancestry to Ireland and Spain, his Latino roots are erased in *TWW*'s narrative.[52] Casting Sheen (whose birth name was Ramon Estevez) as the president offered an excellent opportunity to accentuate cultural and ethnic diversity. Instead, the show's producers opted to further conflate whiteness and Americanism by linking the fictional president's bloodline to America's royalty. Although the president's identity is contested through his mother's Catholicism, she is decidedly absent in the narrative ("Two Cathedrals").[53] The ancestral connection to the Founders comes through Bartlet's father, emphasizing the political and intersectional power of masculinity, whiteness, and privilege.

Equating whiteness with governance is a historical commonplace. López explains that in turn-of-the-twentieth-century America, when the immigration restrictions were most apparent, the widely held assumption was that "Whites qualified for citizenship because they were fit by nature for republican government."[54] For Theodore Roosevelt and many of his peers, democracy was a form of government only fit for Europeans or whites.[55] The preponderance of whites on Bartlet's staff and in his cabinet indicates the legacy of such ideological commitments.

In other ways, though, *TWW* continues to perpetuate similar notions of whiteness. During a second-season episode entitled "The Drop-In," the president's skepticism of a U.S. nuclear defense shield functions as the dominant plotline. As he and Leo banter about its practicality and workability throughout the episode, the president seeks the opinion of Lord John Marbury, the British ambassador. He responds, "I think it [the defense shield] is dangerous, illegal, fiscally irresponsible, technically unsound, and a threat to all people everywhere." Leo argues with Marbury, alleging that because "the world invented a nuclear weapon" we are obliged to "invent something that would make it irrelevant." After listening to the debate President Bartlet interjects, "Well it's a discussion for serious men. They say a statesman is a politician who's been dead for thirty years. I'd like us to be statesmen while we're still live."

Because the president seeks Marbury's opinion on the issue, we assume that Marbury, a rather odd character of frequently unpredictable behavior, ranks among Bartlet's "serious men" who are fit for such serious discussions. Most telling are those not invited into the conversation. Throughout the episode President Bartlet meets with ambassadors from Thailand and Sweden; neither are asked their views on the nuclear defense shield. Instead, Bartlet talks with the ambassador from Thailand about playing golf, concluding, "Golf is not a sport. . . . Let's you and I not confuse it with things men do." As Bartlet demasculinizes the Asian male through sport, he further excludes the ambassador from the circle of serious men by not seeking out his views on nuclear defense shields. When Mrs. Landingham interjects her thoughts on the "preposterous[ness]" of the shield, noting that "in my day we knew how to protect ourselves," Leo offers an ageist response that also demasculinizes Native Americans: "In your day you could pretty much turn back the Indians with a Daniel Boone musket." As Nelson observes, historically "the abstracting identity of white/national manhood found one means for stabilizing its internal divisions and individual anxieties *via* imagined projections into, onto, against Indian territories, Indian bodies, Indian identities."[56] Asians are similarly othered in Western discourse, particularly in popular culture.[57]

The president's authority on matters of governance, and his ability to discern serious men from those incapable of addressing such prominent issues, translates to an authentication of the religiosity of illegal immigrants from developing nations. During the second-season episode entitled "Shibboleth," approximately one hundred Chinese immigrants are captured in San Diego Harbor. The narrative features a Thanksgiving theme and begins with a conversation about pilgrims, the *Mayflower,* and the American Revolution. As Sam explains to C.J., bitter over her role as the "Thanksgiving cruise director," the pilgrims came to "worship according to their own beliefs." Such themes offer meaning to the Chinese immigrants seeking asylum as "Christian evangelicals" escaping persecution. In addressing the conflict, Sam serves as the voice of the Chinese immigrants: "A lot of them left their families. Two months on the water in a container, dead bodies in there. They had to want it." Josh responds, though, that some in the Immigration and Naturalization Service (INS) believe the "refugees feign faith."

The president steps in to help determine the immigrants' authenticity as people of faith. The "Shibboleth" narrative serves as a drama frame as the president searches for such authenticity among the illegal immigrants. Just as true Israelites were discerned from imposters, he acts as a detective with the Chinese immigrants, one of whom is brought to the Oval Office to be authenticated. The president begins by saying that he is assessing the "veracity of your claim for asylum." The elderly man can speak English and identifies Jesus as the "head of our church." He also knows the names of all the apostles, which impresses the president. After a time the man states, "Christianity is not demonstrated through a recitation of facts. You're seeking evidence of faith, a whole hearted acceptance of God's promise of a better world for we hold that man is justified by faith alone . . . faith is the true . . . Shibboleth." "Yes it is," the president responds, "and you sir just said the magic word in more ways than one. Thank you." Even though the man passes the president's test, Leo problematizes the foreign policy basis of the asylum offer, arguing that "you don't want to piss off China and you don't want to send them back so you got to ask yourself how secure is the INS detention facility?" In the end, the president secretly convinces the governor of California to allow the refugees to escape from the detention center, which completes the Thanksgiving parable in a romantic and affirming manner.

The episode is a touching Thanksgiving narrative that demonstrates the president's generosity and morality. It also reminds the audience about the plight of the pilgrims and the religious traditions of charity that are foundational to U.S. national identity. The narrative, though, is also a telling performance of whiteness. Stuart Hall equates the logic of identity to the search for an authenticity to one's experience.[58] That reflects what López details as common-knowledge standards of whiteness. In legal cases, such common-knowledge standards "treated questions of race as matters of common sense, an approach that naturalizes race by insisting it is part of the reality . . . something observed and easily known to all," particularly knowledgeable "white Americans."[59]

In addition to reifying a common-knowledge assessment test for persons of color from developing nations Bartlet is also given the capacity to determine such religious authenticity, which ordains the white president with special powers reminiscent of the royal, white, and colonial monarchy. The bifurcation between China and the "new world" by Bartlet likewise furthers the empowerment of the West over developing regions, normalizing America's international policing role and economic control.

In the end, the president is pleased with his actions. The immigrants are not sent back to China, and the administration avoids an international conflict. Of course the message sent is that welcoming the religious refugees openly would be a public relations debacle that the president must astutely avoid. Although the asylum-seekers are allowed to stay they are also left to fend for themselves, without proper support. They become part of the impoverished immigrants who steal away to the United States every year and are politically silent and virtually ignored. Their story and the Shibboleth drama frame imbue whiteness with images of a benevolent spirit that bolsters traditional concepts of white moral superiority and power.

Whiteness is romanticized in a different way during the opening episodes of season four as Donna, Josh, and Toby are stranded in the Midwest after a campaign rally. The three comically try to make their way back to Washington through numerous encounters with individuals in Indiana. With few exceptions (e.g., the owners of a diner), the people they encounter are white. Toby and Josh are extremely frustrated by the pedestrian behavior of the midwesterners, yet they are also taught a lesson about true Americanism. As they wait for transportation back to D.C., Donna, born in Minnesota but raised in Wisconsin, chastises the two bickering beltway insiders about eastern and urban elitism:

> OK, that's it. I can't take it . . . I'm not kidding. I have such an impulse to knock your heads together. I can't remember the last time I heard you two talk about anything other than how a campaign was playing in Washington.

Kathy needed to take a second job so her dad could be covered by insurance. She tried to tell you how bad things were for family farmers. You told how we already lost Indiana. You made fun of the fair but you didn't see they have livestock exhibitions and give prizes for the biggest tomato. . . . They're proud of what they grow. Eight months of transportation . . . and the kindness of six strangers. Random conversations with twelve more and nobody brought up Bartlet vs. Ritchie but you. . . . Can I have the table please?

Shamed, Toby and Josh leave the table and eventually engage in a conversation at the bar with a white middle-aged male who is in Indiana to visit the University of Notre Dame with his college-aged daughter. For the first time Toby and Josh listen to someone from the Midwest, and they are significantly affected by the man's story: "I never imagined that $55,000 a year and I'd have trouble making ends meet. My wife brings in another $25,000. My son's in public school. It's no good. . . . It should be hard. I like that it's hard. Put your daughter through college. That's a man's job, a man's accomplishment. But it should be a little easier, just a little easier. In that difference is everything." Moved, Toby responds, "I'm Toby Ziegler. I work at the White House. Do you have a minute to talk? We'd like to buy you a beer."

Via their trip through the Midwest the heroic but distracted West Wing staff finally encounter "the people" of the United States—the country's "true Americans"—agrarian, white, economically struggling, and members of households headed by males. Toby and Josh would continue to remember their interaction with the man in the bar and even call him in a subsequent episode to explain their new idea for college tuition tax credits ("College Kids"). Calling whiteness a chimera, López suggests that white identity is "largely a compilation of positive myths that celebrate imagined virtues and conceal real failings."[60] Such myths of whiteness, which include ideologies of individualism, agrarianism, patriarchy, and the American Dream, are articulated powerfully in *TWW*.

The myth of whiteness, of course, is destabilized at the beginning of the second season when we learn that the would-be assassins who fired at the president and his entourage are part of a white supremacist group, West Virginia White Pride. The Secret Service calls the shooting "an act of madmen" trying to kill Charlie, not the president, because of his romantic involvement with the president's daughter ("In the Shadow of Two Gunmen, Part 2"). As *TWW*'s staff attempts to process the assassination in an episode entitled "The Midterms" Toby calls for tougher hate crime laws and greater restrictions on rights for open assembly, suggesting that such groups should be required to "register with the FBI." C.J. represents the voice of free speech and free assembly and questions, "Any problems with the First Amendment?" Ultimately, President Bartlet clarifies the emotional complexity for Toby by first admitting that he wanted to tell the attorney general to "take them" (the West Virginia group). "And then I hang up the phone," the president adds, "because I know it will be better tomorrow and better the day after that. We saw a lynching Toby. That's why it feels like this."

Although the narrative decenters whiteness, such deconstructions take place through the characterizations of white supremacist groups, extreme enactments that neutralize other forms of white racism. The plot implies that white supremacists function as the primary example of such explicit racism; they want "the kind of America . . . where white, European Americans would be able to develop freely their common culture and common political life without hindrance from members of other racial groups."[61]

The question of hate groups and white supremacy is also contextualized in *TWW* through the use of a drama frame that exhibits the ways in which whites are undeserving victims of racism. In the same episode, "The Midterms," Sam convinces his Duke Law School friend Tom Jordan to run for Congress, promising the support of the president. Not long after Jordan agrees to run, C.J. tells Sam that there are problems with his candidacy because Jordan "likes white juries for black defendants." Leo adds that Jordan belonged to an "all-white fraternity." Sam rejects the implication that Jordan was part of an "all-white fraternity," noting that his fraternity did not have "any black pledges," but Leo tells him that the president will no longer support Jordan's candidacy. Sam is outraged. "I told him we would stand behind him. I told him he would have our full support . . . I was asked to ask him. We walk away now, that's it. He's a racist. The White House just said so." Leo responds, "We can't afford all the things we want Sam. It's over."

The president's words of restraint on matters of hate crimes, combined with evidence of white victimization, normalize racism and suggest that white hate groups embody it yet are also its victims. Of course, the imbalance of the crimes is ignored; an attempted murder of a black man in a position of power is implicitly likened to the political defeat of a candidate vying for public office. As *TWW* normalizes racism within the United States it commemorates the protections offered to hate groups. In the concluding segment of "The Midterms," Bartlet's staff gathers on Josh's front steps to drink beer. Josh says to Toby, who argues for stronger hate crimes legislation, "What do you say about a government that goes out of its way to protect even citizens that try to destroy it?" "God bless America," Toby responds. As the show fades to the credits all four staffers toast. Sam, followed by C.J. and then Josh, all individually repeat, "God bless America."

The message of *TWW* in such constructions and others suggests much about the conditions of contemporary racial issues. Whiteness is normalized and is an essence of true Americanism, complete with positive myths that perpetuate the innocence and greatness of white America led by a fallible yet moral white male president. When whiteness is critiqued, white racism is embodied by hate groups that attempt to lynch people of color—far removed from true Americanism. It also suggests that even though such groups espouse hate and may plan for violence their rights for free assembly take precedence over the protection that victims of such crimes could expect.

In describing legal precedents concerning freedom of expression and hate speech Kathleen E. Mahoney asserts that many jurists assume that "the muzzling of hate promoters undeniably detracts from free expression values and that they must attach the highest importance to political speech," even though "harms of hate propaganda to group members included humiliation, degradation, self-hate, isolation, and hostility."[62] The show also suggests that racism permeates the United States, and everyone, regardless of racial grouping, is a potential victim of it. Such constructions not only normalize racism but also ignore the lived realities of white privilege and racism throughout U.S. history and attempt to equate crimes of violence with the realities of electoral politics. These inequitable depictions are furthered through narratives that address issues of color in *TWW* episodes.

## Multiculturalism and Internationalism in *TWW*'s World of Presidential Whiteness

Just as whites are viewed as privileged participants in representative government, people of color assume more contested space. Writing about Theodore Roosevelt's nationalist principles, Gerstle notes that "Roosevelt believed that most non-whites belonged to 'inferior' races with limited capacities for self-government."[63] America's history of immigration restrictions created a culture in which non-whites were constructed as perpetual outsiders and whiteness became the normative standard of identity.[64] When such ideologies interact with depictions of the presidency, complex and often contradictory discourses emerge. As Nelson explains:

> The president embodies democracy as a paradigm of national manhood's unhealthy desires for unity, wholeness, and self-sameness. But the figure of the president is also loaded up with national manhood's ambivalent longings for a more heterogeneous democratic connectedness. These contradictory desires

split the president in our "democratic" imaginary. The hard body of the president offers us a strong guarantee for national boundaries and self-identity. The soft body of the president holds out for us sensations of democratic recognition and equalitarian exchange. We can't seem to imagine having both at the same time and we can't figure out how to live without either one.[65]

There are moments, of course, where otherness is celebrated in *TWW*, yet even at such commemorative moments people of color are marginalized in the political narrative. Many story lines depict issues of race in the United States as political quagmires the president seeks to avoid and political leaders of color as self-interested, single-issue activists. On such matters of race the president voices considerable ambivalence, and whiteness is often articulated by one of the inner circle who further accentuates white victimization and bitterness. Most disturbing is the fact that people of color are often linked with acts of violence. When countries with people of color are written into the story lines, they, too, are frequently associated with violence and seem incapable of controlling chaos.

*TWW* offers moving moments in certain episodes that celebrate the presence of others in electoral politics. In an episode from the first season, "Mr. Willis of Ohio," Joe Willis steps into a political battle over an appropriations bill when he is appointed to fill his late wife's term in the House of Representatives. Willis is an eighth-grade social studies teacher whom Toby lobbies about the need to drop a census amendment from the appropriations bill to assure its quick passage. The West Wing staff wants the amendment dropped because it would incite additional debate over the prohibition of census sampling. Willis is portrayed as a kindly yet naïve man whose wife was politically accomplished and astute. Even he acknowledges, "I'm not nearly as smart as my wife was. I went to night school because I went to work pretty young. And I tried to understand the things Janice brought home from the office, but I wasn't in her league. I never understood what she wanted with a dummy like me."

Willis is othered not only because he is out of place in this political environment but also because of his race. In talking about the census amendment Toby has Mandy read Article 1, section 2 of the Constitution relating to matters of citizenship. Mandy fails to incorporate the words *free person* in her rendering, omitting references to all others. In response, Toby accentuates the "three-fifths of all other persons" clause—and thus the citizenship inequalities for African Americans—when he says to Willis, "They meant you, Mr. Willis, didn't they?" In the end, Joe Willis does not vote for the amendment because he finds that Toby made "a very strong argument." Toby, in the White House, watches the roll-call vote in the House of Representatives and comments to the other West Wing staffers over a poker game, "I met an unusual man . . . didn't walk into the room with a political agenda. He didn't walk in with his mind made up. He genuinely wanted to do what he thought was best. He didn't mind saying the words 'I don't know.'"

Although it is a moving episode that demonstrates the genuineness and eagerness of Willis to vote his conscience, the narrative also accentuates his otherness and portrays him as an outsider to the political process and an incomplete other constitutionally. Joe Willis's wife is portrayed as a strong political leader, but she is dead and thus not part of the episode. His otherness is emphasized, but Toby's political positioning is validated, reifying the central role of whites in governance and the foreignness, or at least awkwardness, of persons of color to the business of representative democracy.

Another example evinces the ideological legacy of Theodore Roosevelt's "true Americanism" as it celebrates a multicultural Congress and makes it an other. In this instance President Bartlet meets with Representative Peter Lien, a newly appointed member of Congress from the Twenty-second District of Texas. Lien's family left Vietnam in 1974 and established a fishing business in Galveston Bay thereafter. Upon meeting Lien, President Bartlet asks, "You think when your folks got you out in '74 they imagined they were taking you to a place that would be willing to make you a Congressman?" Lien responds, "As a matter of fact I think that's exactly what they imagined." The president then reflects, "Me too. . . . Obviously, you have a bigger symbolic responsibility than that. . . . But your biggest responsibility isn't symbolic, right? . . . What is it?" Lien attempts to pass the presidential test, responding, "It's to my district, my country, and the Congress of the United States." The president concludes, "Welcome, my friend, to the show that never ends." After Lien leaves, Bartlet comments, "Isn't that a hell of a thing? What's next?"

Without question Lien's presence in Congress is an aberration, given the president's final words in the scene, which establish Lien's otherness as an Asian American from Texas. More than that, though, Bartlet ensures that Lien passes the loyalty oath in such a way that reflects Roosevelt's and Wilson's assimilationist legacies. As Stanley A. Renshon explains, "You could come from any geographical, ethnic, racial, or religious origin and still be welcome, though not always unambivalently, to develop an American identity and nationality."[66]

The non-white status of those who demonstrate the "psychology" of an American identity is, like women's political role, still acknowledged and at times celebrated. It is also, however, made an other in the on-going white male political world. These narratives marginalize persons of color in electoral politics but nevertheless fashion positive and mythic images of such individuals, providing an ethnically enriched nationalism. Other episodes are more troubling because of the ways in which issues of race are linked to political predicaments and people of color are often associated with violence.

## The Political Quagmires of Race

*TWW,* mirroring the larger political context, tends to portray leaders of color as motivated exclusively by self or group interest and depict their issues in terms of political capital or political landmines to be avoided. In the third-season episode entitled "Ways and Means" the loyalty of African Americans and Latinos to the party is challenged, verifying how their callous self-interest transcends true beliefs about democracy and party allegiance. The confrontations between the West Wing staff and leaders from developing nations function as the dramatic juxtaposition for Bartlet's presidential campaign. Even though the white president is flawed he is nevertheless moral and committed to the good of the people. People of color who organize and collectivize like other congressional or lobbying groups do, however, demonstrate disregard for such noble political practices and seem to be political opportunists.

The first example of this juxtaposition relates to the Congressional Black Caucus's support for repealing the estate tax, a common position among Republicans. Leo explains their position, which counters the president's attempt to ensure that the wealthy pay their fair share of taxes: "The first generation of black millionaires is about to die." Later in the same episode Josh and Toby confront the leader of the Black Caucus, Representative Richardson, who explains that "the African American community doesn't think one way about anything." Josh responds, "You think a few black millionaires justifies a multi-billion-dollar boondoggle?" Demonstrating a more defeatist and self-interested attitude, Richardson comments, "As long as there's a Congress, there are going to be multi-billion-dollar boondoggles. We'd just like to share in them a little bit." "We're bleeding here," Toby pleads. "You can work with us or you can be ignored by a Republican president." Richardson wonders aloud what "happens to the people who got you here" while "you guys are defending yourselves against special prosecutors." Connecting African Americans with problems of poverty, Toby reminds Richardson of all the issues Bartlet supports, which include failing schools, drug treatment, and community policing. In the end Richardson concludes, "The Black Caucus doesn't vote as one mind. I can't promise anything."

Even as *TWW* destabilizes the commonplace that all blacks vote alike, its producers later construct African Americans as a voting block when they consider replacing the current vice president, John Hoynes, with Joint Chiefs Chair Fitzwallace. Of this idea, later dropped, Josh concludes, "Black turnout would explode. It would realign the country," constructing people of color as like-minded political targets ("Stirred"). Suggesting that African Americans "could be exploited in service of all manner of political ends, especially the winning and holding of elective office" represents a political practice and assumption that is on-going and has historical roots in Reconstruction, Riley notes.[67]

The self-interestedness of others is further illustrated in "Ways and Means" when Sam and Connie Tate, a member of Bartlet's campaign team, visit Victor Campos, a political leader in the Latino community. In a heated exchange Sam also lists the issues the president addressed because of campaign promises to Latinos—minimum wage, prenatal care for illegal immigrants, and small-business loans. "That's what I got in the last election," Campos responds. "What do I get in this one?" "What happened to loyalty?" Sam replies, a direct challenge to the Latino's faithfulness to the party. Campos again shows callous disregard for such loyalty, "You can't deposit it in a savings account . . . What do I get?" He eventually asks for "complete amnesty for all undocumented immigrants from the Americas. . . . The Legal Amnesty Fairness Act is in the Senate right now." The request outrages Sam, who insists, "We can't back a bill that treats Hispanic immigrants any different." "Sure we can," says Connie as she cuts him off. When Connie, the political campaign operative, and Sam go over the issue in private she tells him to "suck it up and give him what he wants, which is going to help you in the long run anyway." Once they return, Campos promises Sam "California and its 435 delegates" in return for Bartlet's support of the Legal Amnesty Fairness Act.

Constructing politics in this manner romanticizes the white president's political vision as being grounded in an authentic desire to achieve good against a political philosophy voiced by people of color that reveals their desire to take from the whole, even if only a few benefit from a proposed policy or action. Robert Fine charges, "From the point of view of civic nationalism, ethnic nationalism appears irrational, even pathological, as if the relation between them were one of light against darkness, reason against madness, tolerance against bigotry, freedom against authoritarianism."[68]

*TWW* clearly fosters the bifurcation between its heroic and romanticized white president, who represents the whole, against proponents of identity politics who represent the self-interested few. Nira Yuval-Davis asserts that ethnicity is "primarily a political process which constructs the collectivity and its interests not only as a result of the general positioning of the collectivity in relation to others in the society, but also as a result of the specific relations of those engaged in 'ethnic politics' with others within that collectivity."[69]

The discussion of loyalty seems to accentuate a lack of gratitude on the part of people of color for being invited into the political arena. The argument is similar to the argument Josh makes to Amy about women's support for Bartlet. Even though a Democratic president's policies may not fulfill the political agendas for all marginalized citizens, the reasoning suggests, they go further than the Republican Party in considering "minority" views. Thus, the consent of marginalized citizens to the dominant group's position assumes common-sense characteristics that perpetuate and reify existing positions of power and insubordination in a way reflective of Antonio Gramsci's conception of social hegemony.[70]

Issues linked to identity politics are likewise crafted as political quagmires that legitimate President Bartlet's ambivalence on matters of race. In "The Drop-In," an episode in which Marbury's political opinions are valorized while the president demasculinizes Asian and Native American men, the Bartlet administration also asks the African American comedian Cornelius Sykes not to host an event called the Will Rogers Dinner. Sykes had attracted considerable negative press for a performance two years earlier when he joked, with the president present, about New York police officers shooting a black man. The administration's public response to the incident was that Bartlet "didn't laugh at the joke." "The president laughed" Sykes maintains during an uncomfortable conversation with C.J. The comedian, who helped elect Bartlet by raising funds and appearing in campaign advertising, tells C.J. he is angry about the president's lack of public support. Still, she asks that he decline the invitation so he and Bartlet will not appear in public together, and Sykes agrees.

Although these scenes may reflect an attempt by *TWW* to offer commentary about the troubling political climate concerning matters of race, the episode continues to communicate the contested nature of racial politics and the contentious role that African Americans play within it. As hooks explains this "white supremacist logic," "Rather than using coercive tactics of domination to colonize, it seduces black folks with the promise of mainstream success if only we are willing to negate the value of blackness."[71]

*TWW* also emphasizes the contestation surrounding issues commonly associated with persons of color. As the presidential election heats up in season three, Bartlet's Republican opponent, Robert Ritchie, makes a public statement during the primary in opposition to the use of race as a qualification for college admittance. Toby views such a statement as an opening for President Bartlet to support affirmative action. Even though Toby incorporates a position statement on affirmative action into a campaign speech, Bartlet rewrites it, prompting a hostile reaction from Toby: "Sir, I've read it twice and I don't even know what we're talking about." The president explains, "Yeah, I was trying to avoid a quote . . . it's purposefully nonspecific." When Toby protests Bartlet's lack of specificity the president suggests, "We get the word out to our friends that I was obviously nodding in the direction of affirmative action." Toby pushes the president, who responds, "Nobody's questioning where we stand . . . I don't want to campaign today." Even though Toby reminds the president that they were going to write a "new book" on campaigning, Bartlet concludes, "We will. . . . We don't have to piss people off every day in order to demonstrate that we're not—" (the president redirects his thought in mid-sentence)—"look, we're going to Iowa where we already won . . . and I say thank you for getting me elected in the first place and we're back on the plane and I tell you what else. I don't think it's a good idea for us to be fighting for news coverage with three governors, two senators and the head of the church of 'I hate you.' Let's just stay under the radar."

Toby is still troubled by the president's ambiguity on affirmative action when Bartlet speaks in Iowa: "Now that we've abolished discrimination in our laws, we need to abolish it in our hearts and minds." As before, *TWW* accentuates the president's ambivalence on controversial matters and reinforces his internal struggle over the game of politics. In the process, however, *TWW* furthers the idea that issues linked to people of color (and women) are indeed political quagmires.

Rather than take the opportunity for the president to address the historical legacies of racism (and sexism) in the United States, *TWW* accentuates the logic of whiteness and reverse racism. As Toby tries to convince C.J. that "it's a good time to talk about affirmative action when it comes to admissions" she challenges his support of affirmative action initiatives: "Your father didn't need affirmative action and neither did mine and they were both children of immigrants." "Your father needed the GI Bill," Toby responds, "and so did mine." C.J. then offers a longer assessment of this contested policy:

> I'm the wrong Democrat to talk to about this . . . because after my father fought in Korea, he became what this government begs every graduate to become. He became a teacher and he raised a family on a teacher's salary and he paid his taxes . . . and anytime there was an opportunity for career advancement, it took an extra five years 'cause invariably there was a less qual-

ified black woman in the picture. So, instead of retiring as Superintendent of the Ohio Valley Union Free School District, he retired as head of the math department at William Henry Harrison Junior High.

The subject then immediately turns to the health of C.J.'s father rather than a defense of affirmative action. C.J.'s statement reaffirms the popular conception of white male victimization as an outgrowth of affirmative action and ignores the historical conditions of racism and the data on career advancement and college admissions for groups targeted by affirmative action. The statement is given greater force, and perhaps enhanced irony, because a white woman voices it, and white women are generally the greatest beneficiaries of affirmative action policies. Most troubling though is that the statement also confirms the consternation in *TWW*'s discourse of nationalism over issues of immigration, class, and race on matters of worth and contribution to U.S. culture. African American women in this narrative personify such contestation. As John David Skrentny has written, "Most Euro-Americans never have been generous with social policy to benefit African Americans." He blames Lyndon Johnson and Richard Nixon for not using the "'bully pulpit'" to "explain and advocate the policy to the American people," which created a resentful white population that thinks that affirmative action "was forced on them."[72]

At other times *TWW* furthers the self-interestedness of persons of color, connects such people with overtly racial issues, and accentuates the unresolvable conflict of many racial issues. The show does so in a way, however, that educates viewers about the various positions on controversial matters. Although educational and provocative, issues are not resolved, and action is not taken.

In season one ("Six Meetings before Lunch") *TWW* offers such a debate on the issue of slave reparations and features an informed argument between Josh and Jeff Breckenridge, Bartlet's African American nominee for assistant attorney general for civil rights. The conflict centers around three groups of others, each vying for political retribution. Breckenridge's nomination is seen as uncontroversial until Bartlet's staff learns that he has been quoted as saying "Otis Hastings is a unique and extraordinary historian. This book should be read by everyone and burned into the minds of white America" on the back cover of Hasting's book *The Unpaid Debt*. From the beginning of the controversy Josh, a "white guy from Connecticut," is concerned about speaking to Breckenridge on the matter. Leo urges him on, however, with "remember, you're also Jewish." It is a statement that seems to offer Josh the necessary credibility to address such issues with the civil rights lawyer from Athens, Georgia.

From the beginning of the conversation it is clear Breckenridge favors reparations. "If asked," he says, "I'll tell the Committee that my father's fathers were kidnapped outside a village called Wimbabwa, brought to New Guinea, sold to a slave trader from Boston and bought by a plantation owner in Wadsworth, South Carolina, where they worked . . . for no wages." Josh is more stunned, though, when Breckenridge says that the amount of reparations deserved is "1.7 trillion dollars," based on calculations from an economist of the Manchester Institute who "calculated the number of slaves held, multiplied it by the number of hours worked, multiplied that by the market value of manual labor and came up with a very conservative figure."

In the next segment Breckenridge informs Josh that the debate over slave reparations is nothing new given that African Americans were provided with land and other equipment, including mules, after the Civil War until President Andrew Johnson rescinded the order. In response, Josh reminds Breckenridge that more than "six hundred thousand white men . . . died over the issue of slavery."

In the last segment of the episode Breckenridge brings up the issue of reparations for Japanese Americans interned during World War II. "They were actually in the internment camps," Josh counters, meaning that slave reparations are too late. When Breckenridge asks for reparations in the form of "tax deductions and scholarship funds," Josh reminds him of "affirmative action and empowerment zones and civil rights acts." He is angry by this point and suggests, "I'd love to give you money. . . . But I'm a little short of cash right now. It seems the S.S. officer forgot to give my grandfather his wallet back when he let him out of Birkenau."

Breckenridge offers reasoned arguments to Josh's consternation: "We have laws in this country. You break them, you pay your fine. You break God's laws, that's a different story. You can't kidnap a civilization and sell them into slavery. No amount of money will make up for it, and all you have to do is look, two hundred years later, at race relations in this country." Josh begins to calm down, acknowledging that no amount of money "will make up for it." Breckenridge asks for a dollar bill and informs Josh:

> The seal, the pyramid, it's unfinished. With the eye of God looking over it. And the words *Annuit Coeptis*. He, God, Favors our Undertaking. The seal is meant to be unfinished, because this country's meant to be unfinished. We're meant to keep doing better. We're meant to keep discussing and debating and we're

meant to read books by great historical scholars and then talk about them, which is why I lent my name to a dust cover. I want to be your Assistant Attorney General for Civil Rights. I'll do an outstanding job for all people in this country. You got any problem with me saying all that to the committee?

Josh says no, and they prepare to go to lunch. The exchange is constructive because it gives voice to the different positions on matters of U.S. history and racism. Although emotive and productive, the debate over a contentious matter of race is offered for historical enlightenment and dialectical purposes. There is no way to resolve such historical tensions apart from the correctives that have already been offered.

A similar exchange in a third-season episode entitled "The Indians in the Lobby" offers further engagement with race relations in the United States yet provides even fewer answers than were proffered in the slave reparations issue. In this instance two Native Americans enter the lobby of the White House on the day before Thanksgiving because Jacob Cutler of Intergovernmental Affairs canceled an appointment with them. Maggie Morningstar-Charles and Jack Lonefeather of the Stockbridge-Munsee Indians in Wisconsin are seeking a response to a land request and vow not to leave until they get an answer. As the narrative returns to them throughout the episode they educate C.J. on the U.S. treatment of Native Americans over the past two centuries. They talk about an 1856 treaty, when their tribe was moved from New York to Wisconsin and lost thousands of acres in the process. As the press gathers, C.J. tries to convince them to make an appointment for Monday. Morningstar-Charles responds, "Look, Ms. Cregg. If we give up this land, we lose our one bullet in our gun. We need to be in view of the press." Lonefeather continues that the Dawes Act was supposed to civilize them, teaching them to "cultivate the land, wear civilized clothes . . . and drink whiskey." In 1934, they say, the Indian Relocation Act allowed them to begin buying back the land, something they are trying to do through the application. C.J. continues to emphasize that "there's absolutely nothing I can do for you." As night falls and everyone leaves for Thanksgiving vacation, she tells Morningstar-Charles and Lonefeather that they can either make an appointment for Monday morning and the White House will pay for their weekend expenses or "I'm gonna have the Park Police escort you from the building." They finally opt to make an appointment. As the episode concludes, C.J. laments, "How do you keep fighting these smaller injustices when they're all from the Mother of Injustices?" Morningstar-Charles responds, "What's the alternative?"

As in the slave reparations narrative, *TWW* offers an emotive story about the shameful and historical treatment of persons of color by the U.S. government. And also like the slave reparations discourse, the episode ends with no clear answers to the tragedies of history. The issue functions as an academic matter, reserved for discussion rather than action. Bartlet's major concern is whether it is safe to cook stuffing inside a turkey; he places a call to the Butterball Hotline to find answers to his cooking dilemma.

Just as Josh attends to the slave reparation exigency without presidential involvement, C.J. addresses the issue of Native American land loss with minimal interest from anyone else in *TWW*. The stories educate and incite sympathy, and they also construct the issues as historical, political acts that fall outside the purview of contemporary presidential action, reifying the marginalization of people of color and their grievances once again. Such plots also suggest that African Americans, Native Americans, and other persons of color are always performing race and are subject to the white gaze as they do so.

## "Other" Acts of Violence

The stereotyping of people of color is abundant in *TWW* and becomes even more pervasive as they are noticeably associated with violence. Charlie's mother died from cop-killer bullets in the line of duty as a Washington, D.C., police officer ("A Proportional Response"). Throughout the first season his relationship with the "first daughter" is repeatedly brought up in relation to the violent white supremacists that threaten them and motivate a Secret Service investigation. The assassination attempt that ends the first season is attributed to racial hatred against Charlie. In season two, an African American computer specialist whose young son accompanies him to the West Wing comments to Charlie, "You don't think I know who you are. . . . The one man who almost got the president killed" ("The Midterms").

Leo also conflates violence and blackness during the first season with an African American member of Congress opposing a gun control bill. To him, Leo pleads, "God, Mark. The bodies being wheeled into the emergency room are black. These guns aren't going to Scottsdale, Mark, they're going to Detroit, they're going to Philadelphia. An entire generation of African American men are being eaten alive by drugs and poverty" ("Five Votes Down"). Of such images Carr observes, the "black male body" acts "as a site of confrontation (as criminal, as threat)." Since the Civil Rights movement of the

1950s and 1960s, Carr suggests that the "street" is "masculinized" and also "the site of struggle" for African American men.[73]

Such associations of violence with people of color also transcend domestic political contexts. In most instances developing nations are seldom represented in the show. Instead, *TWW* constructs the distant lands in the narration, reflecting a "third persona" where groups are "objectified," "negated," and/or rejected in the narrative process by the voices of authority.[74] In "The State Dinner" from the first season, for example, Indonesians are characterized as "gangs of roving people beheading those they suspect of being sorcerers." Pakistan and India are linked to nuclear proliferation in season two when Toby says, "We're all going to die." America's use of nuclear weapons, of course, does not influence his fearful thoughts ("The Lame Duck Congress"). In the third season, the president calls "Kashmir . . . the most dangerous place on earth" and the "Taiwan Strait" the "second most dangerous" ("Hartsfield's Landing"). Also in season three, Bartlet is informed about an accident in which two trucks are on fire. Although there is no sign of hazardous material, one of the trucks is stolen. The president wonders, "Was he [the thief] Arab?" In each case people of color are defined in relation to violent or aberrant behavior, reflecting Stuart Hall's conception of racism as "a structure of discourse and representation that tries to expel the Other symbolically—blot it out, put it over there in the Third World, at the margin."[75]

As sites of violence, developing countries, often victims of colonization, are portrayed as being out of control or at least incapable of controlling criminal activity. In "Bad Moon Rising" of the second season, Josh is explaining an economic crisis in Mexico, stating, "It'd be like a two thousand–point drop in the Dow." He argues that the United States should help Mexico pay off its 30 billion dollars worth of loans, accentuating a hierarchal relationship between the two nations, Mexico being economically out of control. In another second-season episode, "In This White House," *TWW* attends to the difficult issue of AIDS in Africa through the fictional Republic of Equatorial Kuhndu. Kuhndu's president Nimbala is visiting the White House to negotiate with American pharmaceutical companies for lower prices on AIDS medications. Toby establishes that he could get the drug companies to "drop their prices," but the "Ministry of Health" and "custom's agents" in Kuhndu must also prevent the influx of "black market drugs" from Pakistan and Korea. With negotiations underway, a coup occurs in the African country, and Nimbala's brother and two sons are killed. In addition to portraying African countries as AIDS-ridden, the region is also depicted as chaotic. Even though President Bartlet is sympathetic, he tells President Nimbala, "You understand, don't you, why I can't offer military assistance?" Although the West Wing staff tries to prevent the African president from returning home, he goes anyway and is killed as soon as he deplanes. When the president receives the notice of Nimbala's death, he tells Toby and Josh, "They executed him in the airport parking lot. OK. I'll see you on Monday." The show ends with a level of considerable despair that nothing can be done in Kuhndu. Disease, violence, and pandemonium is normalized, as is U.S. nonintervention, even if such indifference is never explained. Little can be done on matters of slave reparations or Native American loss of land, and nothing can be done in developing nations ill-equipped for self-rule.[76]

Although offering polysemic texts, *TWW*'s renditions of race reinforce an image of a white male presidency that naturalizes the locus of power for whiteness while reifying the subordinate and, in certain cases, disempowered lives of persons of color who spend time combating violence or are themselves self-serving principal agents in political puzzles. In portrayals of race during the 1980s, Gray suggests, "Television was never just a neutral player, an invisible conduit, in these representations and constructions. Television itself also constituted a significant social site for shaping, defining, contesting, and representing claims about American society."[77] In *TWW*'s world, the United States represents a multicultural and internationalized populace that debates issues of race and reflects some of the more divisive issues of U.S. nationalism. In part, the president functions as the key political actor within such matters, embodying the show's narrative account of the presidency with a stabilized, unquestioned whiteness. In other instances, issues fall outside the presidential purview because they are either removed to the province of history or too inherently complicated for the United States to act on them.

Multiculturalism is contested in many episodes of *TWW*, but presidential masculinity and whiteness are not except in extreme cases of white supremacist violence. As Nelson has explained the persistence of the dominant white, male presidency that incorporates the historical legacy of race and gender ideologies, "People's ability to deal with messier, open-ended, democratic heterogeneity is circulated through national manhood's presidentialism into constitutionally unhealthy longings for wholeness, unity, for 'democratic' homogeneity."[78]

# 4

# Militarized Nationalism and
## *The West Wing*

The eagle on the seal in the carpet. In one talon he's holding
arrows, and in the other an olive branch. Most of the time, the
eagle's facing the olive branch, but when Congress declares war,
the eagle faces the talons. How do they do that? You think
they've got a second carpet sitting around in the basement
someplace? . . . Maybe this piece in the middle cuts out
and they do it like a basketball court.

—Admiral Percy Fitzwallace, "What Kind of Day Has It Been"

ARTICLE 2, section 1, of the Constitution declares, "The executive
Power shall be vested in the President of the United States," who will likewise serve, section 2 commands, as the "Commander in Chief of the Army
and Navy of the United States, and of the militias of the several states, when
called into the actual Service of the United States." From the nation's earliest years the presidency and militarism have been inextricably linked, especially as the nation was born out of war and the country's first presidents
were some of its first war heroes.

The relationship between military experience and presidential qualification
continued well beyond George Washington. Francis A. Beer contends that
"American presidential candidates with military experience have had better
success in getting elected than those without prior military credentials."[1] It
was also common for a president to be occupied at some point with international military excursions; the first century and a half of U.S. history are replete with instances of presidents either sending military forces overseas or
otherwise confronting war crises.[2] The internal threats to the nation, however, are also integral to nationalist ideology. J. Ann Tickner explains that "issues of importance" related to national security "are often exacerbated by the

manipulation of nationalist ideologies that pits ruling groups against 'outsiders' within their own territories." Out of this militarized nationalist context the "valorization of war" occurs.[3]

Early in the history of the United States, precedents were established vesting decisions over the new nation's foreign policy matters in the office of the presidency. Thomas E. Cronin and Michael A. Genovese observe that when President George Washington enacted a pattern for "unilateral executive action" with his issuance of the Neutrality Proclamation of 1793 without congressional consent, "Congress willingly conceded to Washington most of the executive powers he exercised, especially those in foreign policy matters." To lessen "monarchical fears," however, presidents often showed deference to Congress, with most assuming "only necessary executive powers." With such a prudent course, presidents were given latitude on international matters, particularly those involving the negotiation of treaties; they were also mindful, however, of the need for a balance of powers, even on foreign policy issues.[4]

Presidents found themselves embroiled in many external conflicts in the early years of the Republic, and that overseas focus helped fashion U.S. nationalism. In addition to large-scale conflicts such as the War of 1812, which Robert Dallek suggests "turned aside domestic divisions and reestablished American independence from European strife," there were smaller military actions that often involved battles at sea over trading and piracy.[5] Such conflicts, although designed to protect U.S. economic and national interests, can similarly be viewed as the early beginnings of American imperialism. The Monroe Doctrine, issued by President James Monroe on December 2, 1823, was designed to declare America's neutrality in European skirmishes and dissuade future colonialist actions by European powers.[6] It likewise exhibited the country's "imperialist tendency," Michael Hardt and Antonio Negri observe, even if the United States announced its exertion of "control over the Americas" in seemingly "anti-imperialist" terms.[7]

Even before, and certainly after, the United States declared neutrality in European matters and its protectionist interests in the Americas, presidents exhibited expansionist tendencies. By the beginning of the Civil War, the United States had acquired new territory from the Louisiana Purchase (1803) along with the Mississippi (1804), Orleans (1804), Michigan (1805), Illinois (1809), and Indiana (1809) territories. The Texas Annexation occurred in the same year as the acquisition of the Oregon territories (1845), and the Mexican cession followed three years later (1848). Albert K. Weinberg links America's expansionist activities to "the evolution of American nationalism," where "moral doctrines that have been advanced in justification of this extension of the national domain at the expense of other and—usually weaker—peoples."[8]

It was in this expansionist context that the ideology of Manifest Destiny was popularized and a discourse of nationalism flourished during the Civil War era. Manifest Destiny is a concept allegedly developed by John O'Sullivan, yet its ideologies are historically rooted as far back as Thomas Paine's revolutionary *Common Sense*.[9] O'Sullivan, an editor of the *Democratic Review* and ardent supporter of Andrew Jackson, declared in 1839 that "the far-reaching, the boundless future will be the era of American greatness. In its magnificent domain of space and time, the nation of many nations is destined to manifest to mankind the excellence of divine principles. . . . Its floor shall be a hemisphere—its roof the firmament of the star-studded heavens, and its congregation an Union of many Republics . . . governed by God's natural and moral law of equality."[10]

The principles accentuated in O'Sullivan's edict and others who popularized Manifest Destiny were those of Americans who had mostly "Anglo-Saxon, Protestant roots." They articulated "the divine right of 'united white people' to govern the entire continent," sentiments that became "a compelling rationale" in strengthening American nationalism. Such a sense of moral and religious superiority helped propel America's missionary spirit or role as the Benevolence Empire (chapter 2), in which American efforts in a range of areas abroad (including religion, medicine, and humanitarian relief) became a major part of U.S. foreign policy.[11] By the time of the Civil War, Rogan Kersh writes, "Americans turned from a language of localism and states' rights to one emphasizing nationalism during and immediately following the war."[12]

Part of the ideological power of Manifest Destiny and expansionism as key components of U.S. nationalism is linked to what Frederick J. Turner defined as the "frontier thesis" of the nineteenth century. When the superintendent for the census declared in 1890 that frontier areas would no longer be noted in census reports, Turner described that policy shift as "the closing of a great historic movement," when the frontier acted as a "meeting point between savagery and civilization" and "the line of most rapid and effective Americanization." Linking the frontier to militarization and nationalism in 1893, Turner concluded that the frontier, from the Revolutionary War period forward, functioned "as a military training school, keeping alive the power of resistance to aggression, and developing the stalwart and rugged qualities of the frontiersman." Similarly, "The growth of nationalism and the evolution of American political institutions were dependent on the advance of the frontier."[13] Robert H. Wiebe calls Turner's thesis a "fable of democracy" that occurred in "vast spaces awaiting white enterprise" and was "renewed time and again on successive frontiers," which intrinsically linked "democracy and America's colonial rationale."[14]

As the United States entered the twentieth century, the notion of the rugged frontiersman and power of American nationalism were embodied and perpetuated by President Theodore Roosevelt in his visions of U.S. militarism. Relying on the metaphor of family to express his doctrine of U.S. foreign policy, which informed his corollary to the Monroe Doctrine, Governor Roosevelt argued during a speech entitled "The Strenuous Life" on April 10, 1899, that "a man's first duty is to his own home, but he is not thereby excused from doing his duty to the State; for if he fails in this second duty it is under penalty of ceasing to be a free-man. In the same way, while a nation's first duty is within its own borders, it is not thereby absolved from facing its duties in the world as a whole; and if it refuses to do so, it merely forfeits its right to struggle for a place among the peoples that shape the destiny of mankind."[15]

After T.R. became president he expounded further on his masculinist conception of U.S. foreign policy and expanded the parameters of the Monroe Doctrine during a speech in Chautauqua, New York, on August 11, 1905: "In the interest of justice, it is as necessary to exercise the police power as to show clarity and helpful generosity," with Cuba being the key example of U.S. military success that warranted similar actions in Santo Domingo.[16] Roosevelt likewise endorsed military actions outside the Western Hemisphere. When he was vice president, for example, he supported the guerilla war against the Philippines at the turn of the century as well as the effort against the Boxer Rebellion in China.

For Roosevelt, the readiness for battle was the key component of U.S. nationalism, as evidenced in *American Ideals* (1903): "A peaceful and commercial civilization is always in danger of suffering the loss of the virile fighting qualities without which no nation, however cultured . . . and prosperous, can ever amount to anything. Every citizen should be taught . . . that while he must avoid brawling and quarrelling, it is his duty to stand up for his rights." Roosevelt also conflated the skills of the warrior and politician, declaring, "A politician who really serves his country well and deserves his country's gratitude, must usually possess some of the hardy virtues which we admire in the soldier who serves his country well in the field."[17] Throughout, Roosevelt reinforced traditional gender roles, asserting that "the man must be glad to do a man's work, to dare and endure and to labor. . . . The woman must be the housewife . . . the wise and fearless mother of many healthy children." Such roles carried national consequences for Roosevelt: "When men fear work or fear of righteous war, when women fear motherhood, they tremble on the brink of doom; and well it is they should vanish from the earth, where they are fit subjects of scorn of all men and women who are themselves strong and brave and high-minded."[18]

As Roosevelt's discourse reveals, clear conceptions of American nationalism were well formed by the turn of the twentieth century. Such nationalism was dependent on visions of U.S. superiority as ordained by God, justifying American imperialism and expansionism, often against developing countries populated by people of color, and reifying notions of patriarchal instantiation. Kersh maintains that "for the first time apart from actual armed hostilities, patriotic spirit in the late nineteenth century was strongly associated with martial virtue among Americans, especially young men and even boys." National symbols such as the American flag "were increasingly associated with militarism as well."[19]

By the time of Wilson's presidency, competing conceptions of American internationalism were evident in U.S. foreign policy. The president exhibited "crusading moralism," as evidenced by his commitment at times to a nineteenth-century neutrality reflected in the Monroe Doctrine as well as the missionary sentiments and internationalist cooperative spirit of the failed League of Nations. Competing commitments were also valued as expressed in the hyper-militarism of Andrew Jackson and Theodore Roosevelt. As Mead observes, "The United States over its history has consistently summoned the will and the means to compel its enemies to yield to its demands" through a "ruthlessness of war" that attacked "civilian targets" and inflicted "heavy casualties on enemy civilians," playing "a vital part in American war strategies." Moreover, U.S. citizens should all shoulder the burden of such a militarized nationalism as "a significant element of American public opinion supports waging [war] at the highest possible level of intensity."[20]

The persistent militarism of U.S. nationalism helped expand the power of the presidency during the twentieth century; it also reified relationships among war, nationalism, and the presidency. The Civil War, Forrest McDonald writes, "established a potent precedent for the existence of war powers beyond the boundaries of the Constitution but not for the exclusive authority of the president to exercise those powers." Wilson's and Franklin Roosevelt's war powers activities during World War I and World War II came close to—or in the case of FDR, actually achieved—"truly dictatorial powers."[21] Franklin Roosevelt in particular blended the realism of Theodore Roosevelt and the moralistic idealism of Woodrow Wilson. He would exploit the powers of the presidency as if free from constitutional and political restraint.[22] Jeffrey K.

Tulis details the rise of the rhetorical presidency in which presidents like Theodore Roosevelt, Woodrow Wilson, and Franklin Roosevelt used their power as a "way of constituting the people to whom [their discourse] is addressed by furnishing them with the very equipment they need to assess its use."[23] Such presidential prerogatives held extensive consequences for foreign policy matters, which give a president considerable authority.

The post–World War II period also witnessed expansion in the covert operations of the U.S. government as orchestrated by presidential administrations under the authority of the National Security Act of 1947 and the underlying assumption that threats to national security brought on by the cold war justified secret operations. The 1947 act created the Central Intelligence Agency (CIA), formerly known as the Office of Strategic Services (OSS), as well as the National Security Council (NSC), an advisory body to the president on international and domestic political-military strategy. It also revised the structure of the Armed Services.[24]

Only six months after establishing the National Security Act of 1947, the NSC empowered the CIA to conduct "espionage and counter-espionage operations abroad" in such fields as "propaganda, economic warfare, preventative direct action, including sabotage, anti-sabotage . . . subversion against hostile states . . . and support for indigenous anti-communist elements in threatened countries of the free world." The ultimate goal of this presidentially directed action was to sanction covert actions "against hostile foreign states . . . or in support of friendly foreign states . . . but which [were] so planned and executed that . . . if uncovered the U.S. Government [could] plausibly disclaim any responsibility for them."[25] These "covert actions," endorsed by Presidents Truman and Eisenhower and perpetuated by future cold war presidents, "further eroded the checks and balances of congressional review and public scrutiny and aided in the production of more ethically questionable solutions as presidential administrations operated, at least partially, in a covert vacuum."[26]

The cold war era has often been referred to as a realist period in U.S. foreign policy that had significant consequences for the meaning of U.S. nationalism. Francis A. Beer and Robert Hariman talk of realism's "narrative of world politics," which is rooted in classical and medieval governments and appears as a "natural outgrowth of the . . . formation of the nation-state" and expresses the "permanent essence of politics between nations."[27] The common assumptions of a realistic framework are that the struggle for power and security define geopolitical relations, that the world is primarily lawless, and that nations face unlimited and variable perils within this context.[28] As Tickner writes, "Realists believe that, in an anarchical world of sovereign, self-interested states, war is always a possibility; therefore, states must rely on their own power and capabilities rather than international agreements to enhance their national security."[29]

Within this realist philosophy and military practice, research and the search for peace as an important policy formation are often marginalized. As President Eisenhower's NSC directed psychological warfare group noted in July 1953, "No good policy was ever made with either peace or compromise as its main ingredient."[30] During the cold war, the central combatants were viewed as the primary superpowers—the United States and the USSR—given the "age-old threat of great-power conflict" that is often the hallmark of realist thinking. Embedded in such "bipolar" views, often expressed by Europeans and Americans, is a belief that the enemy can be easily identifiable and both superpowers focused on "power balancing" that promotes a sense of stability.[31] Moreover, this cold war mentality, Elaine Tyler May maintains, reified traditional gender relationships that resulted in a "domestic containment" for women and required remasculinization of U.S. nationalism following such military quagmires as Vietnam.[32]

The post–cold war period, in contrast, is often understood in postrealist terms and similarly affects the ideological underpinnings and consequences of U.S. nationalism. Postrealists often challenge the philosophies of realism and believe it is one narrative of many explanations for international relations. They equally hope to move beyond the assumption of the nation-state as the center of authority, recognizing that "power does not grow just from the barrel of a gun." As Beer maintains, "In the twenty-first century, international violence will continue, but the meaning of war will gradually evolve. It will become less physical . . . and more virtual" as national boundaries dissolve and take new shapes.[33] Such a vision sees the enemy as less discernible. War conditions are commonly related to "ethnic wars, which often overlap international borders, [and] are frequently the result of the artificial borders imposed by former colonial powers."[34]

Reading *The West Wing* through a militarized nationalist lens reveals the discursive commitments to many of the same romantic, ideologies of gender, race, and militarization characteristic of the history of U.S. nationalism. Just as such ideological commitments were destabilized historically, so, too, are they in the texts of *TWW*, which at times reveal the discourses of both realism and postrealism. The show's treatment of Russia is the clearest representation of the realist philosophies of the cold war. Here, the legacy of U.S. cold-war sentiments are reinforced through the delegitimation of Russian science dependent on a sexualized and misogynist discourse. Russian women are dismissed, and Russian men are demasculinized, casting suspicion on all Russian policies and public statements. The science of the United States, although flawed, is romanticized through the presidentially backed space program in which white men serve as dreamers and embody hope and white women function as sexualized pragmatists.

As the show plays out military dramas involving developing nations of color, the postrealist ambiguities of the post–cold war era become more apparent. In such engagements the enemy is unclear; the tactics of war that these developing countries employ violate "just-war" principles. Even though the president ultimately engages in military actions that seem to defy the moral codes of war, his ambivalence about doing so combine with his moral sensibilities to demonstrate that he makes the right decisions in the name of U.S. nationalism despite his strict moral code. In the end, the militaristic dilemmas, as they enact discourses of romance, sex, and race, provide the drama frame for the presidential election and ideology of *TWW*'s presidentiality as a whole. The presidential authority as commander-in-chief serves as the metonymy of the office, which suggests that even though presidents may err in judgment (e.g., covering up issues of personal health), the nation's primary leader must, ultimately, exhibit keen intelligence transcending that of the American people in order to make the difficult military decisions required of a commander-in-chief. In addition, the president must embody an appropriate moral code that guides his white, male judgment as he deals with complexities that play out in nationalist and internationalist contexts.

## The International Realism of *The West Wing*

Although the cold war ended in the last decades of the twentieth century, the legacy of its ideological commitments live on in *TWW*. As John Fiske asserts, "The political domains of international affairs, the economy, and the internal politics of everyday life swirl into each other in the general politics of a nation's structure of feeling. This is why the media matter, for their alleged inadequacies in the first two are more than compensated for by their incessant activity in the third."[35] Unlike many media forums, *TWW* does venture into the "political domains of international affairs" and, not unexpectedly, it reifies the same bipolar constructions of the cold war. In the process, *TWW* sexualizes Russian and U.S. women while turning characters like C.J. and Mallory into personifications of pragmatism. *TWW* also has Sam and the president function as the romantic voices that perpetuate a frontier thesis in spite of rather obvious flaws inherent in the U.S. space program. On the program, U.S. moral, scientific, and military superiority is bifurcated against an outmoded and immoral Russia prone to the enticements of Middle Eastern terrorism.

## Cold War Enemies Foreign and Domestic

The good/evil construct that pervaded U.S. cold-war relations with the Soviet Union is still evident in *TWW*'s depictions of Russia. Specifically, the episode entitled "Somebody's Going to Emergency, Somebody's Going to Jail" attends to three separate topics and offers contrary constructions of each. The episode's title derives from a Don Henley song, "In a New York Minute," the refrain of which ("in a New York minute, everything can change") is heard at various points during the show. A cold-war story line of Soviet espionage centers on a granddaughter's attempt to clear the name of her grandfather before her father dies of a terminal illness. The grandfather, Daniel Gault, was a U.S. official charged but never convicted of treason. Two other narratives are offered as more comedic secondary plots. The first, linked to the "Big Block of Cheese Day," deals with the part of Leo's mission that involves throwing open White House doors to groups ordinarily ignored, an event held in tribute to Andrew Jackson, who enticed the American people to the Executive Mansion by disseminating cheese. The staff, without question, despises Leo's annual project, and all groan when he gives a "team morale" speech about the day's significance.

C.J. is particularly annoyed because of having to meet with the Cartographers for Social Equality, a group dedicated to producing more accurate world maps. From them C.J. learns that "third world countries are misrepresented," and Africa is undersized on most maps and North America is oversized. In quoting a famous scholar, one cartographer notes, "In our society, we unconsciously equate size with importance and even power." It is, at one level, a serious topic that offers a new orientation of the world as the cartographers call for inverting the Northern and Southern Hemispheres because of the biases inherent with countries being positioned where they now are on maps. C.J.'s response to the cartographers' proposal is, "But you can't do that . . . because you're freaking me out."

On the one hand, addressing such a socially progressive issue challenges dominant first-world attitudes and reorients thinking about issues of world power and disempowerment as it gains C.J.'s attention in spite of her initial skepticism. On the other hand, and most significant, the issue is marginalized because of being positioned in the "big block of cheese" context. Such issues are usually debased because of the assumption that the staff has to meet with wacky people about wacky issues. In this instance Josh attends the cartographers' meeting momentarily, telling C.J. after he leaves, "When these guys find Brigadoon on this map, you'll call me."

Another comedic moment in the episode relates to its portrayal of protesters and inversion of the mythos surrounding them in a way that also frames Russian exigency. On the same Big Block of Cheese Day, Toby is required to speak to a group protesting the World Bank. From the beginning, he belittles them as "tourists" and suggests that he has "seen better organized crowds at the DMV." Chaos reigns when he enters the room to speak to the protesters, who chant, "We all want justice now." Toby stays onstage, however, reading a newspaper and talking to a police officer as the protesters bicker among themselves. He later calls the protests "activist vacation" and "spring break for anarchist wannabes," suggesting he was almost killed after being hit in the head with bananas. Toby also gives voice to the global capitalist establishment, suggesting that the World Trade Organization (WTO) benefits people and corporations and that "free trade stops wars." Thus he offers an alternative perspective of protesters, who assumed a mythic quality during the 1960s and beyond. Cynthia Enloe notes, however, that the common critique of peace movements is that they "emerge within militarizing nationalist movements [and] are typically treated as though they are hopeless and/or analytically trivial."[36]

These inversions in *TWW* frame the ways in which relations between the United States and Russia after the cold war are understood in the episode. The writers suggest that the hysteria surrounding the evils of communism was justified after all, a reversal of the usual assumptions that the U.S. government engaged in a witch hunt for communists during the McCarthy era. When Donna asks Sam to check into the issue of Daniel Gault's guilt, he eagerly complies because he conducted extensive research on the Gault case in college. Nancy, the national security advisor, tells him to "drop Daniel Gault . . . do it right now," but Sam offers an in-depth analysis of Gault's innocence and refuses to accept her evidence that Gault "was a Soviet spy." "That's crap," he insists. "If the FBI had proof on Gault, they would have told the world about it." Nancy responds by passing him an NSA and CIA file. "He was an agent called Blackwater," she explains. "He was a delegate at Yalta and he returned to the U.S. by way of Rostov where he was awarded the Order of Lenin."

Nancy offers the proof even though sharing the files with Sam violates government policy because the document is "code word classified." She blacks out the classified material, and it is at that point Sam learns of Gault's guilt. "He was a spy," he tells Donna later. "He copied by hand State Department and White House documents and delivered them to the Soviets. They included Roosevelt's plans to enter the war . . . lists of communists and communist sympathizers." Sam also concludes that a Hungarian translator was killed to protect the identity of Blackwater.

The story line is significant because of *TWW*'s suggestion that the panic surrounding communist infiltration of the U.S. government was ultimately justified, a conclusion only reached through the use of covert operations and secret intelligence-gathering sanctioned and practiced by U.S. presidents. As Robert L. Ivie argues, George Kennan and other cold warriors claimed that the real enemy existed within the United States, which was ill-equipped to expel the "external realities" of an "ideological virus infecting unsuspecting victims."[37] Such a position is ironic given the political attacks that many in Hollywood and throughout the nation faced because of those suspicions. After the cold war some indicated that the "United States can eliminate the use of covert operations and restrict itself to gathering intelligence." Stephen F. Knott suggests otherwise, noting that the "United States has a rich history of presidential use of covert intervention" that communicates an integral and unending role for U.S. foreign policy.[38] *TWW* validates this view of covert presidential powers through its depiction of communist espionage and governmental infiltration.

The ways in which the post–cold war plot is framed is likewise significant. Two plotlines provide comedic drama frames as maps for social justice and protesters against global oppression are structured satirically and historical threats of espionage are confirmed and dramatized. Kenneth Burke juxtaposes a comedic frame from a tragic frame in literature, noting that the comedic "converts downward . . . dwarfing the situation" whereas the "tragic" or "heroic . . . converts upward," promoting "acceptance of magnification, making the hero's character as great as the situation he confronts."[39]

The heroes in this situation are not the peace protesters or those fighting for social justice or even countries victimized by domineering world maps. The hero is a clandestine U.S. government that acted correctly to target communists throughout the United States. U.S. nationalism is valorized explicitly when Donna asks, "Why does it matter?" After all, Gault's actions were the work of "people pushing paper around fifty years ago." "It was high treason," Sam responds, "and it mattered a great deal. This country is an idea and one that's lit the world for two centuries and treason against that idea is not just a crime against the living. This ground holds the graves of the people who died for it. Who gave what Lincoln called the last full measure of devotion . . . of fidelity."

Such discourse furthers the ideology of Manifest Destiny. It also fosters loyalty and devotion to the nation through a romantic treatment of a contemporary presidential administration that relies on national nostalgia for heroic past presidents. As Otto Bauer observes, "In the telling of history, the idea of the nation is linked with the idea of its destiny, with the memory of historic struggles. . . . The whole rapport that someone today may feel with the struggling people of the past is then transformed into love for the bearer of this motley fate, the nation."[40]

In addition to reifying the evils of communism, *TWW* also enacts the ongoing cold war *topoi* regarding the nuclear arms race that permeated the East-West conflict. Reflecting the rhetoric of science during the cold war, Robert L. Scott reasons that "all science is military science."[41] Soviet science in the nuclear age was a persistent source of anxiety in the United States.[42] Presidents and their operatives often attended to such fears by portraying the Soviet Union as immoral and its science as intended for evil ends.[43]

In the third-season episode "Enemies Foreign and Domestic," Joint Chiefs Chair Fitzwallace informs the president that "four intelligence agencies" have discovered that the Russians are building a "heavy water reactor" for the Iranians, a facility designed to develop "plutonium," Leo adds. Later, Josh tells President Bartlet and Leo that the Russian atomic energy minister "denies everything" and claims the site is for "commercial power production" only. They note the similarity between the Iranian reactor and one built in Pakistan, and Bartlet points out that "this isn't used to make the lights go on. It's used to make plutonium. . . . The Russians are giving Iran the bomb." As Beer maintains, "During the last half of the twentieth century we became used to the idea of 'cold war.' The crucial adjective here transformed war from a direct, physical, material activity fought with hard, sharp, and bloody weapons . . . into something more extended, more multidimensional, more abstract."[44]

Nevertheless, Russians cannot escape the same level of fear and immoral perceptions of the cold war years when the realist perception of war (the clearly identifiable cold war power) meets postrealism constructions (the messiness of Middle Eastern terrorism) in this one episode of *TWW*. In the end hope is restored because Fitzwallace and others on Bartlet's staff believe the Russian president is sending a message to the president through representatives visiting the United States. The president concludes, "Let's go to Helsinki, but the reactor's the first thing on the agenda."

In the post–cold war context, fear of Russian science is transformed into fear of its aging nuclear equipment overseen by incompetent scientists and military leaders. In a second-season episode entitled "Galileo" the crisis revolves around a fire in a Russian nuclear silo. Once again, proficient U.S. intelligence agencies discover the blaze, which the Russians call an "oil well fire." The cover-up is depicted as naïve given that Russia has no oil wells in the area of the event. Normalizing U.S. covert surveillance activities, the president sarcastically wonders, "Did they think we weren't going to see it, Leo?" Explicitly acknowledging the historical relationship, Leo explains, "It's a cold war mentality." Bartlet is even more incensed when he learns that the fire was caused by "someone draining hydrogen." When the president comes face to face with the Russian ambassador, who rebukes the U.S. offer for help, he asserts:

> Your best trained operators have left or died. The ones you've got aren't paid very much. When they're paid at all, they don't have enough to train with. Your ICBMs are well beyond their warranty life . . . Leo, at the time that the SS19 exploded, it was being drained of its liquid hydrogen in an attempt by deserting soldiers to . . . steal the warhead. When were you going to tell us about that? Do you realize how dangerous that is? . . . You guys fall asleep at the switch in Minsk and I've got a whole hemisphere hiding under the bed. . . . We're sending in NATO inspectors. . . . Get your foreign minister on the phone . . . I really don't know where you guys get the nerve.

President Bartlet's lecture demonstrates how the U.S. president is now the superintendent of the Western Hemisphere, calling forth and extending the scope of the Monroe Doctrine. In addition, it reifies the disintegration of Russia after the cold war, accentuating U.S. military, scientific, and political superiority. Ivie writes that the "vehicle of exaggerated fear reproduced in the post–cold war rhetorical republic" recognized the "tragic identity of a heroic nation which had hardly vanquished the demon of communism only to be confronted by yet another specter of international disorder."[45] The collusion between Russia and Iran brought cold war and post–cold war realities together on *TWW*, delegitimizing the Russian military and scientific system as it rearticulates common fears in a postrealist global terrain.

The same episode sexualizes Russia through the portrayal of the Russian ambassador as a sexually provocative woman. When Leo meets with her about the fire in the nuclear reactor, she attempts to engage him in seductive conversation:

RUSSIAN AMBASSADOR: You look handsome, Leo.

LEO (not looking at her): Thank you. You look very nice yourself.

RUSSIAN AMBASSADOR: You get more handsome every year. And you're having your suits handmade now.

LEO: Are you hitting on me?

RUSSIAN AMBASSADOR: I was sorry to hear about your divorce.

Leo quickly rejects the romantic suggestions. "You have a fire in a missile silo," he scolds—a charge she denies. In a later scene before the president debases the state of Russia's science, he suggests to the ambassador, "Your paranoia was a lot sexier back when you guys were communists." Russia's personification as a sexualized woman furthers repulsive attitudes toward the former communist country by relying on misogyny, which fosters continued hatred and near rebuke of a nation trying to enact democratic reforms. Geoff Eley and Ronald Grigor Suny note that during "situations of crisis . . . the feminine becomes demonized as corruption and threat." Such misogynist constructions are common in nationalist discourse.[46]

Although sexualized in certain plotlines—among them resoundingly rejected romantic advances—Russia is also demasculinized in a debate over the winter attire of the two nation's leaders. In the "Enemies Foreign and Domestic" episode, Sam meets with Russian representatives as President Bartlet readies for a summit with Russia in Helsinki. As they work out the details for the meeting, the Russians demand that Bartlet wear an overcoat and gloves like the Russian president does, earmuffs and a scarf being optional. Sam suggests that the only reason they are trying to control Bartlet's dress code is that "President Shogoren must wear an overcoat and doesn't want to look like a wimp." Leo further demasculinizes male winter clothing, noting that the news about the Russian nuclear reactor being built in Iran is going to "break right next to the picture of [President Bartlet] shaking hands with Shogoren while wearing a coat to protect his MS riddled body from the fierce climate in Finland." President Bartlet likewise rejects the dress code. "Tell me," he asks, "why I can't wear whatever the hell I want?" "Well," Sam replies, "that's not entirely true, the earmuffs are optional." The president concludes, "OK. I probably won't be wearing them."

On one level this comic conflict plays out as tension over American freedom and wealth versus Russian containment. The Russian representatives query, "Why must every American president bound out of an automobile like as at a yacht club . . . while in comparison, our leader looks like, I don't know what the word is?" "Frumpy?" Sam suggests. In other ways the scene contrasts the frontier essence of American males, who are able to bear the cold, with Russian males, who need protection from nature. Even a U.S. president's body "riddled" with disease is stronger than that of a president of Russia. As R. W. Connell argues, "True masculinity is almost always thought to proceed from men's bodies—to be inherent in a male body."[47] As Russia turns toward democracy *TWW* works to accentuate America's continued superiority in the post–cold war context, relying on misogynous and demasculinized antipathies that permeate the national consciousness. Rather than acknowledge Russia's attempts to incorporate democratic commitments, *TWW* puts forth images that invite further contempt.

## Romancing the White, Masculine, and Scientific Nation

A second-season episode, "Galileo," is instructive in demonstrating how American science in a nationalist context is juxtaposed against Russian science in a post–cold war context. The episode centers on a fire at a Russian nuclear site, a contrast to an American space mission to Mars. Even though the U.S. space program has flaws, such errors are embraced; they provide an incentive to try harder in the process of confronting America's unconquered frontier—space—a national enterprise "steeped in myth."[48] NASA's journey to Mars is the romantic drama frame for the U.S. military and for *TWW*'s presidential narrative. The president and his symbolic son Sam, not the astronauts or the NASA staff, perform the romantic roles in this plotline. More specifically, the episode features romantic, white, male dreamers situated against pragmatic white women who are sexualized and portrayed as lacking the knowledge or capabilities of male counterparts. Militarism is further conflated with masculinity, and masculinity with romantic heroism, which are integral components of U.S. nationalism.

From the beginning of "Galileo," President Bartlet, through Sam, is positioned as the voice of the frontier mythos surrounding the space program. Sam bickers with a NASA speechwriter about the content of a speech being prepared for the president to present to school children. NASA wants to write the speech, but Sam, and eventually President Bartlet, reject the staffer's uninspiring prose. In contrast, the emotive speech Sam delivers, which the president wholeheartedly endorses, accentuates Bartlet's role in the romantic space saga. "Good morning," he would say. "Eleven months ago a twelve-hundred-pound space craft blasted off from Cape Canaveral, Florida. Eighteen hours ago . . . it landed on the planet Mars. You, me and sixty thousand of your fellow students across the country along with astro-scientists and engineers from the jet propulsion lab in southern California, NASA, and Houston, and right here at the White House, we're going to be the first to see what it sees and to chronicle the extraordinary voyage of an unmanned ship called Galileo." Sam, the president tells NASA's speechwriter, "got it right." James L. Kauffman notes the limits of the frontier myth's force for the space program, which depends on "manned space programs" to "sustain popular and political support." The president becomes a surrogate, championing the space program, for the heroes who actually pilot spacecraft.[49]

Sam's romance with space is furthered in interactions with Mallory, the sexualized personification of pragmatism and Leo's daughter. Sam is particularly nervous about seeing her after some time and tells Toby about his uncertainty over whether to call Mallory or try to date her again, a relationship carried over from season one. When the two meet accidentally, he is talking on the telephone with Josh, who asks whether Sam "can . . . describe what she's wearing." Sam and Mallory then banter over the funding for Galileo. Deriding Sam, Mallory, a teacher, chastises the space program, given that so many people in the United States are "starving and hungry." He responds as he did in the opening scene of the episode, calling on the nostalgic frontier thesis: "[Mars] is next . . . because we came out of the cave and we looked over the hill and we saw fire and we crossed the ocean and we pioneered the west and we took to the sky. The history of man is on a timeline of exploration and this is what's next."

Such sentiments reflect the frontier discourse of earlier years. Kauffman explains that when selling the space program in the early 1960s, John F. Kennedy's "New Frontier included many of the constituents of the old frontier: adventurous and independent pioneers willing to battle evil enemies and tame a hostile, unknown environment."[50] Mallory eventually admits support of the frontier myth, albeit in much less heroic terms: "I know . . . we're supposed to be explorers. I just like hearing you talk about it. . . . You get all puffed up." Further sexualizing the interaction, they also argue about Mallory's hockey player boyfriend and their "great sex" when Sam insinuates that the hockey player lacks intelligence.

The president's intellectual prowess is also accentuated as C.J. works to temper his elitism. She becomes the voice of those who keep "going to the blackboard," even with the wrong information. The president is excited about returning to the residence and reading about Mars and Galileo. C.J. cautions Bartlet throughout the episode, telling him, "That's fine, just don't show off." Later she tells Toby, "Nobody likes people who know everything," a response to Toby's extensive knowledge of Mars, which rivals that of the president. In the end, NASA loses contact with Galileo, and the staff contemplates whether to drop the conversation with the sixty thousand students. C.J. urges the president to move forward:

> We have at our disposal a captive audience of school children. Some of them don't go to the blackboard or raise their hand because they think they are going to be wrong. I think you should say to these kids, "you think you get it wrong

sometimes, you should come down here and see how the big boys do it." I think you should tell them you haven't given up hope and it may turn up but in the meantime you want NASA to put its best people in the room and you want them to start building Galileo VI. Some of them will laugh and most of them won't care but for some, they might honestly see that it's about going to the blackboard and raising your hand and that's the broader theme.

The president, moved, concludes, "C.J., you said it right that time." As his intellectualism is accentuated and Sam's romance of space emphasized, C.J., conversely, becomes a romantic voice for those who occasionally "get it wrong." In the process the speech romanticizes America's technological errors, although the episode repeatedly emphasizes Russia's scientific faults. As Kauffman says, "Although Americans would sometimes dispute the goals their government ought to pursue, few challenged the faith in technology" that reflected a "technocratic temptation," even in periods of economic concern or in an era of tragedies afflicting the U.S. space program and calls for limited government.[51]

C.J.'s lack of knowledge is further emphasized by the way she is awkwardly sexualized. Not only does she evidence a knowledge deficiency about Mars but her political acumen is also simultaneously challenged when she incorrectly predicts that negative remarks from the president about green beans will not "have legs." When the news media pick up the remarks she confesses to Toby, "Let me say first that you were right and I was wrong. . . . Everybody picked it up. . . . It turns out it's a bit of a deal." C.J.'s intelligence—and intellectual and political insecurity—becomes the center of attention when she suggests that just because "it took me two hours and twenty minutes longer to figure out than it took you [Toby] . . . doesn't mean you're smarter than I am . . . I had fine SAT scores." Later an offhand comment from Sam causes her to snap, "That is like the fourth time I've been called dumb today." Such interactions further the perceived symbiotic relationship between politics and masculinity and reinforce a "politics-as-usual is men's politics" mentality.[52]

In addition to questioning her intellectual capabilities, the episode offers a scene in which a former boyfriend confronts C.J. about a job he did not get at the White House. In case their relationship affected his employment, he wants to stress that even though he broke up with her, "it wasn't because you were bad in bed or anything like that. . . . You're good in bed." C.J. responds, "I'm great in bed." Three men wait for the couple to finish this momentary exchange, gazing from afar and smoking cigarettes. In the last segment of the episode C.J. makes a seemingly strange disclosure to the president, Toby, Josh, and Sam. There might, she says, be a story about her "being good in bed . . . because I am." Kathleen Hall Jamieson notes that as "women gain power" double binds ensure "that they cannot successfully exercise it." Although the writers of *TWW* guarantee that female characters do not sacrifice sexuality (a historical legacy of women's entrance into the political sphere), the women often sacrifice levels of competence in the political sphere as a consequence of empowerment.[53]

Holly Allen writes that "U.S. military conventions are closely linked to a particular, *fraternal* model of U.S. national community."[54] Such conventions marginalize women on *TWW* and its cold war enemy in its realist and mythic renditions of militarized nationalism. Even Nancy's authority as national security advisor is undermined when Sam refuses to believe in Daniel Gault's guilt without documentary proof, an interaction that explicitly erases her credibility as a security expert. Before she and Sam meet to address the Gault situation, her lack of authoritative voice is further destabilized when a colonel is incapable of distinguishing her voice from those of the men on a conference call. She queries, "I'm the only woman on a conference call. [Colonel] Delaney can't tell when it's me talking. Do I have a bizarrely androgynous voice?" Sam responds by shrugging.

George L. Mosse references the historical practice of portraying an androgynous woman as "almost masculine." Such "fear of androgyny," though, is neutralized on *TWW* when the national security advisor's visibility is questioned in her supposed context of authority and power.[55] Frequently, the masculinity of militarism and war require that women be rendered invisible.[56] The female characters on *TWW* are present in plots involving the military, yet their gender is accentuated in more traditional ways and their marginality is apparent.

## The Postrealism of *The West Wing*

In *TWW*'s dealings with countries other than Russia, many of which are developing nations, enemies are at times unclear, and their tactics of war often challenge just-war principles. Because political and military leaders in these countries violate conventional rules of engagement, the Bartlet administration is forced to assume similarly unconventional tactics. Bartlet in particular, the nation's personification, demonstrates considerable ambivalence over using morally disputed tactics as a new reality of modern warfare in a postrealist environment. In the end, these military skirmishes, which rely heavily on covert warfare activities, frame Bartlet's presidential campaign and eventual election. Despite his internal interrogations, he eventually transcends his ambivalence over unjust-warfare measures and fights the new, post–cold war enemies with the righteous fury required of a U.S. president. On *TWW*, nationalism, militarism, and presidentiality assume a symbiotic relationship as historically constituted, complete with romantic, gendered, and racial commitments that reify America's superiority and the president's mythic force.

The president's military actions are a centerpiece of *TWW*'s presidentiality and render Bartlet's personal shortcomings inconsequential when they are situated in a context of military decision making that requires intellectual strength, mental stamina, and personal confidence. Similarly, militarism, the foundation of U.S. nationalism, transcends all other domestic issues of importance, reifies traditional constructions of gender and race, and neutralizes concerns of sexism and racism. Through such commitments *TWW* offers a cathartic rhetoric in a post–cold war global environment that simultaneously embraces the presidential and national faults yet instills a renewed and nostalgic patriotism lost in the aftermath of Vietnam, Watergate, Iran-Contra, the Clinton impeachment, and the 2000 presidential election.

## Presidential Ambivalence and the Postrealist Enemy

*TWW*'s vision of the presidency at times posits a reluctant commitment to military force that further alters the traditional vision of the drama's romantic hero. This ambivalence is established during the first-season episode "Post Hoc, Ergo Propter Hoc" when President Bartlet confides to an aide that he is insecure about his personal military standing: "I'm an accomplished man, Morris. I can sit comfortably with prime ministers and presidents, even the Pope. Why is it every time I sit with the Joint Chiefs, I feel like I'm back at my father's dinner table?" Bartlet even acknowledges that his lack of violent feelings toward the nation's enemies may make him appear weak, which violates masculine constructs often linked to the military.[57]

Neither does Bartlet blindly accept the military's enhanced technology; he spends the entire second-season episode of "Noël," for example, questioning the competence of the Defense Department's missile defense capabilities. The president calls Leo "Charlie Brown" and the Pentagon "Lucy" because even though the defense system usually fails to intercept a target, it tries again and again, just as "Charlie Brown would [always] fall on his butt." Leo and the president visit the Situation Room to see the newest test results of the missile defense system. When the interceptor misses its target by 137 miles Bartlet wonders if the missile will eventually "hit my garage." Leo is furious that the interceptor was so far off-target, and the president responds, "The words you are looking for are, 'Oh good grief.'"

*TWW*'s presidentiality, like the political culture at large, thus questions the commitment to militaristic power from time to time and offers greater ambiguity than is often seen in romantic portrayals of military leaders.[58] As George P. Fletcher contends, "The disdain for war has accumulated slowly since the end of World War II."[59]

In many plots on *TWW* foreign policy exigences in developing countries populated primarily with people of color are difficult to define because the enemy is not easily recognizable and the traditional tactics of war are outmoded. During season two the Bartlet administration confronts the kidnapping of five U.S. drug enforcement agents in Colombia. A conflict erupts in the Situation Room as Leo argues for military intervention: "We are in a war . . . we're sending people down there to fight a war on drugs," justifying the need for "special forces" ("Bartlet's Third State of the Union"). Mickey Troop, an assistant secretary of state for South America who speaks with a Latino accent, becomes the proponent of negotiation, calling for the president "to see how negotiations continue." Bartlet initially supports the continuation of such diplomatic actions yet readies the Special Forces "to kick in the back door." Using a language of war that is normalized in America's "war on drugs" furthers the power of warlike responses over diplomatic ones. As Robin Tolmach Lakoff contends, "Language is just air after all—it is not a gun, it has no power on its own. Yet it changes reality."[60]

It is not surprising that the president eventually sides with Leo and authorizes the Special Forces to engage in a covert rescue of the agents. The action fails, however, because the Colombian hostage-takers entrap the Special Forces, an encounter that leads to the deaths of nine officers after the downing of their Blackhawk helicopter. Colombian President Santos offers to release Juan Aguilar, a drug lord, from prison in "exchange for the hostages." The president, who possesses a strict moral code on matters of justice, vehemently opposes such tactics initially and argues, "I'll share a cell with him before I let him out. I want military options" ("The War at Home").

A contest over military crises in a postrealist context is articulated throughout the episode. As the president explains the futility of the drug war and the unidentifiable enemy to Josh, "I inherited the war on drugs from a president who inherited it from a president who inherited it from a president before that. I'm not 100 percent sure who we're fighting but I know we're not winning." He then discusses military options with Mickey and others, asking what it would take "to wipe them out."

Bartlet's words reflect a mentality often associated with a realist concern that the United States achieve decisive, unequivocal victory. Fletcher suggests recommitment to such a viewpoint in the terrorist context, reigniting America's "incessant drive to maintain our role as a superpower on the stage of world politics."[61] In response to the president's question Mickey declares, "For the kind of victory Americans are used to, for the kind of victory Americans demand from a war, you need a 10 to 1 ratio. It was only after we built up a 10 to 1 ratio in the Gulf that we felt comfortable making a move. Frente has twenty thousand well-armed, well-trained, soldiers. Each of them has a financial stake in heroin and cocaine. We need to put two to three hundred thousand men into a jungle war. And I think we'd lose as many as half." Demonstrating the shifting terrain of power in the post–cold war era, the president replies, "You've really got to ask yourself, 'What's the point in being a superpower anymore?'"

Using the Vietnam debacle as a military compass, Leo and the president ultimately reject the idea of a military response. Bartlet is still adamant that he cannot "possibly reverse our position on negotiating." Leo rationalizes, though, that "no one's going to know . . . Santos is gonna be the one to let him out." Still clinging to his moral conventions, the president says, "You know what Truman Capote said was the bad part about living outside the law? You no longer have the protection of it." Leo continues to justify Santos's offer. "We lost this one, Mr. President," he says. "It was bad intelligence and we lost this one." The president resigns himself to the exchange of the DEA agents for Aguilar. He also resolves to punish the Colombians should they mislead the U.S. government again and experiences angst over the loss of life in a military mishap: "If they so much as experience turbulence on their way out . . . I want to go to Dover later tonight." The president's personal angst, and the show's ambivalence about war at the turn of the twentieth century, are unresolved by the end of the show. Bartlet watches the caskets come home to Dover Air Force Base at 2 A.M., knowing he has negotiated with drug lords.

This story line is significant because it addresses the conflict over racialized nationalism, masculinity, and questions of just war on *TWW*. The conflict plays out in a Central American country where Latino males who are depicted yet not pictured function as the evil drugs lords engaged in unjust acts of war. Nira Yuval-Davis argues that "ethnicity relates to the politics of collective boundaries, and by using identity narratives, dividing the world into 'us' versus 'them.'"[62] Television commonly participates in such identity projects, Michael Curtin suggests, and functions as an "organizer of difference."[63]

The identity narrative of "Bartlet's Third State of the Union" structures Colombia as a site of violence. Questions of U.S. and DEA presence in the region are muted. Also ignored are U.S. historical practices in Latin America involving "covert and direct military operations" to "establish social order and hegemony in the local environment."[64] Making Colombia an other via Latino males creates differences juxtaposed against the white nation via the white president. This location of U.S. nationalism (and its whiteness) serves a "constitutive" role because the "viewer-occupier, the process of viewing, and that which is viewed" further differentiates Colombians and others similarly coded with Latino/a accents.[65]

In addition, the use of negotiation—a practice often associated with weakness—is personified by the Latino male. A military response—a practice often associated with strength—is voiced by two white males. Carol Cohn contends that in "national security discourse . . . you learn that someone is being a wimp if he perceives an international crisis as very dangerous and urges caution."[66] Part of Bartlet's ambivalence about negotiating with the hostage-takers reflects the guilt that commonly accompanies the decision not to engage in a full-fledged counterattack when an individual or a nation is the recipient of violence. "To sit back and suffer attack, without responding in kind," Fletcher advises, "is to accept a form of national humiliation."[67] The president's humiliation is suffered only in private as he wants to attack. Mickey, though, champions less violent forms of conflict resolution, ultimately serving as a scapegoat in the president's masculine redemption. Mickey, not the president, is the site of demasculinization.

Other markers of difference represent the drug lords' use of unjust-warfare tactics. Even though the U.S. government ultimately accepts new rules of engagement, the president's moral code is repeatedly rearticulated and juxtaposed against the perpetrators' inculcation of such tactics. The conflict over just-war principles is centuries old, yet it assumes new attention in the contemporary age of terrorism. Often situated within a discussion of religion and war and traced to the writings of Augustine, a just war centers on "the belief that universal moral reasoning, or what some would call natural moral law, can and should be applied to the activity of war."[68] Beer argues that "speaking just-war discourse is part of how political actors go about creating both war and justice. . . . Just-war doctrine is not only part of the international and domestic struggle for power but also a separate, independent theme in political discourse and culture that helps shape real-world conflict and cooperation."[69] The U.S. involvement in Vietnam altered the ways in which just-war principles were conceived. Richard J. Regan notes, for example, that given the large number of U.S. and Vietnamese causalities, questions were raised over the war in Southeast Asia and whether it was a just one even though reasons for entering the war may have been warranted.

On *TWW* the memory of Vietnam functions as the moral backdrop to prevent large numbers of U.S. casualties, and that memory transcends other questionable tactics of negotiating with hostage takers. For many, "prudence or practical action" is warranted in just-war theory. President Bartlet entertains a military response that conforms to just-war principles but is forced to accept a covert, targeted, and unjust-war solution that lessens the loss of life, emphasizing his religiously inspired morality. He is able to pursue such paths because of presidential authority over covert military matters—options that are part of a "fundamental law" of just-war theory holding that the appropriate ways of war "will change over time."[70] Nevertheless, such tactics suggest the limits of the country's superpower status and accentuate the nation's, and the president's, potential inadequacies in this postrealist condition. As Miriam Cooke suggests, "Postmodern wars [do] not claim so much a substantive as a representational difference from earlier wars. It is not that other wars were more conclusive, but that they seemed to be so."[71]

As the situation in Colombia comes to a close the Bartlet administration faces a new foreign policy crisis in Haiti, where unjust-war principles are again played out in a country of color. In Haiti the new, democratically elected government faces considerable opposition from military leaders such that two bodyguards for President Dessaline have been shot. Even though Bartlet's military advisors serve as the voice of isolationism, arguing that "this is an internal affair in Haiti and the U.S. has no place choosing sides," Leo and Bartlet disagree and articulate the need to intervene in order to support free elections. Leo argues, "Mr. President, there will never be real elections in Haiti if the military thinks it can simply kill the winner." The president concurs. Violence erupts, though, which leads to the evacuation of the American embassy and the Dessaline government when a military general takes over the country ("18th and Potomac").

Foreign policy exigencies carry over into season three. The president eventually calls for sending a message to the general through "the Canadian Prime Minster": "We intend to restore Dessaline." If the leader of the coup "doesn't move out," Bartlet says, "we're willing to move forward with military options" ("Manchester, Part 1"). Evidencing the messiness and immorality of such postrealist exigencies, the general agrees to leave—but only if given amnesty, ten million U.S. dollars, a private aircraft, a guarantee that he will not be prosecuted for war crimes, and a place for him and sixty of his relatives to live. The president, annoyed by this arrogance, determines the conditions of the general's departure himself: "We'll unfreeze his U.S. accounts but he can't remove any money from Haiti. Only his wife, his children, and his parents can seek asylum. If he tries to go back, he'll be under arrest." Leo adds, "And he can screw the private plane . . . and if he's very good, we won't shoot him in the head" ("Manchester, Part 2").

The turmoil in Haiti normalizes the role of violence with the establishment of democracy. The United States, of course, is the source of free elections, reinforcing its role as the sole superpower in internal matters throughout the world, as it did in its dealings with Russia. Bartlet dictates the terms of resolution in Haiti and naturalizes U.S. interventionist policies in the process. As Christopher Dandeker explains this phenomenon, "The West's world leadership in arms manufacture and military organization was a capacity later translated into global, economic, and political supremacy and the spread of the nation-state system as the basis of international society. The upshot of all this was that war created nations, nations created states, and states created further wars."[72]

*TWW*'s international vision conflates violence and nationalism and expands presidential power over the internal affairs of developing nations. Such nations, largely populated by people of color, are shown as incapable of controlling their own affairs, forcing the United States to use unconventional war tactics when dealing with out-of-control nations where unjust-war tactics seemingly originate and abound.

## Just War in the War on Terrorism

The situations in Colombia and Haiti foreshadow the biggest international crisis of the Bartlet administration's first term—the terrorist threat emanating from the fictionalized Middle Eastern country of Qumar, where unjust tactics of war necessitate unconventional and unjust retaliatory responses. The crisis, which begins at the end of season three and continues well into season four, is introduced by Fitzwallace, who tells the president that based on the monitoring of Web sites, cell phone interceptions, and reports from a prisoner held in Chechnya by the Russians, there is reason to believe a "U.S. military installation" is going to be attacked "in the next forty-eight hours." Terrorist blueprints discovered in a Bethesda, Maryland, apartment indicate that other potential targets include the White House, the National Archives, and the Supreme Court.

As the episode "The Black Vera Wang" comes to an end, the president learns that a person has been arrested off the coast of Oakland, California, with a boat full of ammonium nitrate and a gallon of diesel fuel—the Golden Gate Bridge was the intended target. The president also learns that Abdul Shareef, the defense minister of Qumar and a chief U.S. informant, may be involved in the terrorist plot. Shareef is scheduled to visit the United States within two weeks. That such intelligence information now comes from the Russians indicates greater cooperation between the two superpower nations in combating the actions of rogue nations throughout the world.

As the next episode ("We Killed Yamamoto") begins, Shareef's connection with the terrorist plots is confirmed and intelligence initiates a series of covert actions that play out alongside the election campaign. The president talks of indictments for Shareef as he lays out the unjust actions of this newfound enemy: "We're saying he's a terror kingpin. We're saying he's killed, I don't know how many civilians. . . . We're saying he's compromised I don't know how many agents around the world and we're saying he's done it in the clothing of an ally. This isn't a cave dweller. This is Capone."

Such actions without question set up Qumar as a country engaged in unjust terrorist acts against the United States in the manner of an organized crime boss who never plays by the rules. Regan observes, "Terrorism either principally or by definition signifies acts that are intentionally designed to kill (or hold hostage) undeniably innocent individuals in order to achieve political goals." Terrorist immorality is grounded on the assumption that such acts "violate the principle of discrimination as much as their moral equivalents in conventional war, countercity nuclear strategy, and revolutionary war."[73]

As the president visits Mrs. Landingham's grave at Arlington National Cemetery—the most sacred national site in the United States—Leo tells him about a conversation intercepted by an "IR laser beam" between Shareef and "two Muslim clerics": "The enemy imagines he is secure. The bridge did not fall. He looks down from his high or elevated place or places. Our great victory is assured. There will be other moments." Such disregard for just-war tactics, in which the premeditated killing of innocent civilians is forbidden, hastens Bartlet's progression toward retaliatory acts. As Lawrence Freedman asserts in his discussion of 9/11, the assumption in a new terrorist context is that "a direct attack on the United States is likely to produce an extremely strong and unremitting response."[74]

The Bartlet administration's response, though, is not grounded in conventional warfare of massive proportions. It is covert, targeted, and reflective of the underhanded tactics of its terrorist enemies—tactics approved only after considering all other means of retribution. Bartlet calls for Shareef's "arrest" once he "steps off the plane" in Washington, D.C. A State Department official in the room, though, notes that such an action represents a "breach of diplomatic immunity." The White House is also unable to negotiate with the sultan of Qumar because Shareef is part of the royal family—the sultan's brother. Although the State Department tries to resolve the immunity issue, they learn that their evidence would be thrown out of court because it originated from a Chechnyan prisoner after "prolonged physical abuse by Russian soldiers"—other clear acts of unjust warfare.

The president becomes increasingly frustrated by the situation as Fitzwallace attempts to convince Leo of the previously unthinkable option, a reflection of the ambiguities of war and peace in a postrealist context:

FITZWALLACE: Can you tell when it's peacetime and wartime anymore?

LEO: No.

FITZWALLACE: I don't know who the world's leading expert on warfare is but any list of the top [five] has got to include me and I can't tell when it's peacetime and wartime anymore.

LEO: Look, international laws always recognize certain protected persons who you couldn't attack. It's been that way since the Romans.

FITZWALLACE: In peacetime. . . . The international laws that you are talking about . . . were written at a time and place where a person could tell the difference between peacetime and wartime. The idea of targeting one individual was ridiculous. . . . That all changed after Pearl Harbor.

LEO: I don't like where this conversation is going . . .

FITZWALLACE: We killed Yamamoto. We shot the plane down.

LEO: We declared war . . . and the plot to kill Hitler was an international rebellion . . . I'm going back to my office.

FITZWALLACE: We measure the success of a mission by two things. Was it successful and how few civilians did we hurt? They measure success by how many. Pregnant women are delivering bombs. You're talking to me about international laws? The laws of nature don't even apply here. I've been a soldier for thirty-eight years and I found an enemy I can kill. He can't cancel Shareef's trip Leo. You've got to tell him he can't cancel.

As the Bartlet administration moves closer to assassinating Shareef, Fitzwallace, one of the few African Americans in a position of power on *TWW,* functions as the voice of unjust wartime principles. His assignment is to convince the most powerful white men in Bartlet's administration—the chief of staff and the commander-in-chief—of the necessity of questionable tactics based on his intuition about the violent world of the other. bell hooks suggests that representations of "black masculinity" often demonstrate "flagrant disregard for individual rights" and are associated with the notions of "primitive" behavior given historical constructions "where black people were in harmony with nature."[75]

As the voice of the primitive, Fitzwallace also further conflates the use of unethical tactics of war with countries of color (e.g., Qumar and Japan), destabilizing conceptions of just-war tactics. Such repeated destabilizing processes take place through the narratives about Colombia, Haiti, and Qumar on *TWW*. The process also occurs in "War Crimes," an earlier episode about another developing nation, when a military general attempts to move Leo away from supporting international military tribunals by claiming that "all wars are crimes." As evidence he uses Leo's questionable wartime actions in Vietnam, when the barbarity of war involved him in the destruction of civilian targets.

The president's ambivalence over unjust tactics of war is most evident in scenes leading up to his final decision. Even though Leo initially rejects Fitzwallace's once-unthinkable act of war, he eventually works to convince Bartlet of its inevitability. When Leo argues that it is "pretty easy to say this is a war scenario," the president responds, "It's pretty easy to say anything is a war scenario. . . . This is a slippery slope." Leo becomes more forceful, stating, "Stop it. This is the most horrifying part of your liberalism. You think there are moral absolutes." "There are moral absolutes," the president insists. Leo counters by accentuating that the rules of engagement have changed because the people of Qumar, not the United States, changed them: "He's killed innocent people. He'll kill more so we have to end him. The village idiot comes to that conclusion before the Nobel Laureate. . . . This is justified. This is required." The president asks who else thinks the act is justified. "You want to go ask some more people?" Leo responds. "They'll say so too." President Bartlet scoffs at the argument as "mob mentality" that delegitimizes public input into such military actions. At this point the president does not cancel Shareef's trip; as Leo argues, "Let Shareef come here and we have options. Cancel the trip and we have none." Bartlet does continue to argue, however, that "there are moral absolutes."

The legalities of the assassination plot play out in the final episode of season three, "Posse Comitatus." President Bartlet learns that political assassinations are banned by two executive orders and cannot take place on American soil. He also learns that the British support the assassination plot, which, when carried out, will occur on a remote air strip in Bermuda, where Shareef will be assassinated after the airplane lands because of a fictitious mechanical malfunction. The president's ambivalence and morality are furthered when he has to face Shareef in the White House. After they exchange pleasantries, the president refuses to shake Shareef's hand, claiming that he has a rash. The president is also directly involved in the covert operations. As a gift, he presents Shareef with a pen that contains a homing device to be used by the Special Forces. At the end of the evening Leo pushes the president to give the order as Shareef's aircraft nears the assassination location. Leo and Bartlet speak in hushed tones as a song with decidedly religious overtones, "Hallelujah" by Jeff Buckley, plays in the background:

PRESIDENT: Civilians get trials.
LEO: I know . . . he's not a civilian.
PRESIDENT: They're going to find out it's us. We can make it look like the plane went down but they're going to find out it's us and I'm going to be running for reelection while I'm fighting a war against Qumar . . . I want him tried.
LEO: That can't happen. Who is the monk who wrote, "I don't always know the right thing to do Lord but I think the fact that I want to please you, pleases you?" You have two minutes sir.
PRESIDENT: This isn't a matter of religion . . . I recognize that there's evil in the world. . . . Doesn't this mean we join the league of ordinary nations?
LEO: That's your objection? I'm not going to have any trouble saying the Pledge of Allegiance tomorrow.
PRESIDENT: That's not my objection. . . . It's just wrong. It's absolutely wrong.
LEO: I know but you have to do it anyway.
PRESIDENT: Why?
LEO: Because you won.
PRESIDENT (after a long pause with his back to Leo): Take him.

Such discourse reinforces the president's moral code yet normalizes the lack of such ethic in the larger world community—particularly in the "league of ordinary nations." Regan contends that in just-war theory, "A victim nation may also justly target an enemy's political leadership, since that leadership bears the primary responsibility for the war."[76]

Sara Ruddick's insights about just-war principles help explain *TWW*'s construction of war in a terrorist context: "Just-war theory does *not* deny, and indeed insists on, the pain of victims." As the war plays out, however, "There is a frightening disconnection between morality and strategy: might does not make right, but it does make victories." The construction of morality, often expressed in "soft and feminine" terms, is juxtaposed against the "realist . . . instrumentality" imbued with "hard" and "masculine" constructs. Political actors may exude a strict moral code, yet when that individual is situated in the realisms of war, the "realist instrumentality" must overpower any one individual's moral sensibilities, necessitating a painful decision grounded in a sense of moralistic "righteousness, indignation, and (perhaps) shame and guilt" that "conceal as well as license the cruelty and delight in destruction that war provides."[77] A commander-in-chief is required to embody the rational intelligence necessary to discern when the realities of war must take precedence over subjective moral tenets for the sake of national security. Nationalism is thus the highest-order principle that offers stability to the country.

To that end, the military dilemmas involving Colombia, Haiti, and especially Qumar frame the presidential election and resolve ideological dissonance over the reelection of a president who lied to the American people. On the same night that Bartlet orders the assassination of Shareef he gains new determination to defeat his Republican opponent. Also in the finale of season three ("Posse Comitatus"), *TWW* resolves the on-going tension that plays out during the entire campaign regarding whether the president should accentuate his intelligence—a quality his Republican opponent appears to lack. Earlier in the season ("Manchester, Part 2"), Doug, one of political consultant Bruno Gianelli's operatives, argues against using the word *torpor* in Bartlet's announcement speech. The president overhears the argument and challenges the assembled staff: "They can look it up. . . . It's not our job to appeal to the lowest common denominator. . . . It's our job to raise it. If you're going to be the education president, it'd be nice not to hide that you have an education . . . Churchill and FDR. Serious men using big words for a big purpose."

Immediately following the decision to assassinate Shareef, Bartlet comes face to face with Robert Ritchie, his GOP opponent, at a fundraiser performance on Broadway of *The War of the Roses*. The conflict between anti-intellectual populism and intellectual elitism plays out in their conversation. Ritchie explains that he was late getting to the fundraiser because he got stuck in traffic coming back from a New York Yankees baseball game, an activity for "ordinary Americans." The president initially responds "yeah" to Ritchie's comment but then changes his mind and challenges the Republican's assumption: "No, I don't understand that. The center fielder for the Yankees is an accomplished classical guitarist. People who like baseball can't like books?" Ritchie asks, "Are you taking this personally?" The president then explains that "something horrible happened," C.J.'s bodyguard was just killed down the street during an armed robbery at a convenience store in yet another senseless act of unjust violence. Ritchie's response to this tragic news, "Hmmm, crime, boy I don't know," sets off a more explicit argument about intellectual engagement and the presidential election:

PRESIDENT: We should have a great debate Rob. We owe it to everyone. When I was running as a Governor, I didn't know anything. I made them start Bartlet College in my dining room. Two hours every morning on foreign affairs and the military. You could do that.

RITCHIE (laughing): How many different ways do you think you're going to find to call me dumb?

PRESIDENT: I wasn't Rob. But you've turned being unengaged into a Zen-like thing, and you shouldn't enjoy it so much is all, and if it appears at times as if I don't like you, that's the only reason why.

RITCHIE: You're what my friends call a superior sum-bitch. You're an academic elitist and a snob. You're Hollywood. You're weak. You're liberal and you can't be trusted. And if it appears from time to time as if I don't like you, well those are just a few of the many reasons why.

PRESIDENT (as he puffs on a cigarette, rises to leave): They're playing my song. In the future, if you're wondering, "crime, boy I don't know," is when I decided to kick your ass.

As the episode ends the words and music of "Patriot Song" from the play *The Life and Adventures of Nicholas Nickleby* provide a background for a visual display that details what actions take place once a presidential assassination order is issued. Pictures of Shareef being assassinated are spliced with clips from the *War of the Roses* play and shots of Fitzwallace alone in the Situation Room. The ambiguity of the warlike situation is exaggerated as the lines "God will pour his rich increase, And victorious in war shall be made victorious in peace" are repeated. The president looks to the ground and becomes a profiled shadow from behind a curtain after Leo tells him the mission is accomplished.

The season thus fades to a close, simultaneously accentuating while resolving several ideological disputes. On the one hand, the contest over Bartlet's consent to Shareef's murder is highlighted in the words of the song, demonstrating that there is no "glorious[ness] in peace" from victories of war won on the terrorist battlefield. On the other hand, the episode condones Bartlet's decision to assassinate Shareef given the leader's immoral actions in the new world order of global terrorism. Violence is naturalized. It abounds on *TWW*, whether from a Secret Service agent's murder, Russian guards' torture of prisoners, or the killings of innocent Americans by Middle Eastern terrorists. Although the assassination is perhaps unjust, *TWW* suggests no other alternative in the war America is now forced to fight.

Most significant, the episode also resolves the ideological dissonance over the president's reelection, suggesting that his moralism and intellectualism prepare him for wartime necessities and that Ritchie lacks such intellectual prowess. The president, although marked with imperfections, possesses the requisite intellectual capabilities to handle the complex contingencies of postrealist conflicts, removing any anxiety over a second term. Even though the Qumari issue continues in season four (the assassination plot is discovered and Israel is implicated in the act), Bartlet voices the same justifications for his actions. He tells Jordon Kendall, an international lawyer brought in to assist with the situation, that "every nation has a right to wage war to defend itself." After she protests that "the article is incumbent on wars being declared," the president responds, "Wars don't work like that anymore" ("College Kids").[78]

*TWW*, grappling with the complexities of global terrorism, reiterates the commonplace that "Western states have consistently sought to deny that states can commit terrorism." Terrorism is thus enacted by others against a state with unjust means of violence, necessitating a military response by that state that must likewise assume the new rules of engagement.[79] Bartlet embodies romantic nationalism as *TWW* struggles with significant issues facing the United States on domestic and international stages. *TWW*'s presidentiality expresses commitments to moralism, populism, womanism, and multiculturalism while ultimately privileging rationalism, intellectualism, masculinity, and whiteness in its portrayal of the American presidency.

The president's transcendence above all others in the hierarchy of nationalism is reified by the construction of the disempowered populace on military matters and *TWW*'s endorsement of presidential covert warfare. Establishing that foreign policy is the presidency's domain, Bartlet tells Toby when addressing public opinion polls on the test ban treaty, "This is one of those situations where I could give a damn what the people think. The complexities of a global arms treaty. The technological, military, diplomatic nuance is staggering, Toby. Eighty-two percent of the people can't possibly be expected to reach an informed opinion" ("The Lame Duck Congress").

The marginalization of the American people on military and foreign policy issues combines with *TWW*'s commitment to presidential covert operations to lessen congressional control and virtually eliminate many avenues of public accountability. "The military arguably acts as one of the least controversial arms of government in the sense that it operates with limited civilian and public influence. The military also serves as that arm of the government in which the president assumes the most significant and often the least questioned authority" due in large part to an explosion of covert operations in the cold war era.[80]

The symbiotic relationship between the presidency and the military is reified time and time again on *TWW*. During a speech Bartlet gives at Reynolds Air Force Base, America's manifest destiny is likewise reconstituted as the president addresses what he will tell his grandchildren about being president:

> What will I remember? What will I tell my grandchildren? . . . I'll tell them that I stood on the Great Wall of China and that I stood in the well of the U.S. House of Representatives. I'll tell them that I sat with Kings and Cardinals and made an appointment to the Supreme Court. And I'll tell them that one morning in September, I got to spend a few minutes with the men and women of Air Wing One. God bless you and your families and may He continue to shed His magnificent grace upon the United States of America. Thank you so much.

The president walks off to a military rendition of "Battle Hymn of the Republic" ("Twenty Hours in America").

In a post–9/11 context, when a call to war is once again part of the nation's creed, *TWW*'s construction of U.S. nationalism reflects a patriotism that achieves, in spite of the president's and the country's foibles, new levels of emotionality, especially when situated in a traditional song that emphasizes God's truths. Fletcher explains this phenomenon and asserts that even though there was a "disdain for the Romantic view of the world" in the post–Vietnam era that "tends to glorify the nation and war as an expression of patriotism . . . we can now begin to recognize that our national honor matters to us." Fletcher conflates patriotism with a romance of war, suggesting that although we "rarely use the word 'honor,' the virtue still appeals to us."[81]

*TWW* destabilizes conceptions of honor throughout its treatment of U.S. military actions and the president's reaction to world exigencies. Yet that president's moralism, intellectualism, masculinism, and even his whiteness offer catharsis in a time of international and domestic turmoil grounded in a long and storied history of gendered, racialized, and militarized nationalism. As Thomas Farrell, a rhetorical theorist, maintains, catharsis emerges from the "recognition of fate heroically endured [that] is liberating in a lofty way to the individual consciousness, now trapped in an ensemble of others: the audience."[82] In other words, the discursive experience can be constitutive and will provide the individual spectator with a sense of connection to larger publics and communities, and through such collectivization the catharsis of representation is possible. Such catharsis achieves additional power through the ideologically conventional depictions offered in *TWW*.

President Bartlet functions as a significant source of hope in this real world of terrorism and uncertainty. In a season-four episode entitled "Twenty Hours in America," *TWW* addresses this state of the nation through a speech Bartlet makes in the aftermath of a domestic terrorist attack by troubled U.S. youths on a swimming venue at the fictional Kennison State University. Reflective of the rhetoric heard in the aftermath of the 9/11 attacks, Bartlet's words confirm that the United States is not responsible for unjust tactics. Given the severity of the threat, however, the nation must respond in a way that reflects the country's strength and power of years past. At the same time, his speech is rooted powerfully in a mythological sense of U.S. nationalism, which it articulates in ideologically consistent ways. The president speaks of "sustaining hope in this winter of anxiety and fear":

> More than any time in recent history, America's destiny is not of our own choosing. We did not seek nor did we provoke an assault on our freedom, and our way of life. We did not expect nor did we invite a confrontation with evil. Yet the true measure of a people's strength is how they rise to master that moment when it does arise. Forty-four people were killed a couple of hours ago at Kennison State University. Three swimmers from the men's team were killed and two others are in critical condition when, after having heard the explosion from their practice facility, they ran into the fire to help get people out. Ran *into* the fire. The streets of heaven are too crowded with angels tonight. They're our students, and our teachers, and our parents, and our friends. The streets of heaven are too crowded with angels. But every time we think we've measured our capacity to meet a challenge, we look up and we're reminded that that capacity may well be limitless. This is a time for American heroes. We will do what is hard. We will achieve what is great. This is a time for American heroes and we reach for the stars. God bless their memory. God bless you. And God bless the United States of America. Thank you.

# 5

## *The West Wing's* Prime-Time Nationalism

What's next?

—President Josiah Bartlet, "Pilot"

ON THE MORNING of September 11, 2001, a worldwide audience watched in horror as the World Trade Center collapsed, a portion of the Pentagon was destroyed, and another airliner crashed into a Pennsylvania field. That date has joined other extraordinary moments in U.S. history—December 7, 1941, November 22, 1963, and April 19, 1995—dates that signal a shift in the American imaginary of its national identity. Predictably, the presidency, and George W. Bush as the occupant of the office, became a focal point of national attention and a repository of national hopes in the aftermath of September 11. In this role he succeeded Franklin D. Roosevelt, Lyndon B. Johnson, and Bill Clinton before him, who similarly contained and expressed the collective thoughts and feelings of a nation confronting significant trauma. Americans everywhere followed the president's trail across the country on 9/11, joined with him in his eulogistic grieving on September 14 at the National Cathedral, and witnessed his rhetorical stand against terrorism before a joint session of Congress on September 20.[1] For many, George W. Bush confirmed Thomas Langston's conclusion that "the president is not just another political placeholder; to many Americans, he *is* America."[2]

Nationalistic feelings and the wave of emotion that emerged from September 11 coalesced in the person of the president, reflecting the powerful fusion that exists in the American psyche between the sense of national identity and the institution of the American presidency. This fusion beckons considerable scrutiny, if only because "the vulnerability and fluidity of human character are not comfortable foundations for a community's identity."[3] At the very least, the fusion between president and nation requires sustained interrogation so the vagaries of presidential nationalism are exposed. This interrogation is even more important in the patriotic aftermath of September 11.

Increasingly, the imaginary of U.S. nationalism, and the collective understanding of the American presidency as it is critical to that nationalism, are mediated by television and film. Such nationalistic media moments may be sublime, as in the collective viewing of the attacks on September 11.[4] They may also be mundane, as when millions tune in weekly to watch a fictional drama about presidential politics. Similarly, the mass-mediated presidency is an undoubted characteristic of contemporary political culture in the United States wherein popular understandings of presidential behavior, policy, and identity are largely communicated, with a variety of consequences, through the mass medium of television.[5]

Because the American presidency and U.S. nationalism are so inextricably fused, and because both the presidency and the nationalistic imaginary are only real for most via the mass-mediated channels of television, understanding the presidency and U.S. nationalism in the early twenty-first century requires engagement with a range of mass-mediated discourses. The mass media works as "experiential grids or templates through which history can be written and national identity created," conclude Ella Shohat and Robert Stam in their discussion of film. They specifically note that film—and, we would suggest, television—materializes "time in space, mediating between the historical and the discursive, providing fictional environments where historically specific constellations of power are made visible."[6]

Our focus has been a particular popular culture manifestation of the American presidency, *The West Wing*. Our analysis highlights the ability of that program to articulate a nationalistic presidentiality that proffers a specific vision of the United States, its political culture, and the institution of the presidency in the late 1990s and early 2000s. Under the rubric of its nationalism, *TWW* also manifests the intersectionality of component ideological aspects of U.S. nationalism—specifically, romance, gender, race, and militarism. From this analysis, and by drawing upon the show's September 11 special episode entitled "Isaac and Ishmael" ("I&I"), it is possible to illustrate the tensions, resolutions, and ideologies at work in contemporary articulations of U.S. nationalism.

## *The West Wing*'s Complex Presidency

Rarely does contemporary popular culture offer viewers complex characterizations of political leaders or presidents. Presidents in film, specifically, tend to exemplify broadly drawn, stereotypical characteristics. They are heroic in the style of Harrison Ford's president in *Air Force One* or malevolent as with Gene Hackman's president in *Absolute Power*. Perhaps it is because of the medium or preoccupation with special effects and blockbuster moneymakers, but Hollywood, for whatever reason, generally is not able to grasp and portray the "intricacies of the political process" or the complexities of political characters.[7]

*TWW* is different from typical popular culture renditions of U.S. politics in its complexity and ambiguity. Gone is the straightforward, redundant presidential character of Hollywood films. In his place is a multifaceted characterization of the nation's chief executive that complicates and interrogates cultural visions of politics, the presidency, and U.S. nationalism. Specifically, *TWW*'s President Jed Bartlet is a complex romantic hero who presides over an ensemble of other heroic figures pursuing a noble quest for that which is right and just. He is a man of depth and conflict, an atypical romantic hero who faces physical infirmity, professional anxiety, self-doubt, and personal turmoil as he tries to lead the nation. Bartlet's heroism comes not from his courage, although he is depicted as courageous, or his physical strength but from his intellectualism, commitment to pursue the right course, and oratorical and debating skills.

As an embodiment of U.S. nationalism at the end of one century and the start of another, Bartlet enacts a vision of the nation in conflict, confronting turmoil and angst as it navigates in a new and uncertain post–cold war world. Simultaneously, by maintaining a romantic pose for the president *TWW* conveys a romantic nationalism at the foundation of U.S. national identity, offering a vision of the nation rooted in the virtuous quest, fighting the wicked (yet frequently ambiguous and uncertain) villain and sure of the purpose behind its heroism. In this way *TWW* works nationalistically to articulate an "imagined community" for the United States.[8] It is a community that exists as a "constructed landscape of collective aspirations" that is "now mediated through the complex prism of modern media."[9]

As a mediated, imagined articulation of U.S. nationalism *TWW* offers a conflicted, at times contradictory, sense of the country's identity. French philosopher Etienne Balibar suggests that two different discourses of nationalism explain the "ambiguous identities" in postmodern societies. Dominant or oppressive nationalisms are generally invisible and "present themselves, rather, as political and cultural universalisms in which religious and economic components may exist." Nationalisms that offer political and/or cultural resistance to dominant power structures tend to be "over-visible in that, on the one hand, they are generally blind to those causes and determinations that do not stem from the problem of the nation, and on the other, they tend to subsume within themselves . . . all the other ideological schemas, both social and religious."[10] *TWW* articulates both forms of nationalism.

Overvisible nationalisms on *TWW* emerge from its depiction of gender and race and the intersections of these social categories with the U.S. presidency. Both are implicated in contemporary understandings of U.S. nationalism, largely as sites of resistance to dominant power systems ordered primarily around patriarchy and whiteness. Alternative nationalistic discourses emerge from this multiculturalism because such social forces are, to quote Balibar, "present from the outset and are constantly re-forming themselves." In that sense the rhetorics are overly visible. They emerge in greater force and secure more attention because they oppose the dominant, unicultural discourse of national identity. They represent a quest to articulate an alternative sense of their own recognition, and their individual authenticity contrasts with the prevailing nationalistic vision of individuality and identity.[11]

As they challenge prevailing orthodoxies of a broader U.S. nationalism, discourses of multicultural nationalism (including feminist ones promoting gender equality) represent, for some, a dangerous threat to cultural and political unity. Indeed, the overvisibility of multicultural U.S. nationalism intensifies through such a critique. The sociologist and media critic Todd Gitlin laments, for instance, the growth of "identity obsession" in which the United States has become a "stewpot of separate identities." Gitlin considers the rhetoric of multiculturalism—even the word itself—to be "baggy, a mélange of fact and value, current precisely because it is vague enough to serve so many interests."[12] Arthur Schlesinger Jr. worries about the "disuniting of America" as he ponders the threatened breakdown of the "brilliant solution" the United States offers for the inherent disunities of a multiethnic society, "the creation of a brand-new national identity by individuals who, in forsaking old loyalties and joining to make new lives, melted away ethnic differences."[13] Brian Barry, a political theorist who provides an egalitarian critique of multiculturalism, maintains that it, among many other things, articulates an erroneous "endemic tendency to assume that distinctive cultural attributes are the defining features of all groups."[14] These varied voices are all powerful demonstrations of how "the United States still has not come to terms with what it might mean to be a multiethnic and multiracial nation."[15]

Each of these critiques validates Balibar's articulation of the overvisibility of oppositional versions of identity and nationalism. They all specifically highlight threats to the preferred, invisible nationalism of cultural unity and order that multiculturalism presents. In so doing they confirm what Thomas

West calls the "liberal and rationalist rhetorical-political procedures" that screen out "disruptive aspects of emotion, passion, and irreducible differences" and "sell democratic ideals as the norm and attempt to frame partisan debates in nonpartisan ways."[16] Put differently, by attacking the multicultural and feminist as threats to a preferred nationalism of democratic identity and cultural unity, oppositional nationalisms are rendered overvisible; dominant, invisible nationalisms are preserved, naturalized, and dehistoricized.

*TWW* is in many ways a negotiation of tensions between dominant U.S. nationalisms that certify the power of patriarchy and whiteness and multicultural nationalisms that reimagine a different national identity. That is precisely why gendered and racialized discourses of *TWW* are so polyvalent and allow multiple interpretive visions to emerge from the show's rhetoric. Feminists who imagine a United States in which women are equal to men in power and political influence, and who embrace images of strong women in television as an important step in achieving that, may applaud *TWW*'s smart, capable women who function at the seat of political control. They will note that on *TWW* C.J. Cregg is a pivotal member of the president's inner circle, influencing policy and exerting control. They will praise the depiction of a national security advisor as a woman of color who operates at the heart of matters traditionally controlled by men. *TWW* may speak to a feminist nationalism in articulating political issues of specific concern to women and providing positive portrayals of women political leaders.

A feminist nationalism is overly visible, though, and *TWW* never lets its challenge to dominant, patriarchal nationalism prevail. Female characters are regularly sexualized in ways that the male characters are not, and they are frequently the subject of sexualized banter and dialogue. In addition, female characters are dominant in supportive, secretarial roles in which their function is to assist controlling male characters perform important duties. Even when a female character is depicted in an important political role, as C.J. is, she will often rely on male characters for knowledge or insight and will frequently make significant mistakes. At the most basic level of depiction *TWW* generally marginalizes female characters and relegates them to the realm of support and assistance rather than action and decision making. As Lesley Smith, a television critic, has remarked, "To the detriment of the drama [*TWW*], the ongoing delineation of male virtue remains the show's main concern." What results is the message that "women have a place in the White House [but] they serve the boys: they don't initiate."[17]

*TWW* also structures gender dynamics, and the show's narrative, around a family metaphor by positioning the president as a father figure. In so doing the show furthers a patriarchal vision of the presidency and political leadership in the United States and reinforces a patriarchal vision of U.S. nationalism. The family model invokes long-standing gender dynamics and relationships in a powerful depiction of the presidency. George Lakoff argues that American politics are generally ordered around competing familial metaphors—the strict father and the nurturant father. He concludes that "understanding political positions requires understanding how they fit family-based moralities."[18] Jed Bartlet functions paternalistically, and such metaphorical constructions for the gendered nationalism of the show are powerful. More important, Bartlet becomes a receptacle for many emotions that a paternalistic figure evokes, including love, loyalty, and passion. Supporting characters from his family and staff routinely pledge devotion, further reinforcing the presidential-paternalistic link. As with the gendered presidency of *TWW* in general, reliance on a familial metaphor highlights the invisibility of the patriarchal structure of U.S. nationalism by rendering the presidency in consistent, traditional ways.

The drama's treatment of race and a multiethnic nationalism is as complex as its handling of feminist nationalism. The American experience with race is complicated, mostly by virtue of a long history of slavery and forced migration of non-native people to America as well as steady waves of immigration since the early 1800s. In both cases, although in different ways, the U.S. experience with either forced or voluntary immigration reveals that "the majority has lacked the sort of openness that makes it possible for minority groups to integrate," observes philosopher Will Kymlicka.[19] What results is a sense of national identity powerfully constrained by issues of ethnicity and race and a political culture that both embraces and militates against diversity and multiculturalism.

*TWW* pays homage to calls for more diverse casting in television by including people of color and addressing issues typically associated with marginalized communities. The chair of the Joint Chiefs of Staff and the national security advisor are both African Americans, as is the president's personal assistant. There are occasional staffers and other individuals who are Latino or Latina, Asian American, or members of other underrepresented groups. Despite their inclusion, however, *TWW* still relegates people of color and their concerns to its margins, characterizing them typically in violent and unflattering ways. *TWW* manifests what Jack Citrin, a political scientist, calls "weak multiculturalism" in which canons are expanded to include minority voices; months are designated for minority history awareness; and the watchwords are "tolerance, sensitivity, and openness," creating an outlook "that flirts with the idea of group rights without wholly embracing it."[20] That vision coincides with Gary Gerstle's notion of civic nationalism, embracing equality and tolerance without significantly altering or challenging the dominant U.S. nationalism characterized primarily by whiteness.[21] In this way *TWW* reifies the overvisibility of multicultural nationalism and furthers the normalized nature of whiteness in the United States.

Dominant but invisible nationalisms take many forms on *TWW*, some of which we have identified as examples of patriarchy and whiteness. The other governing nationalism on the program is militarism, a powerful force in the formation of U.S. national identity. The ability to invoke military responses to significant problems is evident and reinforces the commander-in-chief role of the presidency. It also positions Bartlet, the primary, heroic possessor of military power and authority, at the center of U.S. nationalism. The messiness of electoral politics, the wrangling with Congress, and the complications of dealing with cabinet officials, government functionaries, or the press are all largely absent as the president sits in the Situation Room. With him are only a few advisors who eagerly await his, and only his, order to attack. Nancy L. Rosenblum has traced the literary and intellectual history of romantic militarism and concludes that within this tradition "the soldier makes his [or her] own opportunity . . . and victory depends upon his [or her] own, sole initiative, courage, and surprise."[22] This same individual autonomy, this same sense of control and power, adheres to the president in *TWW*'s vision of heroic, powerful militarism.

Militarism entails particular ideological and political discourses that figure prominently in *TWW*—loyalty, masculinity, and power. "In most societies," Kjell Skjelsbaek maintains in his attempt to understand the concept of contemporary militarism, "participation in military life is positively valued as a sign of masculinity. It implies strength, endurance, in some cases chivalry, loyalty to comrades in arms."[23] That perspective is confirmed by Alexander DeConde's historical treatment of "presidential machismo" when he concludes that most presidents, upon taking office, "realized that to achieve conventional success in foreign affairs they had to exercise power with strength, virility, and decisiveness."[24]

*TWW*'s militarism is like other militarisms in its relationship to a racialized nationalism endemic in the American experience. Skjelsbaek's analysis of the meanings of militarism reveals the links between racist ethnocentrism and militarism: "A strong conviction about the righteousness of one's own group or cause, combined with a low regard for human life or with an attempt to 'dehumanize' the enemy is conducive to violence. Thus there is a link between militarism and racism."[25] As such, *TWW*'s militarism works alongside the gendered and racialized nationalism in the drama, often reinforcing the dominant, invisible nationalisms of patriarchy and whiteness that frequently emerge from the show's episodes. Militarism is another invisible nationalism, a naturalized source of U.S. identity that suppresses and confines the more emancipatory nationalisms that achieve some level of expression in *TWW*'s discourse. As Patrick Regan suggests, "In a highly militarized society, the symbols that help maintain this [militaristic] patriotic fervor should be evident in any number of media targeted at the general public."[26] *TWW* offers a wealth of such symbols in the militarized presidency that it articulates with increasing frequency.

What results from *TWW* is a complex, varied, polyvalent presidentiality that maintains, despite its presentation of oppositional, counter-hegemonic messages, a predominant message of U.S. nationalism rooted in patriarchy, whiteness, and militarism. The center of all national action, the source of all national identity in *TWW*, comes from a heroic, white, male president who is strongest when exerting military force. Even as viewers see his insecurities, his problems and flaws, and witness his physical infirmities and political errors, they are nonetheless beckoned to endorse Bartlet's leadership because of his intellectualism and capacity for doing right. He actively fights against various villains who live at home and abroad, and he is supported by an active, loyal array of smart and savvy aides who make possible his romantic leadership.

Although its meaning is often complicated, there is an ordering of *TWW*'s nationalism that renders it largely consistent with prevailing visions of U.S. national identity. In this way, presidentiality on *TWW* is a negotiation of the U.S. national imaginary, a delineation of U.S. nationalism that navigates the uncertain terrain of contemporary political reality and ontological uncertainty. Nowhere is that contentious navigation and negotiation more apparent than in *TWW*'s reaction to the attacks of September 11, 2001.

## Reacting to a National Tragedy: *The West Wing*'s Response to 9/11

Most television programming—indeed, most entertainment discourse in general—avoided incorporating the events of September 11, 2001, into their shows in the immediate aftermath of the attacks. The events were so dramatic, so filled with death and terror, and so crammed with meaning and consequence that translating or using them for entertainment purposes appeared unseemly or inappropriate. With only a few exceptions (the NBC show *Third Watch*, for example, glorified the role of firefighters and police in a tribute to the heroism of 9/11's first-responders), reactions to 9/11 were left to journalists and public officials. The exception was "I&I," *TWW*'s special episode at the beginning of its third season.

By even airing a program that was a reaction to the attacks of September 11, *TWW* elevated its status and became more than a television drama about presidential politics. As a program that relies on verisimilitude and offers a hyperreal depiction of the American presidency, *TWW* took its role as a constructed site of presidential authority as license to offer its own "presidential" commentary on dramatic world events. In so doing the show remade its image, forever changing the perceived understanding of the program and its place as a cultural marker, a zeitgeist show about the state of the American presidency and U.S. nationalism.

Rarely do entertainment texts directly engage dramatic events from the real world. They may occasionally draw on stories "ripped from the headlines," but a direct correspondence to actual events is typically obscure because there are significant delays between the actual events and representations of them in fictional television. This convention of entertainment programming makes the decision to produce and present an episode about 9/11 so soon after the events quite remarkable. As Gary Levin noted in *USA Today*, the program's "speedy embrace of the subject is unusual: Several other series, sensitive to public outcry, are deleting even vague references to terrorism or airline travel." As *TWW* producer John Wells explained the rationale for the episode, "It was important that we address the tragic events of the past few weeks in some way. It's affected everyone who works on the show and everyone in the country."[27] Of course the attacks on 9/11 affected many people who work on television programs. Only *TWW*, however, produced an almost immediate response, largely as a function of the symbolic connection between this fictional Hollywood White House and the actual White House, because of the program's capacity to offer an additional vision of the presidency and U.S. nationalism to an eager public.

The episode scored a 16.3 rating, with more than twenty-five million viewers tuned in, ranking the show as the third-most watched for the week in which it aired.[28] "I&I" generated considerable discussion about the meaning of 9/11 from writers, columnists, and everyday viewers. Some saw the episode as television critic Eric Mink did, a "sensible, sensitive, and intelligent" way for television to engage the events of 9/11.[29] The *Fort Worth Star-Telegram*'s critic Ken Parish Perkins called the show "strong and fair" and a "courageous undertaking."[30] Other reviews were less praiseworthy. National Public Radio's television critic David Bianculli called the episode "an hour-long lecture," and Howard Rosenberg at the *Los Angeles Times* reflected a popular sentiment that the program was "preachy."[31] From New Zealand came television critic Jane Bowron's judgment that "Isaac and Ishmael" was a "clumsily executed piece of insanely boring nationalism."[32]

As a text that responds to the events of 9/11, "I&I" offered a different discourse than those offered by President Bush and other public officials. It presented a dialogic rhetoric that symbolically invited participation and disputation about the terrorism confronting the United States.[33] Its narrative was characterized by *methexis* (an invitation to participation and dialogue as a means of cultural understanding and healing).[34] Viewers were interpellated as active agents, with fictional representatives giving voice to their questions and concerns about terrorism to those in power. As a result, "I&I"'s nationalism occurred in more contingent, democratic contexts where uncertainty and anxiety reign although it still located the power to define and respond to national trauma in the White House.

The conflicted and uncertain reactions the episode elicited mirrored its methetic character and ill-defined and complex explanation for the violence of 9/11. At the same time, "I&I" maintained the general ideological focus of *TWW* as it articulated a U.S. nationalism ordered primarily by patriarchy, whiteness, and militarism. Indeed, the dialogic character of the play beckoned viewers to participate in the creation of that nationalism and reify adherence to the common meaning of Americanness in the aftermath of the tragic events of September 11.

### "Isaac and Ishmael": Giving Meaning to 9/11

"I&I"'s plot is rather simple. Two interlocking narratives each involve the show's familiar characters confronting different dimensions of a "lockdown," the situation in the White House when some threat or danger has resulted in the executive compound being completely sealed. One subplot features Deputy Chief of Staff Josh Lyman speaking to a group of teenagers from a program identified as the "Presidential Classroom." As he talks, the lockdown occurs, forcing the students' confinement in the White House. When Josh and his assistant, Donna Moss, take the group to the White House Mess a discussion about terrorism ensues that involves many members of the show's regular cast. The second subplot concerns identification of a possible terrorist on the White House staff. An FBI office has identified a staffer, Ali, who has the same name as an targeted Saudi Arabian terrorist, and Secret Service agents—along with, implausibly, White House Chief of Staff Leo McGarry—detain and interrogate him. The interrogation, we learn, is the reason for the lockdown, which ends when the real terrorist is found in Europe. The staffer is cleared, and the students are released.

A compelling title sequence begins "I&I," replacing the program's regular opening with a series of comments from each of the cast's actors. Direct address is used as they speak to the camera and thus to the audience. Viewers are informed that the episode does not fit within the narrative stream of the program's plot and that they should not "spend a lot of time trying to figure out where this episode comes in the timeline of the series—it doesn't. It's a storytelling aberration if you'll allow." Immediately, the interactive character of "I&I"'s form is established. There is, of course, direct address to the audience. Not only do the show's actors (as actors, not characters) seek viewers' permission to deviate from customary plot and pacing but they also request that viewers donate to relief efforts for victims of the World Trade Center attacks. Viewers are invited into the program via this dialogue, and their sanction is sought. They are also reassured that the episode is an "aberration." Normalcy will be established in the ensuing week, when order is restored by *TWW*'s season premiere. Just as the attacks of 9/11 disrupted and altered the nation's collective life for a brief moment, "I&I"'s opening implies, so, too, the episode will disrupt televiewing only ever so slightly. The future will bring a return to normal lives, and the rhythms of the U.S. national community will be disrupted but temporarily.

"I&I"'s opening is also interactive in its confrontation with the terrorist exigency. It is more subdued, more introspective, than reactions that came from the Bush White House after 9/11, whether the dramatic trip around the nation on the day of the attacks to the faux State of the Union speech to declare "war on terrorism" before a joint session of Congress on September 20. In addition, the episode involves an entire administration, not just a president. While Martin Sheen appears in the opening sequence he is but one of many in the cast who address viewers. The collective presidency of *TWW* will tackle this new public concern, the opening suggests, not just a lone, romantic, heroic president confronting the nation's enemies with resolve and divine guidance.

"I&I" establishes its pattern of involved interaction at the outset of the episode, inviting the audience to participate in its vision of U.S. nationalism in the wake of 9/11. The choice of the White House Mess as a locale launches the conversational, Socratic dynamics of the episode. It is, much like a kitchen, a more intimate and dialogic location than its possible alternatives, an office or one of the formal meeting rooms often used on *TWW* as a site of action. Again, the contrast with the real presidential response is noteworthy. Where George W. Bush opted to confront the terrorism of 9/11 from the stately formal of settings of the White House and the House Chamber, *TWW* places its discourse in a more familiar and personal setting, a kitchen. As if beckoning the audience to join in, the setting personalizes the discussion of terrorism and makes powerful (albeit fictionalized) agents more accessible as they confront national crises.

As Josh begins his interaction with the confined students (who are, in keeping with *TWW*'s symbolic multiculturalism, appropriately diverse), *TWW*'s reorganization of 9/11 occurs almost immediately. Josh begins by articulating the salience of the presidency: "This is the White House, the home of the president and the executive branch, the most powerful of the three branches of the federal government." One senses that he would continue with his lecture were he not immediately interrupted by a student who asks, "Actually . . . isn't it true that the framers made sure that the executive branch was the weakest of the three branches because we were breaking off from the royalists model that put absolute power in just one place? I mean, isn't that why they made the legislative branch, or people's branch, the most powerful?"

In compelling fashion the student (the people's representative) interrogates executive control and articulates the constitutionally prescribed republican character of the balance of power. The agent of executive power in the scene, Josh, is forced to concede, and his concession expresses confidence in the knowledge of an implied audience as represented by the students. Josh becomes more relaxed and personable as he states, "Alright, you already know about the branches of government. I assume you know how a bill becomes a law. What do you want to talk about?"

The high school students become the viewers, who are constructed as smart but in need of leadership and guidance. The students are presented as frightened and anxious, capturing the public anxiety that existed after 9/11. In response to that fear, White House staffers regularly offer reassurances in "I&I" and symbolically express the role of the executive as a therapeutic agent in U.S. political culture. Again, as is so common on *TWW*, the presidency is the locus of security and power but not without a reminder from the people that its power is limited. We have come, the episode implies, to the symbolic location of power and leadership—the White House—to learn and be led.

Even as "I&I" crafts a dialogue about terrorism between fictional leaders and a constructed audience it also implicitly interrogates the Bush White House and Congress's political approach to defining terrorism in the aftermath of 9/11. Following Josh's invitation, he and the students exchange ideas about the meaning and origins of terrorism. He articulates an analogy ("in honor of the SATs they are about to take") that defines Islamic fundamentalist terrorism as equivalent to the Ku Klux Klan. "It's the Klan gone medieval, global," Josh concludes. A female student then asks, "Why are Islamic extremists trying to kill us?" Others answer, "Because we're Americans," and, "It's our freedom . . . freedom and democracy."

Josh's reply is instructive. "Right or wrong," he argues, "it's probably a good idea to acknowledge that they do have specific complaints; I hear them every day. The people we support, troops in Saudi Arabia, sanctions against Iraq, support of Egypt. It's not that they just don't like Irving Berlin." Almost in direct response to Bush's claim on September 20, 2001, that Islamic terrorists are murderers who hate freedom, Josh complicates and interrogates that image only to have his construction challenged by Donna, who becomes the voice of Bush's polarized, nationalistic vision.

What results is that much of the subplot's remaining action involving the students concerns a more nuanced and detailed discussion of the origins of terrorism, its roots in ancient and contemporary history, and its highly contingent and complex quality. The discussion refutes implicitly the explanation of terrorism articulated by George W. Bush in the wake of 9/11. The interactive character of "I&I" is thus multilayered and occurs textually as well as intertextually, offering an alternative "presidential response" to terrorist violence.

## Racialized, Gendered, and Militarized Nationalism on The West Wing

The "Isaac and Ishmael" episode offers a vision of U.S. nationalism that is subtler, less doctrinaire, than the jingoistic nationalism that characterized much public discussion following the attacks of 9/11. "I&I"'s nationalism self-reflexively questions the ethnocentrism inherent in the conventional American mantra about freedom and democracy. Moreover, some viewers might have been reassured by its ideological capacity to reinscribe alternative values to the fervid patriotism of God and freedom, albeit in ways still disturbingly racialized and gendered.

A second subplot of "I&I" involves the questioning of a White House staffer, an Arab suspected of links to a known and captured terrorist. The staffer is detained and queried vigorously and in the process comes to epitomize the injustices of a war on terrorism that subjects individuals to interrogation and scrutiny simply by virtue of ethnicity, background, or name. Although the incident invokes sympathy for the detained suspect, his anger and defiance, along with the events of 9/11 and the emerging national context, invite audience identification with the racism and ethnocentrism that Leo articulates during the interrogation. A type of self-reflection results wherein the prejudices and racisms of the aftermath of 9/11 are legitimated and viewers are simultaneously invited to question and reject the same prejudices.

In the process of the interrogation Leo becomes the voice of American civic nationalism in the face of the Arab terrorist threat. As the dialogue unfolds, Ali expresses many of the objections Josh mentions earlier in the program concerning Islamic fundamentalists' issues with the United States. At one point, for instance, Ali is asked about his participation in a protest against the U.S. presence in Saudi Arabia. He replies, "Saudi Arabia is home to two of our holiest mosques. Mecca is there. How would you like it if I camped out in front of the Vatican with a stockpile of M-16s?" The character credibly expresses the objections held in much of the Arab world to U.S. policy but is rebuffed by Leo, who answers, "I'd like it fine if you were there to protect the Vatican." When Ali asserts, "You sent an army composed of women as well as men to protect a Muslim dynasty where women were not even allowed to drive a car," Leo answers, "Maybe we can teach them."

At virtually every turn Leo ideologically personifies the voice of civic nationalism, portraying the United States imperialistically as the savior of the Arab world and justified in its prejudices. Ali remarks at one point that the perpetual questioning of Arab Americans in the aftermath of terrorism is "horrible." "Well," Leo insensitively concludes, "that's the price you pay." The Arab voice and its anger are sublimated in this exchange to righteous American anger in response to terrorism.

At the same time, the exchange emphasizes nationalism rooted in racial and ethnic differences and gender. His physical appearance makes Ali an other, as do his political convictions; in Balibar's terms, his opposition to U.S. nationalism is overly visible.[35] Moreover, the objections that exist to U.S. policy are rooted in gender, with the presence of U.S. troops in Saudi Arabia working as a threat to Muslim concepts of appropriate gender roles. As such, this plotline of "I&I" questions the simplistic civic nationalism at work in political culture following 9/11 and gives voice to the racialized and gendered quality of U.S. nationalism.

"I&I" reifies the positive connotations associated with the military and positions that vision of U.S. nationalism against the dangers of Islam, understood largely through race and gender. The military, in Leo's opinion, is a source of security and freedom. It is significant that his responses to Ali are all ordered around the security brought to Saudi Arabia by the U.S. military, which keeps the holy places of Islam safe and brings enlightenment and liberation to oppressed Saudi women.

On its surface this subplot would appear to provide a clear and traditional nationalism. Leo, the voice of American outrage in the face of Arab terror, expresses nationalistic thoughts and feelings that invite audience identification. But as on *TWW* generally, the episode does not leave civic nationalism unified and consistent. When it is revealed that Ali is not the terrorist in question, he leaves the interrogation with a parting comment on Leo's behavior: "You have the memory of a gypsy moth. When you and the President and the President's daughter and about a hundred other people, including me by the way, were met with a hail of .44–caliber gunfire in Rosslyn, not only were the shooters white, they were doing it because one of us wasn't."[36] He invokes a previous episode's plot to articulate another dimension of U.S. nationalism, a commitment to diversity and multiculturalism. In the more nuanced discourse of "I&I," nationalism comes to mean more than American exceptionalism and adherence to particular values of freedom and democracy. Instead, the episode asks for a nationalism that is self-reflexive and invites constant interrogation and disputation. It would be an interactive, thoughtful nationalism that upholds the conflicting values that define the American community.

The final scene of "I&I" clearly demonstrates the complexity of *TWW*'s nationalism in response to 9/11. Leo finds Ali at work at his desk later the same evening and issues a measured, limited apology to the young staffer: "Good evening. That's the price you pay for having the same physical features as criminals. That's what I was going to say . . . I'm sorry about that . . . I think if you talk to people who know me, they'd tell you that that was unlike me, you know? We're obviously all under greater than usual amount of you know. And, like you point out with the shooting and everything, yeah, all right. Well, that's all."

Leo is discomforted by the country's projected anxiety about feelings and ethnocentrisms following 9/11. Despite the fact that he is an American citizen, Ali is constructed as the other, and as such he is outside traditional and ideologically powerful conceptions of Americanness. Leo, conversely, largely through his whiteness, gender, and position of authority, embodies Americanness and is the voice of that nationalism. It projects the myth of common origins and highlights threats from outsiders. Such discourse reflects the view that in "the construction of most ethnic and national collectivities, one usually joins the collectivity by being born into it . . . those who are not born into it [the nation] are excluded."[37]

As if to reemphasize its nationalism, "I&I" consistently inscribes conventional U.S. values onto the encounter between Leo and Ali. As Leo walks away from Ali after apologizing, he turns and says, "Hey kid. Way to be back at your desk." With one small comment Leo manages to sublimate Ali's anger and highlight a traditional nationalism based in an all-American work ethic that transcends culture and asserts a larger sense of connectivity and commonality. Leo also deflates Ali's anger by calling him "kid," reifying the chief of staff's authority in the process.

"I&I" is more mature and more complex than the rather straightforward patriotic nationalism of many other responses to the tragedy of 9/11.[38] There is something comforting about absolutes and polarization that "I&I" ignores or rejects. Yet some audiences may respond positively and be comforted by the program's nuance and intellectualism. There is, in other words, a pluralistic polyvalence in "I&I" that offers another vision of presidential leadership in times of difficulty and crisis.

On gendered terms "I&I" also reifies traditional nationalisms. The gendered portrayal of women in "I&I" and the gendered messages of the text are multifarious. The episode assembles a specifically gendered nationalism that is therapeutic given its reinscription of traditional values in the aftermath of 9/11, even as counterintuitive depictions of the episode's female characters problemize that same nationalism's patriarchy.

Women are given powerful roles and voices in "I&I" but are also confined to rigidly stereotyped, often highly patriarchal, portrayals that give voice to the polarization of official Bush administration reactions to 9/11. Donna Moss and C.J. Cregg represent heightened security and ardent nationalism. Facing arguments from many of the male characters upholding civil liberties, cultural tolerance, and a restrained military reaction to terrorism, these women argue for the more militaristic and nationalistic solutions. When Josh tries to demonstrate to the gathered students that Islamic extremists may have legitimate grievances against the United States, it is Donna who replies, "I don't know about Irving Berlin, but the ridiculous search for rational reasons why somebody straps a bomb to their chest is ridiculous."

A bigger platform is accorded C.J. Cregg, who argues with Toby Ziegler about the appropriate responses to terrorism and the civil libertarian implications of those responses. C.J. upholds the need for "human intelligence," saying, "We need spies . . . human spies." When Toby, concerned about civil liberties, confronts her about such intelligence, she replies, "Liberties schmiberties. You know a way to do this without bugging some phones?" A defense of vigorous, extra-constitutional, militaristic responses to terrorism comes in her closing speech:

> Look, I take civil liberties as seriously as anybody, OK? I've been to the dinners. . . . That said, Tobus, we're going to have to do some stuff. We're going to have to tap some phones and we're going to have to partner with people who are the lesser of evils. I'm sorry, but terrorists don't have armies and navies, they don't have capitals. Some of these guys, we're going to have to walk up to them and shoot them. Yeah, we can rout terrorist nests but some of these guys aren't going to be taken by the 105th Armored Tank Division. Some of these guys are going to be taken by a busboy with a silencer. So it's time to give the intelligence agencies the money and the manpower they need. We don't hear about their successes. Guess what? The Soviets never crossed the Elba. The North Koreans stayed behind the 38th Parallel. During the millennium, not one incident. Do you think that's because the terrorists decided that would be a good day to take off, not much action that day? End of song.

There is no immediate reply; Toby and Josh look down at the floor, conceding her point. C.J.'s views are therefore legitimated. In this way "I&I" challenges the nationalism of C.J.'s discourse with Leo's interrogation of Ali and simultaneously upholds that militarized nationalism by giving it a powerful, extended justification so it overrides all other civic concerns such as freedom of speech and freedom of religion.

Adding to the complexity of "I&I"'s gendered nationalism is the way the episode undermines Donna's and C.J.'s nationalistic voices with sexist insults and banter. Donna's credibility is diluted at the episode's opening. In a litany of plotlines to come when "I&I" resumes, the various characters mention such things as reelection, repeal of the estate tax, the embassy in Haiti, and the disclosure of the president's multiple sclerosis. Donna, however, merely comments, "And I get a boyfriend." Furthermore, Josh labels her remarks as "college girlish" after she attacks his rationale for Islamic fundamentalist antipathy toward the United States. He tells the students, "She does have a point, but it certainly doesn't mean you should listen to her." After C.J. suggests that Josh find ways to aid and comfort the "boys in intelligence" he makes a demeaning reply: "You know, they may need some comforting right now. When this crash is over, you'd best get in some fishnets and head to a bar."

C.J.'s comments in support of increased intelligence and her construction of the need to support the "boys in intelligence," moreover, amplify what film critic Robert Burgoyne calls the "relation between male sexual identity and the warrior ethos."[39] Coming as they do from a woman, her comments are counterintuitive to the typical articulation of this relationship and reflect *TWW*'s polyvalent portrayals of women. At the same time, the sexualized banter between C.J. and Josh reestablishes the connection between sexual masculinity and the "warrior ethos." The result is a reinscription of a conventional and patriarchal gendered nationalism, restoring order and providing consistency for viewers struggling for comfort in the aftermath of 9/11's violence.

Ultimately, C.J. and Donna are kept in their gendered places although they voice a masculine, militarized nationalism. Their nationalistic statements may even carry more suasive force because women are often viewed as the "cultural carriers" of the nation's "moral high ground . . . compassion, generosity and a sense of justice" articulating messages of peace, not war.[40] Women thus become the voice of the nation, constructed "in need of protection" and moral guidance in the face of external threats.[41]

In "I&I," women not only supply "girlish" arguments and sexual favors to the men who protect the nation but are also depicted as threats to the American nation-state. Repeatedly throughout the episode women are identified as the problem, or a cause of terrorism. As Toby, for example, explains the history of terrorism to the high school students he notes that eleventh-century followers of the original Islamic terrorist were told they would have unlimited access to concubines if they carried out terrorist attacks. "Ah," Sam interjects, "temptation. I have named thee and thy name is woman."

"I&I" identifies the actions of one woman—Sarah—as the cause of contemporary tensions between Arabs and Jews. When a student asks the First Lady, "How did all of this start?" Abigail Bartlet replies by telling the biblical story of Isaac and Ishmael:

> God said to Abraham, look toward the heaven and number the stars and so shall your descendants be. But Abraham's wife, Sarah, wasn't getting any younger and God wasn't coming through on his promise. . . . Sarah was getting older and she was getting nervous because she didn't have any children. So she sent Abraham to the bed of her maid, Hagar, and Abraham and Hagar had Ishmael. And not long after they did, God kept his promise to Sarah, as He always intended to, and Abraham and Sarah had Isaac. And Sarah said to Abraham, "Cast out this slave woman with her son, for the son of the slave woman will not be heir with my son Isaac." And so it began. The Jews, the sons of Isaac. The Arabs, the sons of Ishmael. But what most people find important to remember is that in the end, the two sons came together to bury their father.

This pivotal moment in the episode reflects its title and offers its clearest statement of the gendered and racialized nationalism of terrorism. On one level the entire Arab-Jewish conflict is understood for its roots in the competition between women over men and in their ability to produce (or not produce) children. In this way the story's plot naturalizes the role of mother and symbolically positions women as giving birth to nations, peoples, and geopolitical conflicts that last for centuries. "Women's bodies . . . not only [function as] symbols of fecundity of the nation and vessels for the nation's reproduction, but also they serve as territorial markers" and as "loci of social conflicts dilemmas."[42]

On still another level, the story's rendition of terrorism locates a source of conflict with a single mother, the dispossessed slave woman who is constructed as the ideological other. Her status is marginalized (like the marginalization of Ali in "I&I"'s other plotline), her voice is absent, and her identity made the central factor in defining her legacy and meaning for centuries. Moreover, it is Hagar's son and his "illegitimacy" that cause perpetual tension between Arabs and Jews. This depiction reflects Mostov's contention that women "who have children with members of other nations [as Hagar did] become potential enemies of the nation, [and] traitors to it."[43] As such, the story dehistoricizes the Arab-Jewish conflict and ignores years of intervening events and persons. The suggestion is that were it not for the petty jealousies and impatience of Sarah, none of the tensions that plague the contemporary world would exist. This threat to American exceptionalism and nationalism is grounded in a situation caused by a woman. American nationalism is thus simultaneously constructed in feminized ways and threatened because of feminized behaviors.

Even as Abigail Bartlet's speech and Sam's comments define the causes of terrorism as female, "I&I" also places the preservation of American nationalism in the hands of men. The "boys of intelligence" in C.J.'s calculus are the hope for the future. In addition, all individuals involved in the interrogation of the suspected terrorist staffer, Ali, are male. And, in the ultimate expression of the masculine, romantic heroism of "I&I," President Bartlet, in a very brief appearance, tells the students, "We don't need martyrs right now. We need heroes. A hero would die for *his* country, but *he'd* much rather live for it." The use of the pronoun is revealing, coming as it does right after the president notes that the gathered women look "bright and lovely" and right before the First Lady instructs the students about the story of Abraham, Sarah, Isaac, Hagar, Ishmael. This depiction reflects the gendered division often promulgated in nationalistic discourse where "women physically reproduce the nation, and men protect and avenge it."[44]

Attending to the gendered and racialized components of nationalistic rhetorics allows for recognition of the systems of identity formation and the role of culture and political loyalty in the formation of collective consciousness.[45] Such a focus makes invisible dominant nationalisms visible by acknowledging their ideological bases. Although the multifaceted character of "I&I"'s gendered nationalism reinforces the methetic, interactive quality of its discourse by inviting the audience into an interrogation of the basis of its nationalistic message, it still resorts to conventional racialized and gendered portrayals, reinforcing ideological adherence to systems of patriarchy and nationalism. The episode, like *TWW* in general, offers a vision of the presidency that is complex and gives viewers messages that appear open and diverse while reinforcing powerful ideologies of patriarchy, whiteness, and militarism.

## *The West Wing*'s Presidentiality

In May 2000 a political digest, *The Hotline,* conducted a survey of attitudes about the pending 2000 election. In the poll, 1,011 "likely voters" were asked for opinions about a variety of topics, from Internet use to presidential preferences to positions on the legality of abortion. When asked their preference between candidates Al Gore and George W. Bush, 43 percent chose Bush whereas 41 percent chose Gore. When a subset of respondents, segmented by their viewing of *TWW,* were asked to chose between Bush, Gore, and fictional president Josiah Bartlet, 14 percent chose Bartlet.[46]

Less startling than the fact that Bartlet attracted as much support as he did is the fact that this poll, asking respondents a series of questions about weighty public policy matters, saw fit to inquire about *TWW* and Bartlet. In so doing, *The Hotline* reflected the ideological and social power of this show in U.S. political culture. *TWW* has buzz, it generates excitement and involvement from viewers, and is a critical success. Its stars appeared at the Democratic national convention in the summer of 2000 and were frequently displayed during the 2000 campaign, most often on behalf of Al Gore and other Democrats. The show has indeed seeped into the national consciousness.

*TWW* works as a discourse of U.S. nationalism and puts forth a complicated presidentiality rooted in romantic narrative forms, offering a vision of national identity based in entrenched ideological systems of gender, race, and militarism. As a discourse of U.S. nationalism, *TWW* contributes to what Balibar calls the formation of the "transindividual" or the "representations of 'us,' or of the relation between self and other, which are formed in social relations, in daily—public and private—activities." The process of creating the transindividual, according to Balibar, "has as a precondition—and operates within—historical *institutions*."[47]

The institution at issue on *TWW* is the American presidency, which is filled with meaning, history, context, and power. *TWW* preserves the invisibility of the presidency's patriarchal identity and makes invisible its whiteness. At the same time, *TWW* opens space and meaning in its text for alternative voices and emphasizes their otherness, making them overvisible, and rendering them marginal. *TWW*'s negotiation between patriarchy and feminism, whiteness and racialized nationalism, ultimately manifests a presidency that promotes, in Balibar's terminology, a "fictive ethnicity" wherein the nation constructs an identity that "distinguishes it from others by perceptible . . . marks, by 'typical' or 'emblematic' behavioural traits."[48]

*TWW* also promotes patriotism as a critical dimension to articulating nationalism; it is a patriotism that constructs the nation as a "transcendent community, implying a common 'destiny,' and at least implicitly linked to the idea of a transhistorical mission."[49] More often than not, that dimension of U.S. nationalism achieves expression via militarism even as the show manifests some ambivalence toward military means for solving problems and achieving policy goals. Militarism ascends as a defining ideology of the presidency and U.S. nationalism, an ordering that addresses Balibar's concern that there is no identity "without the establishment of a *hierarchy* of communal references."[50]

Deeply ambivalent, often self-questioning, powerfully presented, and critically acclaimed, *TWW* and its vision of U.S. nationalism offer a complex and unique sense of the American presidency, one rarely seen before in popular culture or journalistic discourse. Its power and success reside in ambiguity, a capacity to transcend the mundane and overcome the obvious even as it orders and structures a specific hierarchy of ideologically powerful meanings of nationalism and the presidency in an America where such meanings are constantly in flux and under siege.

Even though a different vision of the presidency from the perspective of popular culture, *TWW* still fulfills a larger mission in its duplication of the conventional, the normalized portrayal of the American presidency. Jean Baudrillard remarks that a condition of contemporary political culture is that if "a head of state remains the same or is someone else doesn't strictly change anything, so long as they resemble each other."[51] Despite its backstage view, even with its physically infirm, self-doubting president, *TWW* is largely a duplication of the American presidency and the nation's dominant vision of itself.

# Appendix A:
# The West Wing *Episode Directory*

## Season One

"Pilot," September 22, 1999. Directed by Thomas Schlamme; written by Aaron Sorkin.

"Post Hoc, Ergo Propter Hoc," September 29, 1999. Directed by Thomas Schlamme; written by Aaron Sorkin.

"A Proportional Response," October 6, 1999. Directed by Marc Buckland; written by Aaron Sorkin.

"Five Votes Down," October 13, 1999. Directed by Marc Buckland; written by Aaron Sorkin.

"The Crackpots and These Women," October 20, 1999. Directed by Anthony Drazan; written by Aaron Sorkin.

"Mr. Willis of Ohio," November 3, 1999. Directed by Christopher Misiano; written by Aaron Sorkin.

"The State Dinner," November 10, 1999. Directed by Thomas Schlamme; written by Aaron Sorkin.

"Enemies," November 17, 1999. Directed by Alan Taylor; written by Ron Osborn and Jeff Reno.

"The Short List," November 24, 1999. Directed by Bill D'Elia; written by Aaron Sorkin and Patrick Cadell.

"In Excelsis Deo," December 15, 1999. Directed by Alex Graves; written by Aaron Sorkin and Rick Cleveland.

"Lord John Marbury," January 5, 2000. Directed by Kevin Rodney Sullivan; written by Aaron Sorkin and Patrick Cadell.

"He Shall from Time to Time . . . ," January 12, 2000. Directed by Arlene Sanford; written by Aaron Sorkin.

"Take Out the Trash Day," January 26, 2000. Directed by Ken Olin; written by Aaron Sorkin.

"Take This Sabbath Day," February 9, 2000. Directed by Thomas Schlamme; written by Aaron Sorkin.

"Celestial Navigation," February 16, 2000. Directed by Christopher Misiano; written by Aaron Sorkin.

"Twenty Hours in LA," February 23, 2000. Directed by Alan Taylor; written by Aaron Sorkin.

"The White House Pro-Am," March 22, 2000. Directed by Ken Olin; written by Lawrence O'Donnell Jr., Paul Redford, and Aaron Sorkin.

"Six Meetings before Lunch," April 5, 2000. Directed by Clark Johnson; written by Aaron Sorkin.

"Let Bartlet Be Bartlet," April 26, 2000. Directed by Laura Innes; written by Aaron Sorkin.

"Mandatory Minimums," May 3, 2000. Directed by Robert Berlinger; written by Aaron Sorkin.

"Lies, Damn Lies, and Statistics," May 10, 2000. Directed by Don Scardino; written by Aaron Sorkin.

"What Kind of Day Has It Been," May 17, 2000. Directed by Thomas Schlamme; written by Aaron Sorkin.

## Season Two

"In the Shadow of Two Gunmen, Part 1," October 4, 2000. Directed by Thomas Schlamme; written by Aaron Sorkin.

"In the Shadow of Two Gunmen, Part 2," October 4, 2000. Directed by Thomas Schlamme; written by Aaron Sorkin.

"The Midterms," October 18, 2000. Directed by Alex Graves; written by Aaron Sorkin.

"In This White House," October 25, 2000. Directed by Ken Olin; written by Aaron Sorkin.

"And It's Surely to Their Credit," November 1, 2000. Directed by Christopher Misiano; written by Aaron Sorkin.

"The Lame Duck Congress," November 8, 2000. Directed by Jeremy Kagan; written by Aaron Sorkin.

"The Portland Trip," November 15, 2000. Directed by Paris Barclay; written by Aaron Sorkin.

"Shibboleth," November 22, 2000. Directed by Laura Innes; written by Aaron Sorkin.

"Galileo," November 29, 2000. Directed by Alex Graves; written by Kevin Falls and Aaron Sorkin.

"Noël," December 13, 2000. Directed by Thomas Schlamme; written by Aaron Sorkin.

"The Leadership Breakfast," January 10, 2001. Directed by Scott Winant; written by Aaron Sorkin.

"The Drop-In," January 24, 2001. Directed by Lou Antonio; written by Aaron Sorkin.

"Bartlet's Third State of the Union," February 7, 2001. Directed by Christopher Misiano; written by Aaron Sorkin.

"The War At Home," February 14, 2001. Directed by Christopher Misiano; written by Aaron Sorkin.

"Ellie," February 21, 2001. Directed by Michael Engler; written by Aaron Sorkin.

"Somebody's Going to Emergency, Somebody's Going to Jail," February 28, 2001. Directed by Jessica Yu; written by Paul Redford and Aaron Sorkin.

"The Stackhouse Filibuster," March 14, 2001. Directed by Bryan Gordon; written by Aaron Sorkin.

"Seventeen People," April 4, 2001. Directed by Alex Graves; written by Aaron Sorkin.

"Bad Moon Rising," April 25, 2001. Directed by Bill Johnson; written by Aaron Sorkin.

"The Fall's Gonna Kill You," May 2, 2001. Directed by Bryan Gordon; written by Aaron Sorkin.

"18th and Potomac," May 9, 2001. Directed by Robert Berlinger; written by Aaron Sorkin.

"Two Cathedrals," May 16, 2001. Directed by Thomas Schlamme; written by Aaron Sorkin.


## Season Three

"Isaac and Ishmael," October 3, 2001. Directed by Christopher Misiano; written by Aaron Sorkin.

"Manchester, Part 1," October 10, 2001. Directed by Thomas Schlamme; written by Aaron Sorkin.

"Manchester, Part 2," October 17, 2001. Directed by Thomas Schlamme; written by Aaron Sorkin.

"Ways and Means," October 24, 2001. Directed by Thomas Schlamme; written by Aaron Sorkin.

"On the Day Before," October 31, 2001. Directed by Christopher Misiano; written by Aaron Sorkin.

"War Crimes," November 7, 2001. Directed by Alex Graves; written by Aaron Sorkin.

"Gone Quiet," November 14, 2001. Directed by Jon Hutman; written by Aaron Sorkin.

"The Indians in the Lobby," November 21, 2001. Directed by Paris Barclay; written by Allison Abner, Kevin Falls, and Aaron Sorkin.

"The Women of Qumar," November 28, 2001. Directed by Alex Graves; written by Aaron Sorkin.

"Bartlet for America," December 12, 2001. Directed by Thomas Schlamme; written by Aaron Sorkin.

"H.Con. 172," January 9, 2002. Directed by Vincent Misiano; written by Aaron Sorkin.

"100,000 Airplanes," January, 16, 2002. Directed by David Nutter; written by Aaron Sorkin.

"The Two Bartlets," January 30, 2002. Directed by Alex Graves; written by Kevin Falls and Aaron Sorkin.

"Night Five," February 6, 2002. Directed by Christopher Misiano; written by Aaron Sorkin.

"Hartsfield's Landing," February 27, 2002. Directed by Vincent Misiano; written by Aaron Sorkin.

"Dead Irish Writers," March 6, 2002. Directed by Alex Graves; written by Aaron Sorkin.

"The U.S. Poet Laureate," March 27, 2002. Directed by Christopher Misiano; written by Aaron Sorkin.

"Stirred," April 3, 2002. Directed by Jeremy Kagan; written by Aaron Sorkin and Eli Attie.

"Documentary Special," April 24, 2002. Directed by Bill Coutourie.

"Enemies Foreign and Domestic," May 1, 2002. Directed by Alex Graves; written by Paul Redford and Aaron Sorkin.

"The Black Vera Wang," May 8, 2002. Directed by Christopher Misiano; written by Aaron Sorkin.

"We Killed Yamamoto," May 15, 2002. Directed by Thomas Schlamme; written by Aaron Sorkin.

"Posse Comitatus," May 22, 2002. Directed by Alex Graves; written by Aaron Sorkin.

## Season Four

"Twenty Hours in America, Part 1," September 25, 2002. Directed by Christopher Misiano; written by Aaron Sorkin.

"Twenty Hours in America, Part 2," September 25, 2002. Directed by Christopher Misiano; written by Aaron Sorkin.

"College Kids," October 2, 2002. Directed by Alex Graves; written by Aaron Sorkin.

"The Red Mass," October 9, 2002. Directed by Vincent Misiano; written by Aaron Sorkin.

"Debate Camp," October 16, 2002. Directed by Paris Barclay; written by Aaron Sorkin.

"Game On," October 30, 2002. Directed by Alex Graves; written by Aaron Sorkin and Paul Redford.

"Election Night," November 6, 2002. Directed by Lesli Linka Glatter; written by Aaron Sorkin.

"Process Stories," November 13, 2002. Directed by Christopher Misiano; written by Aaron Sorkin.

"Swiss Diplomacy," November 20, 2002. Directed by Christopher Misiano; written by Eli Attie and Kevin Falls.

"Arctic Radar," November 27, 2002. Directed by John Coles; written by Aaron Sorkin.

"Holy Night," December 11, 2002. Directed by Thomas Schlamme; written by Aaron Sorkin.

"Guns Not Butter," January 8, 2003. Directed by Bill D'Elia; written by Aaron Sorkin.

"The Long Goodbye," January 15, 2003. Directed by Alex Graves; written by John Robin Baitz.

# Appendix B:
## The West Wing *Character Directory*

| Character | Position | Actor |
|---|---|---|
| *The President and His Family* | | |
| Josiah "Jed" Bartlet | President | Martin Sheen |
| Abigail Bartlet | First Lady | Stockard Channing |
| Eleanor Bartlet | Daughter | Nina Siemaszko |
| Zoey Bartlet | Daughter | Elisabeth Moss |
| Dr. Bartlet | President's father | Lawrence O'Donnell |
| *The White House Staff* | | |
| Raqim Ali | Staffer | Ajay Naidu |
| Oliver Babish | Counsel | Oliver Platt |
| Claudia Jean (C.J.) Cregg | Press secretary | Allison Janney |
| Deborah Fiderer | Assistant | Lily Tomlin |
| Mandy Hampton | Media director | Moira Kelly |
| Ainsley Hayes | Associate counsel | Emily Procter |
| Delores Landingham | Assistant to president | Kathryn Joosten |
| Joshua Lyman | Deputy chief of staff | Bradley Whitford |
| Margaret | Assistant to chief of staff | Nicole Robinson |
| Leo McGarry | Chief of staff | John Spencer |
| Donnatella Moss | Assistant to deputy chief of staff | Janel Moloney |
| Sam Seaborn | Deputy communications director | Rob Lowe |

| Character | Position | Actor |
|-----------|----------|-------|
| Charles Young | Personal aide to the president | Dulé Hill |
| Toby Ziegler | Communications director | Richard Schiff |

### Cabinet Secretaries and Other Members of the Administration

| | | |
|-----------|----------|-------|
| Gen. Ed Barrie | Former army chief of staff | Tom Bower |
| Lewis Berryhill | Secretary of state | William Devane |
| Cashmen | Cabinet or sub-cabinet official | not pictured |
| Adm. Percy Fitzwallace | Chair, Joint Chiefs | John Amos |
| John Hoynes | Vice president | Tim Matheson |
| Nancy McNally | National security advisor | Anna Deavere Smith |
| Deborah O'Leary | HUD secretary | CCH Pounder |
| Scott Tate | NASA Public Affairs Officer | Troy Ruptash |
| Morris Tolliver | Naval Office/ presidential physician | Reuben Santiago-Hudson |
| Mickey Troop | Assistant secretary of state | Tony Plana |

### Political Consultants and Operatives

| | | |
|-----------|----------|-------|
| Amy Gardner | Lobbyist | Mary-Louise Parker |
| Bruno Gianelli | Campaign director | Ron Silver |
| Al Kiefer | Democratic pollster | John de Lancie |
| Joey Lucas | Democratic pollster | Marlee Matlin |
| Connie Tate | Political operative | Connie Britton |
| Doug Wegland | Political operative | Evan Handler |

### Members of Congress and Congessional Staff

| | | |
|-----------|----------|-------|
| Clifford Calley | Majority counsel | Mark Feuerstein |
| Peter Lien | U.S. representative (D-Tex.) | Art Chudabala |
| Becky Reeseman | U.S. representative (D-Mich.) | Amy Aquino |
| Mark Richardson | U.S. representative (N.Y.) | Thom Barry |
| Henry Shallick | U.S. representative (R-Mo.) | Corbin Bernsen |
| Matt Skinner | U.S. representative | Charley Lang |

| Character | Position | Actor |
| --- | --- | --- |
| Howard Stackhouse | U.S. senator (Minn.) | George Coe |
| Ann Stark | Senate Minority Leader chief of staff | Felicity Huffman |
| Joe Willis | U.S. representative (Ohio) | Al Fann |
| Jack Wooden | U.S. representative | not pictured |
| Andrea Wyatt | U.S. representative (Md.) | Kathleen York |

*Other Featured Characters*

| | | |
| --- | --- | --- |
| Juan Aguilar | Colombian drug dealer | not pictured |
| Jeff Breckenridge | Assistant attorney general nominee | Carl Lumbly |
| Ron Butterfield | Head, president's secret service detail | Michael O'Neill |
| Victor Campos | California labor leader | Miguel Sandoval |
| Michael Casper | FBI agent | Clark Gregg |
| Danny Concanon | Reporter | Timothy Busfield |
| Talmidge Cregg | Father of press secretary | Donald Moffat |
| Joseph Crouch | Associate justice, Supreme Court | Mason Adams |
| President Dessaline | President of Haiti | not pictured |
| Simon Donovan | Secret Service agent | Mark Harmon |
| Billy Fernandez | Presidential classroom student | Josh Zuckerman |
| Tabitha Fortis | U.S. poet laureate | Laura Dern |
| Stephanie Gault | Friend of Donna Moss | Jolie Jenkins |
| Mark Gottfried | Host, *Capitol Beat* | Ted McGinley |
| Peter Hans | Ambassador from Sweden | Erik Holland |
| Winnifred Hooper | GAO intern | Cara DeLizia |
| Nikolai Ivanovich | Representative of Russian president | Ian McShane |
| Dr. Jenna Jacobs | Radio personality | Claire Yarlett |
| Tom Jordan | Candidate for Congress | Jamie Denton |
| Matt Kelley | Father of college-aged daughter | John P. Connolly |
| Jordon Kendall | Attorney for chief of staff | Joanna Gleason |
| Vasily Konanov | Ukranian parliamentary reformer | Eugene Lazarev |
| Nadia Kozlowski | Russian ambassador to U.S. | Charlotte Cornwell |

| Character | Position | Actor |
|---|---|---|
| Laurie | Call girl/law student | Lisa Edelstein |
| Dr. David Lee | Anethesiologist | Ming Lo |
| Jack Lonefeather | Native American activist | Gary Farmer |
| Lord John Marbury | British ambassador to U.S. | Roger Rees |
| Jenny McGarry | Wife of chief of staff | Sara Botsford |
| Josephine McGarry | Sister to chief of staff | Deborah Hedwall |
| Roberto Mendoza | Supreme Court nominee | Edward James Olmos |
| Maggie Morningstar-Charles | Native American activist | Georgina Lightning |
| President Nimbala | President, Equatorial Kuhndu | Zakes Mokae |
| Mallory O'Brien | Daughter, chief of staff | Alison Smith |
| Robert Ritchie | Governor of Florida/ presidential candidate | James Brolin |
| Clement Rollins | Independent prosecutor | Nicholas Pryor |
| Miguel Santos | President, Colombia | not pictured |
| Abdul Shareef | Defense minister of Qumar | Al No'Mani |
| Tada Sumatra | Ambassador from Thailand | Alberto Isaac |
| Cornelius Sykes | Comedian | Rocky Carroll |
| Gina Toscano | Secret Service agent | Jorja Fox |
| Jhin Wei | Chinese refugee | Henry O |

# Notes

## Introduction

1. In his filmography of all Hollywood films featuring presidents since 1908, John Shelton Lawrence identifies 127 films. Lawrence, "A Filmography for Images of American Presidents," 383–402. For a good review of films that feature presidents in the 1990s, see Prince, "Political Film in the Nineties."

2. John M. Murphy reveals the power of popular culture and its depictions of the presidency when he suggests the possibility of a return to a heroic tradition for presidential rhetoric in his admiration for various mediated presidents such as Morgan Freeman in *Deep Impact,* Harrison Ford in *Air Force One,* Bill Pullman in *Independence Day,* Michael Douglas in *The American President,* Kevin Kline in *Dave,* and Martin Sheen in *TWW.* Murphy, "The Heroic Tradition"; see also Christensen, *Reel Politics; Gianos, Politics and Politicians;* and Giglio, *Here's Looking at You.* For a discussion of the presidency as depicted in popular fiction, see Rochelle, "The Literary Presidency."

3. Parry-Giles and Parry-Giles, *Constructing Clinton,* 3. "Presidentiality" is the discursive manifestation of Bruce Buchanan's discussion of "presidential culture" that involves citizens and the psychological impressions of the presidency that are "imbedded in the public mind." Buchanan, *The Citizen's Presidency,* 26. Our concern, of course, is with how these impressions are expressed rhetorically with ideological resonance for the U.S. political culture.

4. Greenstein, *The Presidential Difference,* 3; see also Ragsdale, "Studying the Presidency."

5. Norton, *Republic of Signs,* 91.

6. Hinckley, *The Symbolic Presidency.*

7. Skowronek, *The Politics That Presidents Make;* see also Abbott, *Strong Presidents;* Cronin and Genovese, *The Paradoxes of the American Presidency;* Hess, *Presidents and*

*the Presidency;* McDonald, *The American Presidency;* and Nelson, ed., *The Presidency and the Political System.*

8. Miroff, "The Presidency and the Public," 300.

9. Farrell, "Rhetorical Resemblance," 17.

10. Gebauer and Wolf, *Mimesis,* 31. An additional commentary on the materiality of mimetic images is offered by Twining, "On Poetry Considered as an Imitative Art," 45–46.

11. Gebauer and Wolf, *Mimesis,* 119. We do not ignore the shifts and changes in the role of mimesis in aesthetic and literary history. For our purposes, however, the constructed process of imitating the U.S. presidency is a component of the ideological meaning of *TWW.* For a fuller discussion of the shifting meanings of mimesis, see Auerbach, *Mimesis,* and Wilson, "The Racial Politics of Imitation."

12. Mikkel Borch-Jacobsen (*The Emotional Tie*) refers to mimetic efficacy in his discussion of the role of hypnosis in psychoanalysis and the relevance of rhetoric to the psychoanalytic process.

13. Discussions of the hyperreal nature of American politics can be found in Fiske, *Media Matters;* Luke, *Screens of Power;* Parry-Giles and Parry-Giles, "Meta-imaging"; Parry-Giles and Parry-Giles, *Constructing Clinton;* and Schram, "The Post-Modern Presidency."

14. Sigelman, "Taking Popular Fiction Seriously," 151. Additional discussions of political fiction are found in *Redefining the Political Novel,* ed. Harris; Howe, *Politics and the Novel;* and Milne, *The American Political Novel.*

15. A study from the University of Missouri demonstrates just how influential programs like *TWW,* and *TWW* in particular, can be to the formation of attitudes about the U.S. presidency. Holbert et al., "*The West Wing* as Endorsement."

16. Edelman, *From Art to Politics,* 66.

17. McBride and Toburen, "Deep Structures," 134.

18. The 2000 election saw an expansion of candidate appearances in various television venues. Al Gore and George W. Bush were featured on *Oprah, Late Night with David Letterman, The Tonight Show,* and *Live with Regis,* just to name the most noteworthy. This, of course, was preceded by Bill Clinton's famous appearances on *The Arsenio Hall Show* and the *Donahue* program in 1992 as well as numerous appearances by both Clinton and Republican Robert Dole in 1996. For discussions of this phenomenon see Davis and Owen, *New Media and American Politics,* and Diamond and Silverman, *White House to Your House.*

19. Mutz, "The Future of Political Communication Research," 231. For a discussion of the persuasive impact of news and entertainment content, see Eveland, "The Impact of News and Entertainment Media."

20. Pierre Bourdieu maintained in his lectures on television that the medium "poses a serious danger for all the various areas of cultural production—for art, for literature, for science, for philosophy, and for law." Bourdieu also argues (*On Television,* 10) that "television poses no less of a threat to political life and to democ-

racy itself." Another example comes from Jürgen Habermas, who observes that electronic mass media is significantly responsible for the disintegration of the public sphere. Habermas, *The Structural Transformation of the Public Sphere*.

21. Newcomb and Hirsch, "Television as a Cultural Forum," 457.

22. Newcomb and Hirsch, "Television as a Cultural Forum," 461.

23. Gross, *Up from Invisibility*, 6–7;see also Walters, who notes in *All the Rage* the cultural, social, political, and economic tensions that accompany the increasing visibility of gay men and lesbians in American life.

24. Street, *Politics and Popular Culture*, 34.

25. Chambers, *Representing the Family*, 93.

26. Projansky, *Watching Rape*, 18.

27. Dow, *Prime-Time Feminism*, 3.

28. There is, regrettably, a tendency at times to overstate the reach and impact of television and specific programs like *TWW*, and we do not want to commit that same error here. Heather Richardson Hayton, for example, asserts that *TWW* and the feature film *The Contender* resulted in lower voter turnout in the 2000 elections because both Al Gore and George W. Bush suffered by comparison to *TWW*'s Jed Bartlet and *The Contender*'s president played by Jeff Bridges. This speculation is interesting but ultimately lacking in evidence and unprovable in any meaningful sense. Hayton, "The King's Two Bodies," 78–79.

29. Miroff, "From 'Midcentury' to *Fin-de-Siècle*," 195.

30. Tulis, *The Rhetorical Presidency*, 203; see also Beasley, *You, the People*. The constitutive, nationalistic quality of language as it functions in the "presidencies" created by Aaron Sorkin is the subject of Quiring, "A Man of His Word."

31. Worthwhile discussions of the public nature of the presidency in the twentieth century are found in Hinckley, *The Symbolic Presidency*; and Kernell, *Going Public*. An extremely useful review of the literature about the rhetorical presidency is found in Stuckey and Antczak, "The Rhetorical Presidency."

32. Not everyone locates the rise of the rhetorical presidency; some scholars argue for a rhetorical focus to the presidency over its entire history. Laracey, *Presidents and the People*; Zarefsky, "The Presidency Has Always Been a Place for Rhetorical Leadership."

33. Ellis, ed., *Speaking to the People*.

34. Miroff, "From 'Midcentury' to *Fin-de-Siècle*."

35. Neustadt, *Presidential Power and the Modern Presidents*; Schlesinger, *The Imperial Presidency*.

36. Hargrove, *The President as Leader*, vii–viii.

37. Stuckey, *The President as Interpreter-in-Chief*, 1. Vanessa B. Beasley makes a similar argument about the important role that the rhetorical president plays ("Engendering Democratic Change").

38. Miller, *The Seventies Now*; Schulman, *The Seventies*; Woodward, *Shadow*.

39. Walsh, *Feeding the Beast*, 245.

40. Roderick Hart ("The End of the American Presidency") asserts that television is to blame for the end of the American presidency, evidenced by the 1988 clash between Dan Rather and George H. W. Bush concerning Iran-contra.

41. For detailed discussions of the public/private distinction and its role in political culture, see *Public and Private*, ed. Passerin d'Entrèves and Vogel; Habermas, *The Structural Transformation of the Public Sphere;* and *Public and Private in Thought and Practice*, ed. Weintraub and Kumar. The erosion of the public/private distinction in presidential politics is discussed in Parry-Giles and Parry-Giles, "Political Scopophilia."

42. Waterman, Wright, and St. Clair, *The Image-Is-Everything Presidency*, 161.

43. Sorkin's other credits include *Sports Night* (an ABC comedy-drama about a twenty-four-hour sports television network), *The American President,* and *A Few Good Men.* At the end of the fourth season of *TWW,* Sorkin announced he would leave the show, along with executive producer Thomas Schlamme, after considerable tension with the program's production company, Warner Brothers. Murphy and Schwed, "Broken Wing."

44. Rob Lowe, Seaborn, left the series in the fourth season when the Sam Seaborn character agreed to run for Congress in a special campaign occasioned by the victory of a dead candidate in the November election. He was replaced by a new speechwriter, Will Bailey (Josh Malina).

45. The show's characters routinely circulate through the offices and corridors of the White House, going in and out of meetings and handling competing tasks and conversations simultaneously. As Lewis Grossberger noted in *MediaWeek,* "the producers realized the show would be big on talk," but conversation is not visually exciting "so the actors have to shout their lines while rushing past each other and racing in and out of each other's offices. Everyone is constantly in motion, spouting political gibberish." Grossberger, "Now and Before," 82. Patrick Finn remarks that the use of a steadicam by *TWW*'s camera operators reinscribes a feeling of order and stability even as the characters constantly move around and through the offices in the White House. Finn, *"The West Wing*'s Textual President," 115–16.

46. Gitlin, *The Whole World Is Watching*, 49.

47. Byrne, "Will NBC Re-Elect 'West Wing'?"

48. Waxman, "Inside *The West Wing*'s New World."

49. Ibid., 94.

50. Rubinstein, "Politically Correct," 74.

51. Murphy, "House Call."

52. Miller, "The Real White House," 88. Miller particularly highlights, as an example of the show's realism, the discussion between Sam and C.J. about the census sampling issue. Miller's conclusion was that NBC's *TWW* "covered it better" than did the news divisions of the same network.

53. Bakhtin, "Forms of Time and of the Chronotope," 84.

54. Levine, *"The West Wing* (NBC) and the West Wing (D.C.)," 62; see also Levine, "The Transformed Presidency." Another author in the same collection worries that

the inaccuracies of *TWW* may interfere with the program's utility as a teaching tool. Beavers, "*The West Wing* as a Pedagogical Tool"; see also Sutin, "The Presidential Powers of Josiah Bartlet."

55. Pompper, "*The West Wing*: White House Narratives That Journalism Cannot Tell," 19. For a discussion of the backstage aspects of politics, see Meyrowitz, *No Sense of Place.*

56. "Aaron Sorkin."

57. Podhoretz, "The Liberal Imagination," 23.

58. Lehmann, "The Feel-Good Presidency."

59. McKisack, "*The West Wing* Is Not a Wet Dream"; see also Mills, "Prime Time White House."

60. This analysis concerns the intersectionality of romance, gender, race, militarism, and nationalism in *TWW* and thus is influenced by our individual subject positions as reader/critics of the text. Trevor Parry-Giles is a Latino/Anglo straight male concerned with progressive politics and a scholar of legal and political communication; Shawn J. Parry-Giles is an Anglo straight female who is a feminist scholar and also a scholar of presidential war discourse. Both of us are university professors and reside in the United States; we are married to each other and have two children. The multicultural identity of our family promotes sensitivity and concern with matters of race and issues affecting developing nations.

61. Bruner, *Strategies of Remembrance,* 1.

62. Anderson, *Imagined Communities,* 6.

63. Beasley, *You, the People,* 7.

64. Anderson, *Imagined Communities,* 22–23.

65. Mayer, "Gender Ironies of Nationalism," 10.

66. Pickering and Kehde, "Introduction," 3.

67. Bonnie Dow defines polyvalence as "the process through which audiences receive essentially similar meanings from television texts but may evaluate those meanings differently depending upon their value systems" (*Prime-Time Feminism,* 12).

68. By using the term *intersectionality,* we acknowledge the "simultaneity of systems" in shaping "experience and identity," which emphasizes the "intersectional nature of hierarchies at all levels of social life. . . . Women and men are differently embedded in locations created by these cross-cutting hierarchies. As a result, women and men throughout the social order experience different forms of privilege and subordination, depending on their race, class, gender, and sexuality." Zinn and Dill, "Theorizing Difference," 327.

69. Lane, "The White House Culture of Gender and Race," 38.

70. During *TWW*'s first season, DeWayne Wickham of *USA Today* maintained that Ben Johnson of President Clinton's Initiative for One America visited with *TWW*'s producers to encourage greater levels of diversity on the program so as to help "this nation escape the bog of our racial division." Wickham, "TV's White House."

71. Gary Gerstle defines civic nationalism as "a people held together by common

blood and skin color and by an inherited fitness for self-government." Gerstle defines "civic nationalism" as a "belief in the fundamental equality of all human beings" (*American Crucible*, 4–5). In chapter 3 we offer a more thorough discussion of civic and racialized nationalism.

72. Lane, "The White House Culture of Gender and Race," 32–36; McKisack, "*The West Wing* Is Not a Wet Dream."

73. Burgoyne, *Film Nation*, 11.

74. Bruner, *Strategies of Remembrance*, 5.

75. Burgoyne, *Film Nation*, 11.


## Chapter 1: *The West Wing* as a Political Romance

1. "Changing Images of Government in TV Entertainment."

2. Jon Roper notes the contrast between the conspiracy films that portray presidents in a negative light (i.e., *All the President's Men, Nixon, Absolute Power*) and the romantic visions of the presidency put forth in films such as *Independence Day* and *Air Force One*. Roper, *The American Presidents*, 211–13.

3. Marlow, *Air Force One*.

4. Devlin and Emmerich, *Independence Day*.

5. Aaron Sorkin, the primary creative force behind *TWW*, also wrote *The American President*. For a discussion of the relationship between *The American President* and *TWW*, see Vest, "From *The American President* to *The West Wing*." It is noteworthy that Sorkin's most successful projects, *A Few Good Men, The American President*, and *TWW* are all structured as romantic narratives and feature romantic heroes on noble quests against some enemy or obstacle. Another of Sorkin's projects, *Sports Night*, although successful with critics, did not do well with viewers, lasting only a short time on ABC. *Sports Night* was not structured as a romantic narrative.

6. Nelson, "Evaluating the Presidency," in *The Presidency and the Political System*, 5. Nelson also notes competing explanations for the presidency that characterize scholarly appraisals, the "satan model" and the "Samson model."

7. Abbott, *Strong Presidents*, 233.

8. Caudwell, *Romance and Realism*, 37.

9. Frye, *The Secular Scripture*, 55.

10. Chesebro, "Communication, Values, and Popular Television Series," 213.

11. Fisher, "Romantic Democracy," 302.

12. Woodrow Wilson, *Constitutional Government*, 68.

13. Hunter, "Dante's Watergate," 305.

14. Frye, *Anatomy of Criticism*, 186. In *Tropics of Discourse*, historian Hayden White explores the role of literary genres in general, and romance in particular, on the ways in which we communicate historical knowledge. In legal discourse, rhetorical analyst William Lewis notes, romance tends to "reinforce the authority and legitimacy

of current legal structures and their related conceptions of order" ("Of Innocence, Exclusion, and the Burning of Flags," 12).

15. Frye, *The Secular Scripture*, 50.

16. Best and Kellner, *The Postmodern Turn*, 132.

17. Lewis, "Of Innocence, Exclusion, and the Burning of Flags," 12.

18. Murphy, "Knowing the President," 30.

19. Bass, "The Romance as Rhetorical Dissociation," 259, 268; Elam, "Feminism and the Postmodern," 196; and Faris, "Scheherazade's Children," 185.

20. Bhabha, "Introduction," in *Nation and Narration*, 2.

21. Sommer is specifically concerned with the role of romance narratives in Latin America. "Irresistible Romance," 84.

22. Fisher, "Romantic Democracy," 300. Rhetorical critics Zagacki and King also reveal the persistence of romantic nationalism in the U.S. context and note that the "key to Reagan's popular success . . . was his ability to exploit the traditional tension between a cultural undercurrent of romantic civic nationalism and the imperatives of techno-scientific advance." Zagacki and King, "Reagan, Romance and Technology," 2.

23. Roper, *The American Presidents*, 5.

24. Sorkin, The West Wing: *The Official Companion*, 260.

25. Roper, *The American Presidents*, 211.

26. Frye, *Anatomy of Criticism*, 187.

27. Meyrowitz, *No Sense of Place*, 268–304.

28. All quotations of dialogue from *TWW* are derived from the authors' transcriptions of the program as aired. When possible, transcriptions were checked against available transcript versions of the program's episodes.

29. Cawelti, *Adventure, Mystery, and Romance*, 40.

30. Chesebro, "Communication, Values, and Popular Television Series," 206.

31. Burton, *The Learned Presidency*, 13–15.

32. Waterman, Wright, and St. Clair, *The Image-as-Everything Presidency*.

33. Abbott, *Strong Presidents*, 1–4.

34. Frye, *Anatomy of Criticism*, 187.

35. Deming, "*Hill Street Blues* as Narrative," 15.

36. Johnson, "As Housewives We Are Worms," 478.

37. White, *Figural Realism*, 68.

38. Schwartz, "The Character of Washington," 217–18; see also Hay, "George Washington," 780–91.

39. Hart, *Seducing America*; see also Meyrowitz, *No Sense of Place*; and Meyrowitz, "New Sense of Politics," 117–38.

40. Edwards, *On Deaf Ears*; Tulis, *The Rhetorical Presidency*.

41. Fisher, "Romantic Democracy," 301.

42. Norton, *Republic of Signs*, 105. In their analysis of FDR's rhetorical management

of his physical disabilities, Houck and Kiewe (*FDR's Body Politics*) articulate the importance of physical strength, or the appearance of physical prowess, to the presidency.

43. The relationship between presidential health, public trust, and the full disclosure of presidential health crises is the subject of Ferrell, *Ill-Advised;* see also Gilbert, *The Mortal Presidency.*

44. Beavers, "*The West Wing* as a Pedagogical Tool," 184.

45. Thompson, *Political Scandal,* 245; see also Dunn, *The Scarlet Thread of Scandal.*

46. O'Connor and Rollins, "Introduction," 5–6.

47. Edelman, *Constructing the Political Spectacle,* 45.

48. Langston, *With Reverence and Contempt,* 13.

49. The translation comes from http://www.televisionwithoutpity.com/story.cgi?show=4&story=1718&limit=all&sort=.

50. Thompson, *Political Scandal,* 235; see also Lee and Barton, "Clinton's Rhetoric of Contrition," 219–46.

51. Thompson, *Political Scandal,* 12.

52. The most immediate impact on *TWW* of the September 11 attacks was the airing of a special episode in lieu of the season premiere. Entitled "Isaac and Ishmael," it implicitly addressed questions about terrorism and Islamic fundamentalism through the plot of a fictionalized terrorist attack on the Bartlet White House (chapter 5).

53. Popkin, *The Reasoning Voter;* Windt Jr., "Presidential Rhetoric," 24–34.

54. Parry-Giles and Parry-Giles, *Constructing Clinton,* 66–75.

55. Edelman, *Constructing the Political Spectacle,* 74.

56. This impression of the presidency was especially popular in describing the Clinton administration. For instance, John Zaller notes Clinton's use of public opinion polling in the policy shifts made by his administration following the 1994 midterm elections. Zaller, "Monica Lewinsky and the Mainsprings of American Politics," 261–62. Most commentators who reach this impression rely heavily on Dick Morris's account of working with the Clinton White House—a relatively short tenure ended by the revelations of Morris's dalliances with a prostitute. Morris, *Behind the Oval Office.*

57. Roper, *The American Presidents,* 116.

58. Stuckey and Wabshall, "Sex, Lies, and Presidential Leadership," 520.

59. Ibid., 526.

60. Ezell, "The Sincere Sorkin White House," 162.

61. Cronin and Genovese, *The Paradoxes of the American Presidency,* 150–51.

62. Edelman, *Constructing the Political Spectacle,* 67.

63. Hargrove, *The President as Leader,* 26.

64. Silberstein, *War of Words,* 14.

65. Burton, *The Learned Presidency,* 198.

66. Stuckey and Wabshall, "Sex, Lies, and Presidential Leadership," 518.

67. Sammyjoe1984, on-line posting, Dec. 21, 2002, http://groups.msn.com/TheWestWing/.

68. Han_yang, "Best Show on TV," on-line posting, Jan. 15, 2004, http://us.imdb.com/.

69. Whiteotter, "Brilliant," on-line posting, Aug. 27, 2003, http://www.us.imdb.com/.

70. Sloop, *Disciplining Gender,* 22.

71. Fisher, "Reaffirmation and Subversion of the American Dream," 167.

72. Langston, *With Reverence and Contempt,* 134.

73. Barger, "The Incredible Shrinking Image," 57–80.

## Chapter 2: Gendered Nationalism and *The West Wing*

1. Pickering and Kehde, *Narratives of Nostalgia, Gender, and Nationalism,* 6.

2. Eley and Suny, "Introduction," 9.

3. Mosse, *Nationalism and Sexuality,* 18.

4. Blom, "Gender and Nation in International Comparison," 8.

5. Kersh, *Dreams of a More Perfect Union,* 26, 44, 94, 118.

6. McClintock, "'No Longer in a Future Heaven,'" 91.

7. Yuval-Davis, *Gender and Nation,* 92.

8. Mayer, "Gender Ironies of Nationalism," 1–2, 6.,

9. Smith-Rosenberg, "Political Camp," 275.

10. Connell, *Masculinities,* 68.

11. Beynon, *Masculinities and Culture,* 27, 28, 33.

12. Blom, "Gender and Nation in International Comparison," 17.

13. Mostov, "Sexing the Nation/Desexing the Body," 91.

14. Arendt reminds us that such discernments between the public political sphere versus private domestic space have roots in antiquity: "The *polis* was distinguished from the household in that it knew only 'equals,' whereas the household was the center of the strictest inequality" (*The Human Condition,* 32).

15. Mayer, "Gender Ironies of Nationalism."

16. Smith-Rosenberg, "Political Camp," 275.

17. Kerber, *Women of the Republic.*

18. Hardesty, *Women Called to Witness,* 90. For additional insight into the impact of benevolence ideology, see Ginzberg, *Women and the Work of Benevolence.* Joyce Hope Scott also notes that "Black women had . . . positioned themselves firmly at the forefront of the nationalist movement as early as the late eighteenth century with their benevolent and mutual relief societies followed by antislavery societies in the 1830s" ("From Foreground to Margin," 298).

19. Parry-Giles and Blair, "The Rise of the Rhetorical First Lady," 586.

20. Mayer, "Gender Ironies of Nationalism," 6; Werbner, "Political Motherhood and the Feminisation of Citizenship," 221–22.

21. Ibid.; Enloe, *The Morning After,* 238.

22. Beynon, *Masculinities and Culture,* 65; Mostov, "Sexing the Nation/Desexing the Body," 91.

23. Eley and Suny, "Introduction," 26.

24. Mostov, "Sexing the Nation/Desexing the Body."

25. Eley and Suny, "Introduction," 26–27.

26. Mostov, "Sexing the Nation/Desexing the Body," 92, 100.

27. Kersh, *Dreams of a More Perfect Union,* 2. Kersh's study centers on the constructions of "union," a term he believes holds "meaningful analytic distinctions" from conceptions of nationalism even though studies of nationalism and federalism "in the U.S. context are important sources of inspiration" for conceptions of union.

28. Tickner, *Gendering World Politics,* 54.

29. Eley and Suny, "Introduction," 32.

30. Bonnie Dow provides a useful definition of post-feminism: "[it] represents . . . a hegemonic negotiation of second-wave ideals, in which the presumption of equality for women in the public sphere has been retained. This presumption, serving as the 'essence' of feminism, requires the least ideological adjustment from men [and women] and from the culture at large. . . . At the same time, the most radical aspects of feminism, those centered in sexual politics and a profound awareness of power differences between the sexes at all levels and in all arenas, have been discarded as irrelevant or threatening" (*Prime-Time Feminism,* 87–88).

31. Kersh, *Dreams of a More Perfect Union,* 28.

32. Welter, "The Cult of True Womanhood," 151–74.

33. Sorkin, The West Wing: *The Official Companion,* 47.

34. Abbott, *Strong Presidents.*

35. Beynon, *Masculinities and Culture,* 65–66. Hegemonic masculinity is defined by Carrigan, Connell, and Lee as "centrally connected with the institutionalization of men's dominance over women" and relates to the ways that "groups of men inhabit positions of power and wealth, and how they legitimate and reproduce the social relationships that generate their dominance" ("Toward a New Sociology of Masculinity," 592).

36. McClintock, "'No Longer in a Future Heaven,'" 93.

37. Edelman, *Constructing the Political Spectacle,* 61.

38. Anthias and Yuval-Davis, "Introduction," 9–10.

39. For more information on the ways in which the republican motherhood frames the role of the first lady, see Parry-Giles and Blair, "The Rise of the Rhetorical First Lady," 565–99.

40. For more information on the relationship between women's political activities and health issues, see Parry-Giles and Blair, "The Rise of the Rhetorical First Lady," 576–85.

41. Anderson, "Introduction," 12.

42. Vavrus, *Postfeminist News,* 23.

43. Whelehan, *Modern Feminist Thought,* 221.

44. Burke, *The Rhetoric of Religion*, 174–78.

45. Doane and Hodges, *Nostalgia and Sexual Difference*, 133.

46. Imelda Whelehan explains that the beginnings of the second-wave of feminism are traced to the 1960s when women found themselves excluded from the leadership of many "left-wing" political groups. As many white women began creating their own seemingly "non-hierarchical women's liberation's groups" they started to "interrogate the social and material conditions of individual women's existence, often with the longer term aim of creating an agenda for political transformation of the social and economic status of women." The second-wave gained strength throughout the 1970s and began to lose force in the early 1980s as the New Right gained political power and the constitutional battle over the Equal Rights Amendment failed. Whelehan, *Modern Feminist Thought*, 4.

47. McClintock, "'No Longer in a Future Heaven,'" 91, emphasis in the original.

48. Casey et al., *Television Studies*, 48.

49. Mostov, "Sexing the Nation/Desexing the Body," 102.

50. Jasinski, "(Re)constituting Community," 480.

51. Mulvey, *Visual and Other Pleasures*, 20.

52. Grosz, *Volatile Bodies*, 14.

53. Griffin, "The Great War Photographs," 147.

54. Mayer, "Gender Ironies of Nationalism," 16–18. Portraying women without pants may not seem unusual, but imagine plotlines in which male staffers appear in bathrobes or coats only while on the job. Such actions would seem antithetical for men in *TWW* yet they are normalized for women, who are commonly sexualized.

55. Norton, *Republic of Signs*, 3, 60, 126.

56. Yuval-Davis, *Gender and Nation*, 67.

57. Eley and Suny, "Introduction," 26.

58. Even though Simon is not killed in the line of duty, he is in New York because of his commitment to the nation, protecting one of the key female figures of this nationalism romance. The staff and the president all communicate significant signs of grief upon hearing of Simon's death, evidencing his role in the nationalist narrative.

59. Mayer, "Gender Ironies of Nationalism," 18.

60. Wenk, "Gendered Representations of the Nation's Past and Future," 68.

61. French, "Is There a Feminist Aesthetic?" 71.

62. Jasinski, "(Re)constituting Community," 480; see also Arendt, *The Human Condition*.

63. Beiner, *Political Judgment*, 125.

64. Jasinski, "(Re)constituting Community," 468–69.

65. Enloe, *The Morning After*, 237. Enloe is specifically referring to women as traitors in postwar contexts.

66. Breuilly, "Approaches to Nationalism," 149.

67. Kress and van Leeuwen, *Reading Images*, 81.

68. Connell, *Masculinities,* 77–78.

69. Burgoyne, *Film Nation,* 15.

70. Trujillo, "Hegemonic Masculinity on the Mound," 291.

71. Brownmiller, *Femininity,* 16.

72. Dow, *Prime-Time Feminism,* 149.

73. For a discussion of the demands facing women in politics see Witt, Paget, and Matthews, *Running as a Woman.*

74. Gatens, *Imaginary Bodies,* 54, emphasis in the original.

75. Hosken, "Female Genital Mutilation and Human Rights," 13.

76. Okin, "Feminism, Women's Human Rights, and Cultural Differences," 30.

77. Mohanty, "Under Western Eyes," 260.

78. For more discussion of the fear popularly associated with images of strong women, see Jamieson, *Beyond the Double Bind;* and Parry-Giles, "Mediating Hillary Rodham Clinton," 205–26.

79. Norton, *Republic of Signs,* 127–28.

80. Dow, *Prime-Time Feminism,* 92, 95.

81. Enloe, *The Morning After,* 239.

82. Eley and Suny, "Introduction," 27.

83. Connell, *Masculinities,* 37.

84. Yuval-Davis, *Gender and Nation,* 47.

85. Stec, "Female Sacrifice," 140.

86. Norton, *Republic of Signs,* 121.

87. Yuval-Davis, *Gender and Nation,* 39.

88. Blom, "Gender and Nation in International Comparison," 8.

## Chapter 3: Racialized Nationalism and *The West Wing*

1. Act of March 26, 1790 (Naturalization Law of 1790), 1 Stat. 103–4.

2. Light and Chaloupka, "Angry White Men," 333, 336.

3. López, *White by Law,* 31.

4. Marx, *Making Race and Nation,* 268.

5. Gerstle, *American Crucible,* 4–5.

6. Marx, *Making Race and Nation,* 3.

7. Ibid., 60.

8. Goodman, *Of One Blood,* 6–7.

9. Riley, *The Presidency and the Politics of Racial Inequality,* 50–51.

10. Goodman, *Of One Blood,* 10–11, 15, 21–22; Marx, *Making Race and Nation,* 59. Although the organizers of the American Colonization Society first met in 1816, the group officially formed in 1817.

11. Zarefsky, "Consistency and Change in Lincoln's Rhetoric," 29.

12. Rathbun, "The Debate over Annexing Texas," 467.

13. Goodman, *Of One Blood,* 21–22.

14. Carr, *Black Nationalism in the New World*, 14.

15. Kersh, *Dreams of a More Perfect Union*, 6, 116.

16. Fields, *Union of Words*, 196–98.

17. Kersh, *Dreams of a More Perfect Union*, 115.

18. Zarefsky, "Consistency and Change in Lincoln's Rhetoric," 39.

19. Zarefsky, "The Continuing Fascination with Lincoln," 339.

20. Marx, *Making Race and Nation*, 135; *Plessy v. Ferguson*, 163 U.S. 537 (1896).

21. Pierson, "Nations," 49–50.

22. Kersh, *Dreams of a More Perfect Union*, 263; Chinese Exclusion Act, 47th Cong., lst sess, 1882, chpt. 126.

23. Kersh, *Dreams of a More Perfect Union*, 263.

24. Immigration Act of 1907, 34 Statutes-at-Large 898.

25. Gerstle, *American Crucible*, 96–98; López, *White by Law*, 37–39.

26. López, *White by Law*, 38,

27. Roosevelt, *American Ideals*, 28.

28. Pickus, "Which America?" 36.

29. Gerstle, *American Crucible*, 8–9.

30. Wilson, "An Address in Philadelphia," 148.

31. Andrews, "Presidential Leadership," 141.

32. For more information on presidential advancements on race see Carcasson and Rice, "The Promise and Failure of President Clinton's Race Initiative," 243–74; Fields, *Union of Words*; Gerstle, *American Crucible*; Goldzwig, "Civil Rights and the Cold War," 143–69; Goldzwig and Dionisopoulos, "Crisis at Little Rock"; and Murphy, "Inventing Authority," 71–89.

33. Pauley, *The Modern Presidency*, 220.

34. Riley, "The Presidency, Leadership, and Race," 71.

35. O'Reilly, *Nixon's Piano*, 9.

36. Fields, *Union of Words*, 199.

37. Parry-Giles and Parry-Giles, *Constructing Clinton*, 9.

38. Marx, *Making Race and Nation*, 5, 270.

39. Swain and Nieli, eds., "Forging a Common Identity," 5.

40. Fine, "Benign Nationalism?" 159.

41. Fiske, *Media Matters*, 42.

42. Seshadri-Crooks, *Desiring Whiteness*, 3–4.

43. Fiske, *Media Matters*, 42; see also Winant, *Racial Conditions*.

44. López, *White by Law*, xiii, 190.

45. Gerstle, *American Crucible*, 42–43.

46. Gray, *Watching Race*, 168.

47. hooks, *Black Looks*, 19.

48. Fiske, *Media Matters*, 47–48.

49. Nelson, *National Manhood*, 181–82.

50. Fields, *Union of Words*, 127, 132.

51. Dorsey and Harlow, "'We Want Americans Pure and Simple,'" 69, 71 (emphasis in original).

52. Baynes, "White Out," 317.

53. In a season-three episode, "The Two Bartlets," President Bartlet's mother is depicted as no longer living.

54. López, *White by Law*, 162.

55. Gerstle, *American Crucible*, 23.

56. Nelson, *National Manhood*, 67, emphasis in the original.

57. Nakayama, "Show/Down Time," 162–79; Said, *Orientalism*.

58. Hall, "Ethnicity: Identity and Difference," 339. This essay was originally published in *Radical America* 23 (Oct.–Dec. 1989): 9–20.

59. López, *White by Law*, 163.

60. Ibid., 167.

61. Swain, *The New White Nationalism*, 19.

62. Mahoney, "Recognizing the Constitutional Significance of Harmful Speech," 283–84.

63. Gerstle, *American Crucible*, 79.

64. López, *White by Law*, 169–71.

65. Nelson, *National Manhood*, 226.

66. Renshon, ed., "Dual Citizenship + Multiple Loyalties = One America?" 258.

67. Riley, *The Presidency and the Politics of Racial Inequality*, 122.

68. Fine, "Benign Nationalism?," 151.

69. Yuval-Davis, *Gender and Nation*, 44.

70. Gramsci, *Selections from the Prison Notebooks of Antonio Gramsci*, 12–13.

71. hooks, *Black Looks*, 17.

72. Skrentny, "Affirmative Action and the Failure of Presidential Leadership," 112–13, 122, 135.

73. Carr, *Black Nationalism in the New World*, 187, 191.

74. Wander, "The Third Persona," 209–10.

75. Hall, "Ethnicity," 345.

76. López, *White by Law*, 162.

77. Gray, *Watching Race*, 15.

78. Nelson, *National Manhood*, 204–5.

## Chapter 4: Militarized Nationalism and *The West Wing*

1. Beer, *Meanings of War and Peace*, 5; Fields, *Union of Words*, 36.

2. Mead, *Special Providence*, 17.

3. Tickner, *Gendering World Politics*, 49, 56.

4. Cronin and Genovese, *The Paradoxes of the American Presidency*, 69–70.

5. Dallek, *Hail to the Chief*, vxiii. Forrest McDonald explains, for example, that in February 1802 Congress empowered President Thomas Jefferson to use armed ves-

sels to attack ships near Tripoli, an act that helped Jefferson fight piracy in Algiers and Morocco. McDonald, *The American Presidency*, 264–65; see also Boot, *The Savage Wars of Peace*.

6. Monroe, "Seventh Annual Message," 218. It is also important to understand that Monroe's secretary of state, John Quincy Adams, was the primary author of the Monroe Doctrine. Stephanson, *Manifest Destiny*, 59.

7. Hardt and Negri, *Empire*, 177–78.

8. Weinberg, *Manifest Destiny*, x.

9. Sanford, ed., *Manifest Destiny and the Imperialism Question*, 26.

10. O'Sullivan, "The Great Nation of Futurity," 427. The essay most often attributed with creating the phrase *manifest destiny* was published in 1845 by O'Sullivan, who wrote that those who opposed the annexation of Texas did so "for the avowed object of thwarting our policy and hampering our power, limiting our greatness and checking the fulfillment of our manifest destiny to overspread the continent allotted by Providence for the free development of our yearly multiplying millions." O'Sullivan, "Annexation," 5.

11. Mead, *Special Providence*.

12. Kersh, *Dreams of a More Perfect Union*, 228.

13. Turner, "The Significance of the Frontier," 199–201, 210–11, 217.

14. Wiebe, *Who We Are*, 75.

15. Roosevelt, "The Strenuous Life," 328. Roosevelt fashioned the Roosevelt Corollary throughout his presidency and articulated it during his "Annual Message to Congress" on December 6, 1904, when the exigence of U.S. intervention in Latin America represented an important public issue. Roosevelt, "Message of the President," 1–40.

16. Roosevelt, "Address of President Roosevelt," 16.

17. Roosevelt, *American Ideals*, 46–47.

18. Roosevelt, "The Strenuous Life," 321.

19. Kersh, *Dreams of a More Perfect Union*, 268.

20. Mead, *Special Providence*, 220–21.

21. McDonald, *The American Presidency*, 402.

22. Hargrove, *The President as Leader*.

23. Tulis, *The Rhetorical Presidency*, 203.

24. Simpson, *Science of Coercion*, 37.

25. "A Report to the National Security Council," 1–3.

26. Parry-Giles, *The Rhetorical Presidency*, 185.

27. Beer and Hariman, eds., *Post-Realism*, 4–5; Beynon, *Masculinities and Culture*, 89–93.

33. Beer and Hariman, *Post-Realism*, 6–10; Beer, *Making War and Peace*, 84, 165, 167.

34. Tickner, *Gendering World Politics*, 41–42.

35. Fiske, *Media Matters*, 11.

36. Enloe, *The Morning After*, 248.

37. Ivie, "Realism Masking Fear," 64–65.

38. Knott, *Secret and Sanctioned,* 4, 9.

39. Burke, *Attitudes toward History,* 42–43.

40. Bauer, "The Nation," 63.

41. Scott, "Cold War and Rhetoric," 12.

42. Holloway, "The Strategic Defense Initiative and the Technological Sublime."

43. Parry-Giles, *The Rhetorical Presidency,* 151–82. See a discussion of Eisenhower's construction of the "Atoms for Peace" campaign that accentuated the immorality of the Soviet Union, which was designed to cast suspicion on a Soviet-engineered nuclear program.

44. Beer, *Making War and Peace,* 170.

45. Ivie, "Tragic Fear and the Rhetorical Presidency," 172.

46. Eley and Suny, eds., "Introduction," in *Becoming National,* 26; see also Beynon, *Masculinities and Culture,* 67.

47. Connell, *Masculinities,* 45.

48. Kauffman, *Selling Outer Space,* 1.

49. Ibid., 4, 136.

50. Ibid., 5.

51. Ibid., 1, 4.

52. Connell, *Masculinities,* 204.

53. Jamieson, *Beyond the Double Bind,* 18, 57.

54. Allen, "Gender, Sexuality and the Military Model," 309.

55. Mosse, *Nationalism and Sexuality,* 103–4.

56. Tickner, *Gendering World Politics,* 57.

57. Connell, *Gender and Power;* see also Parry-Giles and Parry-Giles, "Gendered Politics and Presidential Image Construction," 337–53.

58. The Clinton administration worked with Hollywood to lessen the amount of violence aired through television and film, and the president called on the entertainment industry to work with the administration to create more positive television shows for children in his 1996 State of the Union address. Clinton, "1996 State of the Union Address."

59. Fletcher, *Romantics at War,* 10.

60. Lakoff, *The Language War,* 21.

61. Fletcher, *Romantics at War,* 14.

62. Yuval-Davis, *Gender and Nation,* 44; see also Azzi, "From Competitive Interests, Perceived Injustice, and Identity Needs."

63. Curtin, "Organizing Difference on Global TV," 342.

64. Robinson, "Promoting Capitalist Polyarchy," 308–14.

65. Fiske, *Media Matters,* 42.

66. Cohn, "Wars, Wimps, and Women," 234.

67. Fletcher, *Romantics at War,* 13.

68. Barry, *The Sword of Justice,* 15; see also Regan, *Just War,* 14; and Elshtain, *Just War against Terror,* 202–3.

69. Beer, *Making War and Peace,* 91.

70. Regan, *Just War,* 20–23.

71. Cooke, "Wo-man, Retelling the War Myth," 181.

72. Dandeker, "Nationalism, Nation-States, and Violence," 27.

73. Regan, *Just War,* 94.

74. Freedman, "A New Type of War," 46.

75. hooks, *Black Looks,* 26, 102.

76. Regan, *Just War,* 88.

77. Ruddick, "Notes Toward a Feminist Peace Politics," 115–16.

78. During season four, we learn that after Shareef was shot his airplane was crashed into the Bermuda Triangle. Despite the destruction of evidence, the Qumaris discover the plane and allege publicly that Israel downed it, even though, privately, they believe the United States was responsible. The Israelis counterattack when the Qumaris retaliate by downing an Israeli jet, killing an Israeli leader who visited Leo and knew the truth about the U.S. involvement. In the end, the Bartlet administration pressures Qumari leaders to stop any further attacks against Israel. The situation is resolved, at least for the moment, by the episode "Game On."

79. Booth and Dunne, eds., "Worlds in Collision," 8–13.

80. Parry-Giles, *The Rhetorical Presidency,* 192.

81. Fletcher, *Romantics at War,* 11–12.

82. Farrell, "Rhetorical Resemblance," 13.

## Chapter 5: *The West Wing*'s Prime-Time Nationalism

1. For an analysis of Bush's various rhetorical performances in the aftermath of September 11, see Silberstein, *War of Words.* A discussion of the composition of Bush's September 20 speech before Congress is found in Max, "The Making of the Speech," 32–37. A more compelling critical analysis is offered in Murphy, "'Our Mission and Our Moment,'" 607–32.

2. Langston, *With Reverence and Contempt,* xii (emphasis in original).

3. Parry-Giles, "Character, the Constitution, and the Ideological Embodiment of 'Civil Rights,'" 377.

4. Nye, *American Technological Sublime.*

5. Diamond and Silverman, *White House to Your House;* Hart, *Seducing America;* Meyrowitz, *No Sense of Place;* Parry-Giles and Parry-Giles, *Constructing Clinton;* Schram, "The Post-Modern Presidency," 210–16.

6. Shohat and Stam, "From the Imperial Family to the Transnational Imaginary," 154.

7. Giglio, *Here's Looking at You,* 115.

8. Anderson, *Imagined Communities.*

9. Appadurai, "Disjuncture and Difference," 273.

10. Balibar, *Politics and the Other Scene,* 61. For a discussion of Balibar and his con-

ception of ambiguous universality, with specific attention to the September 11 attacks and some mention of *TWW*, see Mailloux, "Contingent Universals," 1583–604.

11. For a full discussion of the role of identity and authenticity in multiculturalism, see Taylor, "The Politics of Recognition," 25–73; see also Levy, *The Multiculturalism of Fear* and Vincent, *Nationalism and Particularity.*

12. Gitlin, *The Twilight of Common Dreams,* 227–28. A series of essays that uphold the value of multiculturalism is offered in *Multi-America,* ed. Reed.

13. Schlesinger Jr., *The Disuniting of America,* 17; see also Wilkinson, *One Nation Indivisible.*

14. Barry, *Culture and Equality,* 305.

15. Smith, "Photographing the 'American Negro,'" 78.

16. West, *Signs of Struggle,* 107.

17. Smith, "Reigning Men."

18. Lakoff, *Moral Politics,* 384.

19. Kymlicka, *Politics in the Vernacular,* 178.

20. Citrin, "The End of American Identity?" 289.

21. Gerstle, *American Crucible.*

22. Rosenblum, "Romantic Militarism," 263.

23. Skjelsbaek, "Militarism, Its Dimensions and Corollaries," 221.

24. DeConde, *Presidential Machismo,* 285.

25. Skjelsbaek, "Militarism, Its Dimensions and Corollaries," 221.

26. Regan, *Organizing Strategies for War,* 96; see also Carlton, *Militarism.*

27. Levin, "'West Wing' Mirrors Attacks," 1D. The self-importance of the show's producers is also expressed by the president of NBC Entertainment, Jeff Zucker, who said about the episode: "Aaron [Sorkin] is a brilliant writer who has something he wants to say. We have great faith in his abilities to interpret last week's events in a manner that make this an important hour of television" ("*The West Wing* Controversy").

28. The ratings for *The West Wing* come from http://www.boxofficemojo.com/tv/2001/1001.htm. Only ahead of this episode were installments of *Friends* and *ER.*

29. Mink, "'Wing' Gets It Just Right," 112.

30. Perkins, "Timely Topic Fits U.S. Mood," 15.

31. "Fresh Air," National Public Radio, Oct. 4, 2001, http://web.lexis-nexis.com; Rosenberg, "Wishful Thinking in 'West Wing,'" http://www.latimes.com/.

32. Bowron, "A Truly Surreal Piece of Nationalism," 2.

33. Robert Jones and George Dionisopoulos see the episode as a parable that holds potential for television storytelling in general and invites audience thought about its topic rather than simple answers to explain international terrorism. Jones and Dionisopoulos, "Scripting a Tragedy," 21–40.

34. Case, *Feminism and Theatre;* Giles, "Methexis vs. Mimesis"; Maranhao, *Therapeutic Discourse.*

35. It is telling that the actor playing Ali, Ajay Naidu, is of Indian descent and was

NOTES TO PAGES 165–71 · 201

born in Illinois. He has appeared with some frequency in films including *Chutney Popcorn, American Chai,* and *The Guru* as an Indian or Indian American character.

36. "I&I" invokes the audience's memory of the program and its previous episodes and plots even as it holds out this episode as special and outside the stream of *The West Wing*'s regular story lines. This rather disingenuous dimension to the program's introduction is reminiscent of the marketing and commercialism inherent in the program's treatment of terrorism in the wake of 9/11.

37. Yuval-Davis, *Gender and Nation,* 26–27.

38. Contrast the praise cited earlier for this episode of *The West Wing* with Tom Shales's reaction as evidence of this installment's polyvalence. Shales wrote in his review that "even in this moment of pain, trauma, heartbreak, destruction, assault and victimization, Hollywood liberals can still find some excuse to make America look guilty. For what it's worth, that's crap." Shales, "'The West Wing' Assumes the Role of Moral Compass," C1.

39. Burgoyne, *Film Nation,* 70.

40. Yuval-Davis and Anthias, eds., *Woman-Nation-State,* 9; Werbner, "Political Motherhood and the Feminisation of Citizenship, 241; see also Yuval-Davis, *Gender and Nation,* 94.

41. Mayer, "Gender Ironies of Nationalism," 10.

42. Mostov, "Sexing the Nation," 90; Sered, "Replaying the Rape of Dinah," 193.

43. Mostov, "Sexing the Nation," 91.

44. Ibid., 89.

45. Peterson, "Gendered Nationalism."

46. "Today's National Polls."

47. Balibar, *Politics and the Other Scene,* 66–67 (emphasis in original).

48. Ibid., 68.

49. Ibid.

50. Ibid., 69 (emphasis in original).

51. Baudrillard, *Simulacra and Simulation,* 25.

# Bibliography

## Books, Book Chapters, and Archival Sources

Abbott, Philip. *Strong Presidents: A Theory of Leadership.* Knoxville: University of Tennessee Press, 1996.

Allen, Holly. "Gender, Sexuality and the Military Model of U.S. National Community." In *Gender Ironies of Nationalism: Sexing the Nation,* edited by Tamar Mayer, 309–27. London: Routledge, 2000.

Anderson, Benedict. *Imagined Communities: Reflections on the Origin and Spread of Nationalism.* London: Verso Press, 1991.

———. "Introduction." In *Mapping the Nation,* edited by Gopal Balakrishnan, 1–16. London: Verso Press, 1996.

Andrews, James R. "Presidential Leadership and National Identity: Woodrow Wilson and the Meaning of America." In *The Presidency and Rhetorical Leadership,* edited by Leroy G. Dorsey, 129–44. College Station: Texas A&M University Press, 2002.

Anthias, Floya, and Nira Yuval-Davis. "Introduction." In *Woman—Nation—State,* edited by Nira Yuval-Davis and Floya Anthias, 1–15. New York: St. Martin's Press, 1989.

Appadurai, Arjun. "Disjuncture and Difference in the Global Cultural Economy." In *The Phantom Public Sphere,* edited by Bruce Robbins, 269–95. Minneapolis: University of Minnesota Press, 1993.

Arendt, Hannah. *The Human Condition.* Chicago: University of Chicago Press, 1958.

Auerbach, Erich. *Mimesis: The Representation of Reality in Western Literature.* Translated by Willard R. Trask. Princeton: Princeton University Press, 1953.

Azzi, Assaad E. "From Competitive Interests, Perceived Injustice, and Identity Needs to Collective Action: Psychological Mechanisms in Ethnic Nationalism." In *Nationalism and Violence,* edited by Christopher Dandeker, 73–138. New Brunswick: Transaction Publishers, 1998.

Bakhtin, Mikhail. "Forms of Time and of the Chronotope in the Novel." In *The Dialogic Imagination: Four Essays by M.M. Bakhtin,* edited by Michael Holquist, translated by Caryl Emerson and Michael Holquist, 84–258. Austin: University of Texas Press, 1981.

Balakrishnan, Gopal, ed. *Mapping the Nation.* London: Verso Press, 1996.

Balibar, Etienne. *Politics and the Other Scene,* translated by Christine Jones, James Swenson, and Chris Turner. London: Verso Press, 2002.

Barger, Harold M. "The Incredible Shrinking Image: From Cold War to Globalist Presidency." In *The Post-Cold War Presidency,* edited by Anthony J. Eksterowicz and Glenn P. Hastedt, 57–80. Lanham: Rowman and Littlefield, 1999.

Barry, Brian. *Culture and Equality: An Egalitarian Critique of Multiculturalism.* Cambridge: Harvard University Press, 2001.

Barry, James A. *The Sword of Justice: Ethics and Coercion in International Politics.* Westport: Praeger, 1998.

Baudrillard, Jean. *Simulacra and Simulation,* translated by Sheila Faria Glaser. Ann Arbor: University of Michigan Press, 1994.

Bauer, Otto. "The Nation." In *Mapping the Nation,* edited by Gopal Balakrishnan, 34–77. London: Verso Press, 1996.

Beasley, Vanessa B. *You, the People: American National Identity in Presidential Rhetoric.* College Station: Texas A&M University Press, 2004.

Beavers, Staci. *"The West Wing* as a Pedagogical Tool: Using Drama to Examine American Politics and Media Perceptions of Our Political System." In The West Wing: *The American Presidency as Television Drama,* edited by Peter C. Rollins and John E. O'Connor, 175–86. Syracuse: Syracuse University Press, 2003.

Beer, Francis A. *Meanings of War and Peace.* College Station: Texas A&M University Press, 2001.

Beer, Francis A., and Robert Hariman, eds. *Post-Realism: The Rhetorical Turn in International Relations.* East Lansing: Michigan State University Press, 1996.

Beiner, Ronald. *Political Judgment.* Chicago: University of Chicago Press, 1983.

Best, Steven, and Douglas Kellner. *The Postmodern Turn.* New York: Guilford, 1997.

Beynon, John. *Masculinities and Culture.* Buckingham, U.K.: Open University Press, 2002.

Bhabha, Homi K., ed. *Nation and Narration.* London: Routledge, 1990.

Blom, Ida. "Gender and Nation in International Comparison." In *Gendered Nations: Nationalisms and Gender Order in the Long Nineteenth Century,* edited by Ida Blom, Karen Hagemann, and Catherine Hall, 3–26. Oxford, U.K.: Berg, 2000.

Boot, Max. *The Savage Wars of Peace: Small Wars and the Rise of American Power.* New York: Basic Books, 2002.

Booth, Ken, and Tim Dunne. "Worlds in Collision." In *Worlds in Collision: Terror and the Future of Global Order,* edited by Ken Booth and Tim Dunne, 1–23. London: Palgrave Macmillan, 2002.

Borch-Jacobsen, Mikkel. *The Emotional Tie: Psychoanalysis, Mimesis, and Affect,* translated by Douglas Brick and others. Stanford: Stanford University Press, 1993.

Bourdieu, Pierre. *On Television,* translated by Priscilla Parkhurst Ferguson. New York: New Press, 1998.

Breuilly, John. "Approaches to Nationalism." In *Mapping the Nation,* edited by Gopal Balakrishnan, 146–74. London: Verso Press, 1996.

Brownmiller, Susan. *Femininity.* New York: Linden Press, 1984.

Bruner, M. Lane. *Strategies of Remembrance: The Rhetorical Dimensions of National Identity Construction.* Columbia: University of South Carolina Press, 2002.

Buchanan, Bruce. *The Citizen's Presidency: Standards of Choice and Judgment.* Washington: CQ Press, 1987.

Burgoyne, Robert. *Film Nation: Hollywood Looks at U.S. History.* Minneapolis: University of Minnesota Press, 1997.

Burke, Kenneth. *Attitudes toward History.* Berkeley: University of California Press, 1984.

———. *The Rhetoric of Religion: Studies in Logology.* Berkeley: University of California Press, 1970.

Burton, David H. *The Learned Presidency: Theodore Roosevelt, William Howard Taft, Woodrow Wilson.* Rutherford: Fairleigh Dickinson University Press, 1988.

Carlton, Eric. *Militarism: Rule without Law.* Aldershot, U.K.: Ashgate, 2001.

Carr, Robert. *Black Nationalism in the New World: Reading the African-American and the West Indian Experience.* Durham: Duke University Press, 2002.

Case, Sue-Ellen. *Feminism and Theatre.* New York: Routledge, 1988.

Casey, Bernadette, et al. *Television Studies: The Key Concepts.* London: Routledge, 2002.

Caudwell, Christopher. *Romance and Realism: A Study in English Bourgeois Literature,* edited by Samuel Hynes. Princeton: Princeton University Press, 1970.

Cawelti, John G. *Adventure, Mystery, and Romance: Formula Stories as Art and Popular Culture.* Chicago: University of Chicago Press, 1976.

Chambers, Deborah. *Representing the Family.* London: Sage Publications, 2001.

Chilton, Paul A. "The Meaning of Security." In *Post-Realism: The Rhetorical Turn in International Relations,* edited by Francis A. Beer and Robert Hariman. East Lansing: Michigan State University Press, 1996.

Christensen, Terry. *Reel Politics: American Political Movies from Birth of a Nation to Platoon.* New York: Basil Blackwell, 1987.

Citrin, Jack. "The End of American Identity?" In *One America? Political Leadership, National Identity, and the Dilemmas of Diversity,* edited by Stanley A. Renshon, 285–307. Washington: Georgetown University Press, 2001.

Cohn, Carol. "Wars, Wimps, and Women: Talking Gender and Thinking War." In *Gendering War Talk,* edited by Miriam Cooke and Angela Woollacott, 227–46. Princeton: Princeton University Press, 1993.

Connell, R. W. *Gender and Power: Society, the Person, and Sexual Politics.* Stanford: Stanford University Press, 1987.

———. *Masculinities.* Berkeley: University of California Press, 1995.

Cooke, Miriam. "Wo-man, Retelling the War Myth." In *Gendering War Talk,* edited by Miriam Cooke and Angela Woollacott, 177–204. Princeton: Princeton University Press, 1993.

Cronin, Thomas, and Michael A. Genovese. *The Paradoxes of the American Presidency.* New York: Oxford University Press, 1998.

Curtin, Michael. "Organizing Difference on Global TV: Television History and Cultural Geography." In *Television Histories: Shaping Collective Memory in the Media Age,* edited by Gary R. Edgerton and Peter C. Rollins, 335–356. Lexington: University Press of Kentucky, 2001.

Dallek, Robert. *Hail to the Chief: The Making and Unmaking of American Presidents.* New York: Hyperion, 1996.

Dandeker, Christopher. "Nationalism, Nation-States, and Violence at the End of the Twentieth Century: A Sociological View." In *Nationalism and Violence,* edited by Christopher Dandeker, 21–46. New Brunswick: Transaction Publishers, 1998.

Davis, Richard, and Diana Owen. *New Media and American Politics.* New York: Oxford University Press, 1998.

DeConde, Alexander. *Presidential Machismo: Executive Authority, Military Intervention, and Foreign Relations.* Boston: Northeastern University Press, 2000.

d'Entrèves, Maurizio Passerin, and Ursula Vogel, eds. *Public and Private: Legal, Political, and Philosophical Perspectives.* London: Routledge, 2000.

Diamond, Edwin, and Robert A. Silverman. *White House to Your House: Media and Politics in Virtual America.* Cambridge: MIT Press, 1997.

Doane, Janice, and Devon Hodges. *Nostalgia and Sexual Difference: The Resistance to Contemporary Feminism.* New York: Methuen, 1987.

Dow, Bonnie J. *Prime-Time Feminism: Television, Media Culture, and the Women's Movement since 1970.* Philadelphia: University of Pennsylvania Press, 1996.

Dunn, Charles W. *The Scarlet Thread of Scandal: Morality and the American Presidency.* Lanham: Rowman and Littlefield, 2000.

Edelman, Murray. *Constructing the Political Spectacle.* Chicago: University of Chicago Press, 1988.

———. *From Art to Politics: How Artistic Creations Shape Political Conceptions.* Chicago: University of Chicago Press, 1995.

Edgerton, Gary R. "Television as Historian: A Different Kind of History Altogether." In *Television Histories: Shaping Collective Memory in the Media Age,* edited by Gary R. Edgerton and Peter C. Rollins. Lexington: University Press of Kentucky, 2001.

Edwards, George C. III. *On Deaf Ears: The Limits of the Bully Pulpit.* New Haven: Yale University Press, 2003.

Elam, Diane. "Feminism and the Postmodern: Theory's Romance." In *The Feminist Reader: Essays in Gender and the Politics of Literary Criticism,* 2d ed., edited by Catherine Belsey and Jane Moore, 182–202. Malden, U.K.: Blackwell, 1997.

Eley, Geoff, and Ronald Grigor Suny, eds. *Becoming National: A Reader.* New York: Oxford University Press, 1996.

Ellis, Richard J., ed. *Speaking to the People: The Rhetorical Presidency in Historical Perspective.* Amherst: University of Massachusetts Press, 1998.

Elshtain, Jean Bethke. *Just War against Terror: The Burden of American Power in a Violent World*. New York: Basic Books, 2003.

Enloe, Cynthia. *The Morning After: Sexual Politics at the End of the Cold War*. Berkeley: University of California Press, 1993.

Eveland, Jr., William P. "The Impact of News and Entertainment Media on Perceptions of Social Reality." In *The Persuasion Handbook: Developments in Theory and Practice*, edited by James Price Dillard and Michael Pfau, 691–727. Thousand Oaks: Sage, 2002.

Ezell, Pamela. "The Sincere Sorkin White House, or, the Importance of Seeming Earnest." In The West Wing: *The American Presidency as Television Drama*, edited by Peter C. Rollins and John E. O'Connor, 159–74. Syracuse: Syracuse University Press, 2003.

Faris, Wendy B. "Scheherazade's Children: Magical Realism and Postmodern Fiction." In *Magical Realism: Theory, History, Community*, edited by Lois Parkinson Zamora and Wendy B. Faris, 163–90. Durham: Duke University Press, 1995.

Ferrell, Robert H. *Ill-Advised: Presidential Health and Public Trust*. Columbia: University of Missouri Press, 1992.

Fields, Wayne. *Union of Words: A History of Presidential Eloquence*. New York: Free Press, 1996.

Fine, Robert. "Benign Nationalism? The Limits of the Civic Ideal." In *People, Nation and State: The Meaning of Ethnicity and Nationalism*, edited by Edward Mortimer, 149–61. London: I. B. Tauris, 1999.

Finn, Patrick. "*The West Wing*'s Textual President: American Constitutional Stability and the New Public Intellectual in the Age of Information." In The West Wing: *The American Presidency as Television Drama*, edited by Peter C. Rollins and John E. O'Connor, 101–24. Syracuse: Syracuse University Press, 2003.

Fiske, John. *Media Matters: Everyday Culture and Political Change*. Minneapolis: University of Minnesota Press, 1996.

Fletcher, George P. *Romantics at War: Glory and Guilt in the Age of Terrorism*. Princeton: Princeton University Press, 2002.

Frankel, Benjamin, ed. *Roots of Realism*. London: Frank Cass, 1996.

Freedman, Lawrence. "A New Type of War." In *Worlds in Collision: Terror and the Future of Global Order*, edited by Ken Booth and Tim Dunne, 37–47. London: Palgrave Macmillan, 2002.

French, Marilyn. "Is There a Feminist Aesthetic?." In *Aesthetics in Feminist Perspective*, edited by Hilde Hein and Carolyn Korsmeyer, 68–76. Bloomington: Indiana University Press, 1993.

Frye, Northrop. *Anatomy of Criticism: Four Essays*. New York: Atheneum, 1967.

———. *The Secular Scripture: A Study of the Structure of Romance*. Cambridge: Harvard University Press, 1976.

Gatens, Moira. *Imaginary Bodies: Ethics, Power and Corporeality*. London: Routledge, 1996.

Gebauer, Gunter, and Christoph Wolf. *Mimesis: Culture, Art, Society,* translated by Don Reneau. Berkeley: University of California Press, 1992.

Gerstle, Gary. *American Crucible: Race and Nation in the Twentieth Century.* Princeton: Princeton University Press, 2001.

Gianos, Phillip L. *Politics and Politicians in American Film.* Westport: Praeger, 1998.

Giglio, Ernest. *Here's Looking at You: Hollywood, Film, and Politics.* New York: Peter Lang, 2000.

Gilbert, Robert E. *The Mortal Presidency: Illness and Anguish in the White House.* New York: Fordham University Press, 1998.

Giles, Freda Scott. "Methexis vs. Mimesis: Poetics of Feminist and Womanist Drama." In *Race/Sex: Their Sameness, Difference, and Interplay,* edited by Naomi Zack, 175–82. New York: Routledge, 1997.

Ginzberg, Lori D. *Women and the Work of Benevolence: Morality, Politics, and Class in the Nineteenth-Century United States.* New Haven: Yale University Press, 1990.

Gitlin, Todd. *The Twilight of Common Dreams: Why America Is Wracked by Culture Wars.* New York: Metropolitan Books, 1995.

———. *The Whole World Is Watching: Mass Media in the Making and Unmaking of the New Left.* Berkeley: University of California Press, 1980.

Goldzwig, Steven R. "Civil Rights and the Cold War: A Rhetorical History of the Truman Administration's Desegregation of the United States Army." In *Doing Rhetorical History: Concepts and Cases,* edited by Kathleen J. Turner, 143–69. Tuscaloosa: University of Alabama Press, 1998.

Goldzwig, Steven R., and George N. Dionisopoulos. "Crisis at Little Rock: Eisenhower, History, and Mediated Political Realities." In *Eisenhower's War of Words: Rhetoric and Leadership,* edited by Martin J. Medhurst, 189–221. East Lansing: Michigan State University Press, 1994.

Goodman, Paul. *Of One Blood: Abolitionism and the Origins of Racial Equality.* Berkeley: University of California Press, 1998.

Gramsci, Antonio. *Selections from the Prison Notebooks of Antonio Gramsci,* translated by Quintin Hoare and Geoffrey Nowell Smith. New York: International Publishers, 1999.

Gray, Herman. *Watching Race: Television and the Struggle for "Blackness."* Minneapolis: University of Minnesota Press, 1995.

Greenstein, Fred I. *The Presidential Difference: Leadership Style from FDR to Clinton.* New York: Martin Kessler Books, 2000.

Griffin, Michael. "The Great War Photographs: Constructing Myths and History and Photojournalism." In *Picturing the Past: Media, History, and Photography,* edited by Bonnie Brennen and Hanno Hardt, 122–57. Urbana: University of Illinois Press, 1999.

Gross, Larry. *Up from Invisibility: Lesbians, Gay Men, and the Media in America.* New York: Columbia University Press, 2001.

Grosz, Elizabeth. *Volatile Bodies: Toward a Corporeal Feminism.* Bloomington: Indiana University Press, 1994.

Habermas, Jürgen. *The Structural Transformation of the Public Sphere,* translated by Thomas Burger. Cambridge: MIT Press, 1992.

Hall, Stuart. "Ethnicity: Identity and Difference." In *Becoming National: A Reader,* edited by Geoff Eley and Ronald Grigor Suny, 339–49. New York: Oxford University Press, 1996.

Hardesty, Nancy. *Women Called to Witness: Evangelical Feminism in the Nineteenth Century,* 2d ed. Knoxville: University of Tennessee Press, 1999.

Hardt, Michael, and Antonio Negri. *Empire.* Cambridge: Harvard University Press, 2000.

Hargrove, Edwin C. *The President as Leader: Appealing to the Better Angels of Our Nature.* Lawrence: University Press of Kansas, 1998.

Harris, Sharon M. ed. *Redefining the Political Novel: American Women Writers, 1797–1901.* Knoxville: University of Tennessee Press, 1995.

Hart, Roderick P. *Seducing America: How Television Charms the Modern Voter.* New York: Oxford University Press, 1994.

Hayton, Heather Richardson. "The King's Two Bodies: Identity and Office in Sorkin's *West Wing.*" In The West Wing: *The American Presidency as Television Drama,* edited by Peter C. Rollins and John E. O'Connor, 63–79. Syracuse: Syracuse University Press, 2003.

Hess, Stephen. *Presidents and the Presidency.* Washington: Brookings Institution, 1996.

Hinckley, Barbara. *The Symbolic Presidency: How Presidents Portray Themselves.* New York: Routledge, 1990.

Holloway, Rachel L. "The Strategic Defense Initiative and the Technological Sublime: Fear, Science, and the Cold War." In *Critical Reflections on the Cold War: Linking Rhetoric and History,* edited by Martin J. Medhurst and H. W. Brands, 209–32. College Station: Texas A&M University Press, 2000.

hooks, bell. *Black Looks: Race and Representation.* Boston: South End Press, 1992.

Houck, Davis W., and Amos Kiewe. *FDR's Body Politics: The Rhetoric of Disability.* College Station: Texas A&M University Press, 2003.

Howe, Irving. *Politics and the Novel.* New York: Horizon Press, 1957.

Ivie, Robert L. "Realism Masking Fear: George F. Kennan's Political Rhetoric." In *Post-Realism: The Rhetorical Turn in International Relations,* edited by Francis A. Beer and Robert Hariman, 55–74. East Lansing: Michigan State University Press, 1996.

———. "Tragic Fear and the Rhetorical Presidency: Combating Evil in the Persian Gulf." In *Beyond the Rhetorical Presidency,* edited by Martin J. Medhurst, 153–78. College Station: Texas A&M University Press, 1996.

Jamieson, Kathleen Hall. *Beyond the Double Bind: Women and Leadership.* New York: Oxford University Press, 1995.

Johnson, Lesley. "'As Housewives We Are Worms': Women, Modernity, and the Home Question." In *Feminism and Cultural Studies,* edited by Morag Shiach, 475–91. New York: Oxford University Press, 1999.

Kauffman, James L. *Selling Outer Space: Kennedy, the Media, and Funding for Project Apollo, 1961–1963.* Tuscaloosa: University of Alabama Press, 1994.

Kerber, Linda K. *Women of the Republic: Intellect and Ideology in Revolutionary America.* Chapel Hill: University of North Carolina Press, 1980.

Kernell, Samuel. *Going Public: New Strategies of Presidential Leadership,* 3d ed. Washington: CQ Press, 1997.

Kersh, Rogan. *Dreams of a More Perfect Union.* Ithaca: Cornell University Press, 2001.

Knott, Stephen F. *Secret and Sanctioned: Covert Operations and the American Presidency.* New York: Oxford University Press, 1996.

Kress, Gunther, and Theo van Leeuwen. *Reading Images: The Grammar of Visual Design.* London: Routledge, 2000.

Kymlicka, Will. *Politics in the Vernacular: Nationalism, Multiculturalism, and Citizenship.* Oxford, U.K.: Oxford University Press, 2001.

Lakoff, George. *Moral Politics: What Conservatives Know that Liberals Don't.* Chicago: University of Chicago Press, 1996.

Lakoff, Robin Tolmach. *The Language War.* Berkeley: University of California Press, 2000.

Lane, Christina. "The White House Culture of Gender and Race in *The West Wing:* Insights from the Margins." In The West Wing: *The American Presidency as Television Drama,* edited by Peter C. Rollins and John E. O'Connor, 32–41. Syracuse: Syracuse University Press, 2003.

Langston, Thomas S. *With Reverence and Contempt: How Americans Think about Their President.* Baltimore: Johns Hopkins University Press, 1995.

Laracey, Mel. *Presidents and the People: The Partisan Story of Going Public.* College Station: Texas A&M University Press, 2002.

Lawrence, John Shelton. "A Filmography for Images of American Presidents in Film." In *Hollywood's White House: The American Presidency in Film and History,* edited by Peter C. Rollins and John E. O'Connor, 383–402. Lexington: University Press of Kentucky, 2003.

Lee, Ronald, and Matthew H. Barton. "Clinton's Rhetoric of Contrition." In *Images, Scandal, and Communication Strategies of the Clinton Presidency,* edited by Robert E. Denton Jr. and Rachel L. Holloway, 219–46. Westport: Praeger, 2003.

Levine, Myron A. "The Transformed Presidency: People and Power in the *Real* West Wing." In The West Wing: *The American Presidency as Television Drama,* edited by Peter C. Rollins and John E. O'Connor, 235–58. Syracuse: Syracuse University Press, 2003.

———. *"The West Wing* (NBC) and the West Wing (D.C.): Myth and Reality in Television's Portrayal of the White House." In The West Wing: *The American Presidency as Television Drama,* edited by Peter C. Rollins and John E. O'Connor, 42–62. Syracuse: Syracuse University Press, 2003.

Levy, Jacob T. *The Multiculturalism of Fear.* Oxford, U.K.: Oxford University Press, 2000.

Light, Andrew, and William Chaloupka. "Angry White Men: Right Exclusionary Nationalism and Left Identity Politics." In *Gender Ironies of Nationalism: Sexing the Nation,* edited by Tamar Mayer, 329–50. London: Routledge, 2000.

López, Ian F. Haney. *White by Law: The Legal Construction of Race*. New York: New York University Press, 1996.

Luke, Timothy W. *Screens of Power: Ideology, Domination, and Resistance in Informational Society*. Urbana: University of Illinois Press, 1989.

Mahoney, Kathleen E. "Recognizing the Constitutional Significance of Harmful Speech: The Canadian View of Pornography and Hate Propaganda." In *The Price We Pay: The Case against Racist Speech, Hate Propaganda, and Pornography*, edited by Laura Lederer and Richard Delgado, 277–89. New York: Hill and Wang, 1995.

Maranhão, Tullio. *Therapeutic Discourse and Socratic Dialogue*. Madison: University of Wisconsin Press, 1986.

Marx, Anthony W. *Making Race and Nation: A Comparison of South Africa, the United States, and Brazil*. Cambridge, U.K.: Cambridge University Press, 1998.

May, Elaine Tyler. *Homeward Bound: American Families in the Cold War Era*. New York: Basic Books, 1999.

Mayer, Tamar. "Gender Ironies of Nationalism: Setting the Stage." In *Gender Ironies of Nationalism: Sexing the Nation*, edited by Tamar Mayer, 1–22. London: Routledge, 2000.

McBride, Allen, and Robert K. Toburen. "Deep Structures: Polpop Culture on Primetime Television." In *Culture and Politics*, edited by Lane Crothers and Charles Lockhart, 133–49. New York: St. Martin's Press, 2000.

McClintock, Anne. "'No Longer in a Future Heaven': Gender, Race and Nationalism." In *Dangerous Liaisons: Gender, Nation, and Postcolonial Perspectives*, edited by Anne McClintock, Aamir Mufti, and Ella Shohat, 89–112. Minneapolis: University of Minnesota Press, 1997.

McDonald, Forrest. *The American Presidency: An Intellectual History*. Lawrence: University Press of Kansas, 1994.

Mead, Walter Russell. *Special Providence: American Foreign Policy and How It Changed the World*. New York: Routledge, 2002.

Meyrowitz, Joshua. *No Sense of Place: The Impact of Electronic Media on Social Behavior*. New York: Oxford University Press, 1985.

Miller, Stephen Paul. *The Seventies Now: Culture as Surveillance*. Durham: Duke University Press, 1999.

Milne, Gordon. *The American Political Novel*. Norman: University of Oklahoma Press, 1966.

Miroff, Bruce. "The Presidency and the Public: Leadership as Spectacle." In *The Presidency and the Political System*, edited by Michael Nelson, 299–322. Washington: CQ Press, 1998.

Mohanty, Chandra Talpade. "Under Western Eyes: Feminist Scholarship and Colonial Discourses." In *Dangerous Liaisons: Gender, Nation, and Postcolonial Perspectives*, edited by Anne McClintock, Aamir Mufti, and Ella Shohat, 255–77. Minneapolis: University of Minnesota Press, 1997.

Monroe, James. "Seventh Annual Message." In *A Compilation of the Messages and Papers of the Presidents, 1789–1897.* Volume 1. Washington: Government Printing Office, 1896.

Morris, Dick. *Behind the Oval Office: Getting Reelected against All Odds.* Los Angeles: Renaissance Books, 1999.

Mosse, George L. *Nationalism and Sexuality: Respectability and Abnormal Sexuality in Modern Europe.* New York: Howard Fertig, 1985.

Mostov, Julie. "Sexing the Nation/Desexing the Body: Politics of National Identity in the Former Yugoslavia." In *Gender Ironies of Nationalism: Sexing the Nation,* edited by Tamar Mayer, 89–110. London: Routledge, 2000.

Mulvey, Laura. *Visual and Other Pleasures.* Bloomington: Indiana University Press, 1989.

Nelson, Dana D. *National Manhood: Capitalist Citizenship and the Imagined Fraternity of White Men.* Durham: Duke University Press, 1998.

Nelson, Michael, ed. *The Presidency and the Political System.* Washington: CQ Press, 1998.

Neustadt, Richard E. *Presidential Power and the Modern Presidents: The Politics of Leadership from Roosevelt to Reagan.* New York: Free Press, 1990.

Newcomb, Horace, and Paul M. Hirsch. "Television as a Cultural Forum." In *Television: The Critical View,* 4th ed., edited by Horace Newcomb, 455–70. New York: Oxford University Press, 1987.

Norton, Anne. *Republic of Signs: Liberal Theory and American Popular Culture.* Chicago: University of Chicago Press, 1993.

"Notes for a General Policy Approach to the Lodge Project," July 1953, White House Office, NSC Staff: Papers, 1953–61, PSB central files series, box 23, Dwight D. Eisenhower Presidential Library.

Nye, David E. *American Technological Sublime.* Cambridge: MIT Press, 1994.

O'Connor, John E., and Peter C. Rollins. Introduction. In The West Wing: *The American Presidency as Television Drama,* edited by Peter C. Rolllins and John E. O'-Connor. Syracuse: Syracuse University Press, 2003.

Okin, Susan Moller. "Feminism, Women's Human Rights, and Cultural Differences." In *Decentering the Center: Philosophy for a Multicultural, Postcolonial, and Feminist World,* edited by Uma Narayan and Sandra Harding, 26–46. Bloomington: Indiana University Press, 2000.

O'Reilly, Kenneth. *Nixon's Piano: Presidents and Racial Politics from Washington through Clinton.* New York: Free Pres, 1995.

Parry-Giles, Shawn J. *The Rhetorical Presidency, Propaganda, and the Cold War, 1945–1955.* Westport: Praeger, 2002.

———, and Trevor Parry-Giles. *Constructing Clinton: Hyperreality and Presidential Image-Making in Postmodern Politics.* New York: Peter Lang, 2002.

Pauley, Garth E. *The Modern Presidency and Civil Rights: Rhetoric on Race from Roosevelt to Nixon.* College Station: Texas A&M University Press, 2001.

Peterson, V. Spike. "Gendered Nationalism: Reproducing 'Us' versus 'Them.'" In *The Women and War Reader,* edited by Lois Ann Lorentzen and Jennifer Turpin, 41–49. New York: New York University Press, 1998.

Pickering, Jean, and Suzanne Kehde, eds. *Narratives of Nostalgia, Gender, and Nationalism.* New York: New York University Press, 1997.

Pickus, Noah M. W. "Which America? Nationalism among the Nationalists." In *One America? Political Leadership, National Identity, and the Dilemmas of Diversity,* edited by Stanley A. Renshon, 28–66. Washington: Georgetown University Press, 2001.

Pierson, Ruth Roach. "Nations: Gendered, Racialized, Crossed with Empire." In *Gendered Nations: Nationalisms and Gender Order in the Long Nineteenth Century,* edited by Ida Blom, Karen Hagemann, and Catherine Hall, 41–61. Oxford, U.K.: Berg, 2000.

Pompper, Donnalyn. "*The West Wing:* White House Narratives That Journalism Cannot Tell." In The West Wing: *The American Presidency as Television Drama,* edited by Peter C. Rollins and John E. O'Connor, 17–31. Syracuse: Syracuse University Press, 2003.

Popkin, Samuel L. *The Reasoning Voter: Communication and Persuasion in Presidential Campaigns.* Chicago: University of Chicago Press, 1991.

Prince, Stephen. "Political Film in the Nineties." In *Film Genre 2000: New Critical Essays,* edited by Wheeler Winston Dixon, 63–75. Albany: State University of New York Press, 2000.

Projansky, Sarah. *Watching Rape: Film and Television in Postfeminist Culture.* New York: New York University Press, 2001.

Quiring, Loren P. "A Man of His Word: Aaron Sorkin's American Presidents." In *Hollywood's White House: The American Presidency in Film and History,* edited by Peter C. Rollins and John E. O'Connor, 234–47. Lexington: University Press of Kentucky, 2003.

Ragsdale, Lyn. "Studying the Presidency: Why Presidents Need Political Scientists." In *The Presidency and the Political System,* edited by Michael Nelson, 29–61. Washington: CQ Press, 1998.

Reed, Ishmael, ed. *Multi-America: Essays on Cultural Wars and Cultural Peace.* New York: Viking, 1997.

Regan, Patrick M. *Organizing Strategies for War: The Process and Consequences of Societal Militarization.* Westport: Praeger, 1994.

Regan, Richard J. *Just War: Principles and Cases.* Washington: Catholic University of American Press, 1996.

Renshon, Stanley A. "Dual Citizenship + Multiple Loyalties = One America?" In *One America? Political Leadership, National Identity, and the Dilemmas of Diversity,* edited by Stanley A. Renshon, 232–82. Washington: Georgetown University Press, 2001.

"A Report to the National Security Council by the Executive Secretary of Office of

Special Projects," June 1948, Records of Organizations in the Executive Office of the President, record group 429, Harry S Truman Presidential Library.

Riley, Russell L. *The Presidency and the Politics of Racial Inequality: Nation-Keeping from 1831 to 1965.* New York: Columbia University Press, 1999.

———. "The Presidency, Leadership, and Race." In *One America? Political Leadership, National Identity, and the Dilemmas of Diversity,* edited by Stanley A. Renshon, 69–90. Washington: Georgetown University Press, 2001.

Robinson, William. "Promoting Capitalist Polyarchy: The Case of Latin America." In *American Democracy Promotion: Impulses, Strategies, and Impacts,* edited by Michael Cox, G. John Ikenberry, and Takashi Inoguchi, 308–24. New York: Oxford University Press, 2000.

Roosevelt, Theodore. *Address of President Roosevelt at Chautauqua, New York, August 11, 1905.* Washington: Government Printing Office, 1905.

———. *American Ideals and Other Essays, Social and Political.* Philadelphia: Gebbie and Company, 1903.

———. "Message of the President of the United States Communicated to the Two Houses of Congress." In *Theodore Roosevelt Papers,* series 5C, reel 426, Library of Congress.

———. "The Strenuous Life." In *The Works of Theodore Roosevelt.* Volume 13. New York: Charles Scribner's Sons, 1926.

Roper, Jon. *The American Presidents: Heroic Leadership from Kennedy to Clinton.* Edinburgh, U.K.: Edinburgh University Press, 2000.

Ruddick, Sara. "Notes toward a Feminist Peace Politics." In *Gendering War Talk,* edited by Miriam Cooke and Angela Woollacott, 109–27. Princeton: Princeton University Press, 1993.

Said, Edward W. *Orientalism.* New York: Pantheon, 1978.

Sanford, Charles L., ed. *Manifest Destiny and the Imperialism Question.* New York: John Wiley and Sons, 1974.

Schlesinger, Arthur M. Jr. *The Disuniting of America: Reflections on a Multicultural Society.* Revised and enlarged edition. New York: W. W. Norton, 1998.

———. *The Imperial Presidency.* Boston: Houghton Mifflin, 1989.

Schulman, Bruce J. *The Seventies: The Great Shift in American Culture, Society, and Politics.* New York: Free Press, 2001.

Scott, Joyce Hope. "From Foreground to Margin: Female Configurations and Masculine Self-Representation in Black Nationalist Fiction." In *Nationalisms and Sexualities,* edited by Andrew Parker et al., 296–312. New York: Routledge, 1992.

Scott, Robert L. "Cold War and Rhetoric: Conceptually and Critically." In *Cold War Rhetoric: Strategy, Metaphor, and Ideology,* edited by Martin J. Medhurst et al., 1–16. East Lansing: Michigan State University Press, 1997.

Sered, Susan. "Replaying the Rape of Dinah: Women's Bodies in Israeli Cultural Discourse." In *Jews and Gender: The Challenge to Hierarchy,* edited by Jonathan Frankel, 191–208. New York: Oxford University Press, 2000.

Seshadri-Crooks, Kalpana. *Desiring Whiteness: A Lacanian Analysis of Race.* London: Routledge, 2000.

Shohat, Ella, and Robert Stam. "From the Imperial Family to the Transnational Imaginary: Media Spectatorship in the Age of Globalization." In *Global/Local: Cultural Production and the Transnational Imaginary,* edited by Rob Wilson and Wimal Dissanayake, 145–72. Durham: Duke University Press, 1996.

Sigelman, Lee. "Taking Popular Fiction Seriously." In *Reading Political Stories: Representations of Politics in Novels and Pictures,* edited by Maureen Whitebrook, 149–63. Lanham: Rowman and Littlefield, 1992.

Silberstein, Sandra. *War of Words: Language, Politics and 9/11.* London: Routledge, 2002.

Simpson, Christopher. *Science of Coercion: Communication Research and Psychological Warfare, 1945–1960.* New York: Oxford University Press, 1994.

Skowronek, Stephen. *The Politics That Presidents Make: Leadership from John Adams to Bill Clinton.* Cambridge: Harvard University Press, 1997.

Skrentny, John David. "Affirmative Action and the Failure of Presidential Leadership." In *One America? Political Leadership, National Identity, and the Dilemmas of Diversity,* edited by Stanley A. Renshon, 111–40. Washington: Georgetown University Press, 2001.

Sloop, John M. *Disciplining Gender: Rhetorics of Sex Identity in Contemporary U.S. Culture.* Amherst: University of Massachusetts Press, 2004.

Smith, Shawn Michelle. "Photographing the 'American Negro': Nation, Race, and Photography at the Paris Exposition of 1900." In *With Other Eyes: Looking at Race and Gender in Visual Culture,* edited by Lisa Bloom, 58–87. Minneapolis: University of Minnesota Press, 1999.

Smith-Rosenberg, Carroll. "Political Camp or the Ambiguous Engendering of the American Republic." In *Gendered Nations: Nationalisms and Gender Order in the Long Nineteenth Century,* edited by Ida Blom, Karen Hagemann, and Catherine Hall, 271–92. Oxford, U.K.: Berg, 2000.

Sommer, Doris. "Irresistible Romance: The Foundational Fictions of Latin America." In *Nation and Narration,* edited by Homi K. Bhabha, 71–98. London: Routledge, 1990.

Sorkin, Aaron. The West Wing: *The Official Companion.* New York: Pocket Books, 2002.

Stec, Loretta. "Female Sacrifice: Gender and Nostalgic Nationalism in Rebecca West's *Black Lamp and Grey Falcon.*" In *Narratives of Nostalgia, Gender, and Nationalism,* edited by Jean Pickering and Suzanne Kehde, 138–58. New York: New York University Press, 1997.

Stephanson, Anders. *Manifest Destiny: American Expansionism and the Empire of Right.* New York: Hill and Wang, 1995.

Street, John. *Politics and Popular Culture.* Philadelphia: Temple University Press, 1997.

Stuckey, Mary E. *The President as Interpreter-in-Chief.* Chatham: Chatham House, 1991.

Swain, Carol M. *The New White Nationalism in America: Its Challenge to Integration.* Cambridge, U.K.: Cambridge University Press, 2002.

Swain, Carol M., and Russ Nieli, eds. *Contemporary Voices of White Nationalism in America*. New York: Cambridge University Press, 2003.

Taylor, Charles. "The Politics of Recognition." In *Multiculturalism: Examining the Politics of Recognition*, edited and introduced by Amy Gutmann, 25–74. Princeton: Princeton University Press, 1994.

Thompson, John B. *Political Scandal: Power and Visibility in the Media Age*. Cambridge, U.K.: Polity, 2000.

Tickner, J. Ann. *Gendering World Politics: Issues and Approaches in the Post-Cold War Era*. New York: Columbia University Press, 2001.

Tulis, Jeffrey K. *The Rhetorical Presidency*. Princeton: Princeton University Press, 1987.

Turner, Frederick J. "The Significance of the Frontier in American History." In *American Historical Association Annual Report*. Washington: Government Printing Office, 1894.

Twining, Thomas. "On Poetry Considered as an Imitative Art." In *Aristotle's "Poetics" and English Literature: A Collection of Critical Essays*, edited by Elder Olson, 42–75. Chicago: University of Chicago Press, 1965.

Vavrus, Mary Douglas. *Postfeminist News: Political Women in Media Culture*. Albany: State University of New York Press, 2002.

Vest, Jason P. "From *The American President* to *The West Wing*: A Scriptwriter's Perspective." In The West Wing: *The American Presidency as Television Drama*, edited by Peter C. Rollins and John E. O'Connor, 136–56. Syracuse: Syracuse University Press, 2003.

Vincent, Andrew. *Nationalism and Particularity*. New York: Cambridge University Press, 2002.

Walsh, Kenneth T. *Feeding the Beast: The White House versus the Press*. New York: Random House, 1996.

Walters, Suzanna Danuta. *All the Rage: The Story of Gay Visibility in America*. Chicago: University of Chicago Press, 2001.

Waterman, Richard W., Robert Wright, and Gilbert St. Clair. *The Image-Is-Everything Presidency: Dilemmas in American Leadership*. Boulder: Westview, 1999.

Weinberg, Albert K. *Manifest Destiny: A Study of Nationalist Expansionism in American History*. Gloucester, U.K.: Peter Smith, 1958.

Weintraub, Jeff, and Krishan Kumar, eds. *Public and Private in Thought and Practice: Perspectives on a Grand Dichotomy*. Chicago: University of Chicago Press, 1997.

Wenk, Silke. "Gendered Representations of the Nation's Past and Future." In *Gendered Nations: Nationalism and Gender Order in the Long Nineteenth Century*, edited by Ida Blom, Karen Hagemann, and Catherine Hall, 63–77. Oxford, U.K.: Berg, 2000.

Werbner, Pnina. "Political Motherhood and the Feminisation of Citizenship: Women's Activisms and the Transformation of the Public Sphere." In *Women, Citizenship, and Difference*, edited by Nira Yuval-Davis and Pnina Werbner, 221–45. London: Zed Books, 1999.

West, Thomas R. *Signs of Struggle: The Rhetorical Politics of Cultural Difference.* Albany: State University of New York Press, 2002.

*The West Wing, Created by Aaron Sorkin: The Official Companion.* New York: Pocket Books, 2002.

Whelehan, Imelda. *Modern Feminist Thought: From the Second Wave to "Post-Feminism."* New York: New York University Press, 1995.

White, Hayden. *Figural Realism: Studies in the Mimesis Effect.* Baltimore: Johns Hopkins University Press, 1999.

———. *Tropics of Discourse: Essays in Cultural Criticism.* Baltimore: Johns Hopkins University Press, 1978.

Wiebe, Robert H. *Who We Are: A History of Popular Nationalism.* Princeton: Princeton University Press, 2002.

Wilkinson, J. Harvie III. *One Nation Indivisible: How Ethnic Separatism Threatens America.* Reading: Addison-Wesley, 1997.

Wilson, Woodrow. "An Address in Philadelphia to Newly Naturalized Citizens." In *The Papers of Woodrow Wilson,* edited by Arthur S. Link. Princeton: Princeton University Press, 1980.

———. *Constitutional Government in the United States.* New York: Columbia University Press, 1908.

Winant, Howard. *Racial Conditions: Politics, Theory, Comparisons.* Minneapolis: University of Minnesota Press, 1994.

Witt, Linda, Karen M. Paget, and Glenna Matthews. *Running as a Woman: Gender and Power in American Politics.* New York: Free Press, 1995.

Woodward, Bob. *Shadow: Five Presidents and the Legacy of Watergate.* New York: Simon and Schuster, 1999.

Yuval-Davis, Nira. *Gender and Nation.* London: Sage, 1997.

———, and Floya Anthias, eds. *Woman—Nation—State.* New York: St. Martin's Press, 1989.

Zaller, John. "Monica Lewinsky and the Mainsprings of American Politics." In *Mediated Politics: Communication in the Future of Democracy,* edited by W. Lance Bennett and Robert M. Entman, 252–78. New York: Cambridge University Press, 2001.

Zarefsky, David. "The Presidency Has Always Been a Place for Rhetorical Leadership." In *The Presidency and Rhetorical Leadership,* edited by Leroy G. Dorsey, 20–41. College Station: Texas A&M University Press, 2002.

## Articles and On-line Sources

"Aaron Sorkin." *MacNeill Lehrer Newshour,* Sept. 27, 2000.

Bass, Jeff D. "The Romance as Rhetorical Dissociation: The Purification of Imperialism in *King Solomon's Mines.*" *Quarterly Journal of Speech* 67 (1981): 259–69.

Baynes, Leonard M. "White Out: The Absence and Stereotyping of People of Color by the Broadcast Networks in Prime Time Entertainment Programming." *Arizona Law Review* 45 (2003): 293–369.

Beasley, Vanessa B. "Engendering Democratic Change: How Three U.S. Presidents Discussed Female Suffrage." *Rhetoric and Public Affairs* 5 (2002): 79–103.

Bowron, Jane. "A Truly Surreal Piece of Nationalism." Wellington, N.Z., *Evening Post*, Oct. 13, 2001, 2.

Byrne, Bridgit. "Will NBC Re-Elect 'West Wing'?" *E!Online*, Oct. 10, 2002. http://att .eonline.com/News/Items/O,1,10670,00.html.

Carcasson, Martín, and Mitchell F. Rice. "The Promise and Failure of President Clinton's Race Initiative of 1997–1998: A Rhetorical Perspective." *Rhetoric and Public Affairs* 2 (1999): 243–74.

Carrigan, Tim, Bob Connell, and John Lee. "Toward a New Sociology of Masculinity." *Theory and Society* 14 (1985): 551–604.

"Changing Images of Government in TV Entertainment." Council for Excellence in Government, June 5, 2001. http://www.trustingov.org/research/govtv/index.htm.

Cherry, Kristin L., and Amy R. Daulton. "*The West Wing* as Endorsement of the U.S. Presidency: Expanding the Bounds of Priming in Political Communication." *Journal of Communication* 53 (2003): 427–43.

Chesebro, James W. "Communication, Values, and Popular Television Series: A Seventeen-Year Assessment." *Communication Quarterly* 39 (1991): 197–225.

Clinton, William Jefferson. "1996 State of the Union Addres," Jan. 23, 1996. http:// clinton4.nara.gov/textonly/WH/New/other/sotu.html.

Deming, Caren J. "*Hill Street Blues* as Narrative." *Critical Studies in Mass Communication* 2 (1985): 1–22.

Devlin, Dean, and Roland Emmerich. *Independence Day.* http://www.script-o-rama .com/snazzy/dircut.html.

Dorsey, Leroy G., and Rachel M. Harlow. "'We Want Americans Pure and Simple': Theodore Roosevelt and the Myth of Americanism." *Rhetoric and Public Affairs* 6 (2003): 55–78.

Farrell, Thomas B. "Rhetorical Resemblance: Paradoxes of a Practical Art." *Quarterly Journal of Speech* 72 (1986): 1–19.

Fisher, Walter R. "Reaffirmation and Subversion of the American Dream." *Quarterly Journal of Speech* 59 (1973): 160–67.

———. "Romantic Democracy, Ronald Reagan, and Presidential Heroes." *Western Journal of Speech Communication* 46 (1982): 299–310.

Grossberger, Lewis. "Now and Before." *Mediaweek*, Oct. 18, 1999, 82.

Hart, Roderick P. "The End of the American Presidency." http://comm.colorado .edu/default_news.aspx?page=HartLecture.

Hay, Robert P. "George Washington: American Moses." *American Quarterly* 21 (1969): 780–91.

Holbert, R. Lance et al. "*The West Wing* as Endorsement of the U.S. Presidency: Expanding the Bounds of Priming in Political Communication." *Journal of Communication* 53 (2003): 427–43.

Hosken, Fran P. "Female Genital Mutilation and Human Rights." *Feminist Issues* 1 (1981): 3–23.

Hunter, Mark. "Dante's Watergate: *All the President's Men* as a Romance Narrative." *American Journalism* 14 (1997): 303–16.

Jasinski, James. "(Re)constituting Community through Narrative Argument: *Eros* and *Philia* in *The Big Chill.*" *Quarterly Journal of Speech* 79 (1993): 467–86.

Jones, Robert, and George N. Dionisopoulos. "Scripting a Tragedy: The 'Isaac and Ishmael' Episode of *The West Wing* as Parable." *Popular Communication* 2 (2004): 21–40.

Lehmann, Chris. "The Feel-Good Presidency." *Atlantic Monthly,* March 2001, 93–96.

Levin, Gary. "'West Wing' Mirrors Attacks in New Episode." *USA Today,* Sept. 24, 2001, 1D.

Lewis, William. "Of Innocence, Exclusion, and the Burning of Flags: The Romantic Realism of the Law." *Southern Communication Journal* 60 (1994): 4–21.

Mailloux, Steven. "Contingent Universals: Religious Fundamentalism, Academic Postmodernism, and Public Intellectuals in the Aftermath of September 11." *Cardozo Law Review* 24 (2003): 1583–604.

Marlow, Andrew. *Air Force One.* http://blake.prohosting.com/awsm/script/AirForceOne_TXT.htm.

Max, D. T. "The Making of the Speech." *New York Times Magazine,* Oct. 7, 2001, 32–37.

McKisack, Fred. "*The West Wing* Is Not a Wet Dream." *The Progressive,* May 2000, 39.

Meyrowitz, Joshua. "New Sense of Politics: How Television Changes the Political Drama." *Research in Political Sociology* 7 (1995): 117–38.

Miller, Matthew. "The Real White House." *Brill's Content,* March 2000, 88–95, 113.

Mills, Nicholas. "Prime Time White House." *Dissent* 47 (Winter 2000): 89–90.

Mink, Eric. "'Wing' Gets It Just Right." *Daily News,* Oct. 4, 2001, 112.

Miroff, Bruce. "From 'Midcentury' to *Fin-de-Siècle:* The Exhaustion of the Presidential Image." *Rhetoric and Public Affairs* 1 (1998): 185–199.

Murphy, John M. "The Heroic Tradition in Presidential Rhetoric." *Rhetoric and Public Affairs* 3 (2000): 466–70.

———. "Inventing Authority: Bill Clinton, Martin Luther King, Jr., and the Orchestration of Rhetorical Tradition." *Quarterly Journal of Speech* 83 (1997): 71–89.

———. "Knowing the President: The Dialogic Evolution of the Campaign History." *Quarterly Journal of Speech* 84 (1998): 23–40.

———. "'Our Mission and Our Moment': George W. Bush and September 11th." *Rhetoric and Public Affairs* 6 (2003): 607–32.

Murphy, Mary. "House Call." *TV Guide,* July 22–28, 2000, 15–24.

———, and Mark Schwed. "Broken Wing." *TV Guide,* May 31–June 6, 2003, 37–39.

Mutz, Diana C. "The Future of Political Communication Research: Reflections on the Occasion of Steve Chaffee's Retirement from Stanford University." *Political Communication* 18 (2001): 231–36.

Nakayama, Thomas K. "Show/Down Time: 'Race,' Gender, Sexuality, and Popular Culture." *Critical Studies in Mass Communication* 11 (1994): 162–79.

O'Sullivan, John L. "Annexation." *United States Magazine and Democratic Review,* July 1845, 5–10.

———. "The Great Nation of Futurity." *United States Magazine and Democratic Review,* Nov. 1839, 426–30.

Parry-Giles, Shawn J. "Mediating Hillary Rodham Clinton: Television News Practices and Image-Making in the Postmodern Age." *Critical Studies in Media Communication* 17 (2000): 205–26.

———. "Meta-imaging, *The War Room,* and the Hyperreality of U.S. Politics." *Journal of Communication* 49 (1999): 28–45.

———, and Diane M. Blair. "The Rise of the Rhetorical First Lady: Politics, Gender Ideology, and Women's Voice, 1789–2002." *Rhetoric and Public Affairs* 5 (2002): 565–600.

———, and Trevor Parry-Giles, "Gendered Politics and Presidential Image Construction: A Reassessment of the 'Feminine Style.'" *Communication Monographs* 63 (1996): 337–53.

Parry-Giles, Trevor. "Character, the Constitution, and the Ideological Embodiment of 'Civil Rights' in the 1967 Nomination of Thurgood Marshall to the Supreme Court." *Quarterly Journal of Speech* 82 (1996): 364–82.

———, and Shawn J. Parry-Giles. "Political Scopophilia, Presidential Campaigning, and the Intimacy of American Politics." *Communication Studies* 47 (1996): 191–205.

Perkins, Ken Parish. "Timely Topic Fits U.S. Mood." *Fort Worth Star-Telegram,* Oct. 4, 2001, 15.

Podhoretz, John. "The Liberal Imagination." *Weekly Standard,* March 27, 2000, 23.

Rathbun, Lyon. "The Debate over Annexing Texas and the Emergence of Manifest Destiny." *Rhetoric and Public Affairs* 4 (2001): 459–93.

Rochelle, Warren G. "The Literary Presidency." *Presidential Studies Quarterly* 29 (1999): 407–20.

Rosenberg, Howard. "Wishful Thinking in 'West Wing.'" Oct. 5, 2001 http://www.latimes.com/.

Rosenblum, Nancy L. "Romantic Militarism." *Journal of the History of Ideas* 43 (1982): 249–68.

Rubenstein, Julian. "Politically Correct." *Us* (Nov. 1999): 74.

Schram, Sanford F. "The Post-Modern Presidency and the Grammar of Electronic Electioneering." *Critical Studies in Mass Communication* 8 (1991): 210–6.

Schwartz, Barry. "The Character of Washington: A Study in Republican Culture." *American Quarterly* 38 (1986): 202–22.

Shales, Tom. "'The West Wing' Assumes the Role of Moral Compass." *Washington Post,* Oct. 5, 2001, C1.

Skjelsbaek, Kjell "Militarism, Its Dimensions and Corollaries: An Attempt at Conceptual Clarification." *Journal of Peace Research* 16 (1979): 213–29.

Smith, Lesley. "Reigning Men." *Pop Matters.* www.popmatters.com/tv/reviews/w/west-wing.html.

Stuckey, Mary E., and Frederick J. Antczak. "The Rhetorical Presidency: Deepening Vision, Widening Exchange." *Communication Yearbook* 21 (1998): 405–41.

———, and Shannon Wabshall. "Sex, Lies, and Presidential Leadership: Interpretations of the Office." *Presidential Studies Quarterly* 30 (2000): 514–33.

Sutin, L. Anthony. "The Presidential Powers of Josiah Bartlet." *Northern Kentucky University Law Review* 28 (2001): 560–72.

"Today's National Polls." *The Hotline,* May 26, 2000. http://nationaljournal.com /members/polltrack/2000/todays/hp000526.htm (subscription service).

Trujillo, Nick. "Hegemonic Masculinity on the Mound: Media Representations of Nolan Ryan and American Sports Culture." *Critical Studies in Mass Communication* 8 (1991): 290–308.

Wander, Philip. "The Third Persona: An Ideological Turn in Rhetorical Theory." *Central States Speech Journal* 35 (1984): 197–216.

Waxman, Sharon. "Inside *The West Wing*'s New World." *George* (Nov. 2000): 54–59, 94–96.

Welter, Barbara. "The Cult of True Womanhood: 1820–1860." *American Quarterly* 18 (1966): 151–74.

"*The West Wing* Controversy." http://www.etonline.com/.

Wickham, DeWayne. "TV's White House Is Just Too White." *USA Today,* March 21, 2000. http://www.usatoday.com/news/comment/columnists/wickham/wick073 .htm.

Wilson, Kirt H. "The Racial Politics of Imitation in the Nineteenth Century." *Quarterly Journal of Speech* 89 (2003): 89–108.

Windt, Theodore O. Jr. "Presidential Rhetoric: Definition of a Field of Study." *Central States Speech Journal* 35 (1984): 24–34.

Zagacki, Kenneth S., and Andrew King. "Reagan, Romance and Technology: A Critique of 'Star Wars.'" *Communication Studies* 40 (1989): 1–12.

Zarefsky, David. "Consistency and Change in Lincoln's Rhetoric about Equality." *Rhetoric and Public Affairs* 1 (1998): 21–44.

———. "The Continuing Fascination with Lincoln." *Rhetoric and Public Affairs* 6 (2003): 337–71.

Zinn, Maxine Baca, and Bonnie Thornton Dill. "Theorizing Difference from Multiracial Feminism." *Feminist Studies* 22 (1996): 321–31.

Trevor Parry-Giles is an associate professor in the Department of Communication at the University of Maryland, where he is also an affiliated scholar with the Center for American Politics and Citizenship.

Shawn J. Parry-Giles is an associate professor in the Department of Communication and an affiliated associate professor in the Department of Women's Studies at the University of Maryland, where she also serves as director of the Center for Political Communication and Civic Leadership.

The University of Illinois Press
is a founding member of the
Association of American University Presses.

---

Composed in 10.5/13 Minion
with Minion display
by Type One, LLC
for the University of Illinois Press
Designed by Dennis Roberts
Manufactured by Thomson-Shore, Inc.

University of Illinois Press
1325 South Oak Street
Champaign, IL 68820-6903
www.press.uillinois.edu